HITLER'S MIRACLE WEAPONS

HITLER'S MIRACLE WEAPONS

*The Secret History of the Rockets and Flying Craft
of the Third Reich Volume 2:
From the V-1 to the A-9: Unconventional short-
and medium-range weapons*

Friedrich Georg

Translated by C. F. Colton MA

HELION & COMPANY LTD

Helion & Company Limited
Unit 8 Amherst Business Centre
Budbrooke Road
Warwick
CV34 5WE
England
Tel. 01926 499619
Email: info@helion.co.uk
Website: www.helion.co.uk
X (formerly Twitter): @Helionbooks
Facebook: @HelionBooks
Visit our blog at https://helionbooks.wordpress.com/

Published by Helion & Company 2003. This new edition 2024
Originally published as *Hitlers Siegeswaffen Band 1: Luftwaffe und Marine* by AMUN-Verlag in co-operation with
Heinrich-Jung-Verlagsgesellschaft mbH, Germany, 2000
German edition © AMUN-Verlag & Agentur Pegasus 2000
This English edition © Helion & Company 2003
Images and artwork © as individually credited
Designed and typeset by Carnegie Publishing Ltd, Lancaster, Lancashire
Cover designed by Paul Hewitt, Battlefield Design (www.battlefield-design.co.uk)

Legal notice: This book contains potentially controversial material. To avoid misunderstandings, nothing in this book should be misconstrued as an attack on the elected government or constitutional order of any country in the world. Similarly, no attacks are intended upon any persons, living or dead, or upon any social groups. The content of this book was compiled to the best of the author's knowledge and is intended purely to serve the purpose of providing historical information. The interpretations expressed in the book are the personal opinion of the author.

Every reasonable effort has been made to trace copyright holders and to obtain their permission for the use of copyright material. The author and publisher apologise for any errors or omissions in this work, and would be grateful if notified of any corrections that should be incorporated in future reprints or editions of this book.

ISBN 978-1-804517-26-0

British Library Cataloguing-in-Publication Data.
A catalogue record for this book is available from the British Library.

For details of other military history titles published by Helion & Company Limited, contact the above address, or visit our website: http://www.helion.co.uk

We always welcome receiving book proposals from prospective authors.

Contents

Acknowledgements

When work began on volume 2 of *Hitler's Miracle Weapons*, the author never dreamed of the quantity of material and information which was to come his way.

I must first thank AMUN-Verlag for making it possible to cover the subject of rocketry and missiles over two volumes. I should like to thank Mr Igor Shestakov for the colour profiles and Mr Richard Lewis Mendes (USA) for the cover picture and other outstanding artwork. Many photographs of models of rockets as well as important information were sent by Daniel and Herminio from the company of Aescala (Mexico). The text of this volume was helped in many ways by Mr Henry Stevens (USA), Mr Pat Flannery (USA), Mr Antonio Chover (Spain) and m Kristian Knaack, to whom I send my thanks. For countless pieces of additional information, much of it submitted anonymously, I must also give my thanks. Your help was an incentive to me! Of course, this book would also not have been possible without the patience and diligence of my secretary, Uschi.

Last but not least, I send my thanks to my family for their patience and understanding in allowing me to again carry out my work for this book.

INTRODUCTION

The Search for the Hidden Truth about Hitler's Rockets and Missiles

If we had had these rockets in 1939, there would not have been a war.
From now on, Europe and the world are too small for a war.
With these weapons, humanity will not be able to withstand a war...
Adolf Hitler on 7 July 1943 in the Führer Headquarters[1]

The Germans were preparing rocket surprises for the whole world in general
and England in particular which would have, it is believed, changed the course of the war.
US Colonel Donald Leander Putt[2]

Were the general public kept in the dark for decades about what really went on at Peenemünde?

Today, Germany's *Vergeltungswaffen*, the V-1 and V-2, are commonly seen as a symbol of the armaments policy of the Third Reich. Technically decades in advance of the competition, it is alleged that they were too expensive, were deployed much too late and were produced in far too small numbers to affect the war in any decisive way. According to the prevalent view today, the only effect that they did have was to serve in the post-war years as a basis for further developments carried out by the Allies, because they were no longer of any military use for their real creators in the Third Reich. Indeed, on the contrary, so popular opinion maintains, they were actually detrimental to the German war effort.[3] [4]

The persistence of this view is also due to the fact that, in the years after the war, the German scientists who worked on the development of these weapons almost all continued working for the former Allies in both East and West, and, as a result, later evinced little interest in drawing attention to their activities during the Third Reich.

There is therefore no doubt that the complete truth about the German missile and rocket programme, its intentions, plans and products, has never been told to this day.

During many years of research I succeeded in evaluating previously inaccessible sources and documents which prove that Hitler's V-weapons had a great influence on events during the last stages of the war - an influence which justified the cost of their development. But it appears that the real aim of Hitler's missile and rocket programme was ultimately to transport weapons of mass destruction which would decide the outcome of the war. The myth of the rocket scientists who would rather have been producing space vehicles, misused by the Third Reich, will no longer be tenable following the publication of this book. Under the direction of Hitler's 'Rocket Tsar', *SS-Obergruppenführer* Dr Hans Kammler, instead of researching the possibility of producing space vehicles, they were carrying out research into producing decisive weapons systems which, if they had been deployed during the last stages of the war, could have cost millions more in terms of war casualties.

The V-1 and the V-2, numerous variants of which have until now remained carefully hidden from the eyes of the public, were not the only weapons - not by a long way! According to Allied documents, at the end of the war there were 138 different types of German rockets and guided missiles, at varying stages of production and development. Today, we still have no information on over 80 types.

Since work on the second volume of *Hitler's Miracle Weapons* began, so much important information has emerged that the author and the publishing company have decided to make this information available to the reader in comprehensive form. The available material became so extensive that it became necessary to divide the single second volume initially planned into two separate volumes.

The present volume deals with the rockets and guided missiles which, used as short and medium-range weapons, could have decisively helped to turn the war in Hitler's favour. Some of these weapons, which to this day officially never existed, were within only days or weeks of being ready for deployment, or, if they were already available, were simply not deployed.

Even if a great deal of information will continue to remain in the obscurity of history, the conclusion of this book is to call for a new - for many people, even revolutionary - way of looking at Hitler's most expensive armaments project.

Friedrich Georg

PART I

Pioneers and Early Robot Weapons: Hitler was not 'the first'

Harbingers of the Inferno? Kaiser Wilhelm's flying bombs and intercontinental offensive plans

In December 1921, the Dutch aircraft manufacturers Fokker exhibited a small high wing glider at the Paris Aero Salon.[1] The similarity of this glider with the Fokker D VIII was immediately evident. They had simply moved the cockpit forward to the place which was normally occupied by the Fokker D VIII's radial engine. The rest of the aircraft was almost exactly the same as the First World War fighter. This modified aircraft had the designation Fokker V.30, and was equipped for aerial tow. Fokker himself explained that he had built this aircraft for his own enjoyment.

However, despite the fact that it only had its official debut at the Aero Salon, the story of the V.30 went back to the First World War. At that time, the English, the Americans and also the Germans were all working under great secrecy on remote controlled unmanned aircraft which could be used as aerial torpedoes or flying bombs.

In Germany, the Siemens-Schuckert company had been experimenting since the outbreak of the war in 1914 with large gliders which would be able to cover great distances under remote control after being released from airships or aircraft.[2] [3] Following a direct proposal by Dr Wilhelm von Siemens, the first work began in October 1914, and by January 1915, flight tests with gliders of increasing size were being carried out under the direction of Dipl. -Ing. Donner. Between 1915 and 1918, Siemens-Schuckert built more than 100 different glider bombs of greatly varying shapes and sizes, some of which scarcely resembled aircraft at all. By the end of the war, two principal types capable of deployment had been developed -one 300-kilogram and one 1000-kilogram glider bomb. Launch trials of the 300-kilogram glider aircraft were carried out in Jüterbog with Zeppelin L.35 and the Parseval airship PL.25. In August 1918, a range of 7.6 kilometres was achieved after a launch from a height of 1220 metres. The guided weapon could be remote controlled by line guidance until it was 60 metres above the target, and then the twin guidance lines were detached.

In 1918, they succeeded in developing a 1000-kilogram glider bomb model, which, there is no doubt, represents the predecessor of today's guided missiles. The first trial launches were made from the roof of the Siemens-Schuckert hangar in Biesdorf. But after this there were also successful launches from airships. Thus, on 2 August 1918, it was possible to launch one of these 1000-kilogram glider bombs from Zeppelin L.35 and guide it over a distance of 7.5 kilometres. It was hoped that these guided weapons with a wingspan of 4.20 metres could be launched not only from airships but also from bombers. It was intended that the Siemens-Schuckert R.VIII heavy bomber could serve for this purpose. The R.VIII was the largest bomber in the First World War and could carry the glider bomb under its wings without any problem. In February 1918, work was begun on the two aircraft of this type, designated R.23/16 and R.24/16, but neither of these aircraft was completed before the war came to an end.

There were no more successful attempts to launch the 1000-kilogram glider bomb from other aircraft before the Entente in December 1918 ordered the work to be abandoned.

Quite independently of the work carried out by Siemens on line-guided glider bombs, the German Army Air Force had established a special unit in Döberitz which was working on a similar idea. This involved a system of remote control by radio which could be carried out either from the ground or from aircraft. Thus, in collaboration with the Mannesmann company (*Direktor* Forsmann), the experimental radio unit F.T.V.A. developed the unmanned remote-controlled aircraft 'Fledermaus'. This was about as large as a C-aircraft (a two-seater single-engined bomber or reconnaissance aircraft). The 'Fledermaus' was launched using a winch, and afterwards was controlled by radio, automatic steering equipment and by two direction-finding stations. Over the target, wireless commands released the bombs and steered the aircraft. Over the home airfield, the engine was switched off, a radio command turned the aircraft on its head, and released a gigantic parachute from the stern, on which the 'Fledermaus' would safely land.

Even today, this concept dating from 1918 still has a modern appeal!

When revolutionary unrest broke out in Germany in the autumn of 1918, all this work was brought to nothing, and the aircraft destroyed. By this time, at least two models of the 'Fledermaus' had been constructed. Other sources suggest that four of these aircraft had already flown.

In 1918, very successful work on remote controlled aircraft was also being carried out by the Merkur factory.

Unfortunately, it has not been possible to find any photographs or plans of the F.T.V.A. and Merkur developments.

Since Fokker were the leading aircraft designers of the Kaiser's empire, in 1916, in the Fokker company in Schwerin, feverish activity began to develop a cheap, simple disposable aircraft. It was intended that the aircraft should first prove its suitability as a test aircraft, and then be developed into its final form as a weapon. The intention was that the winged glider bomb should be towed into the air by a mother aircraft. Fokker was promised that, if the idea proved practicable, he could expect larger contracts for the production of this model, and that he would later play a leading role in the development of a self-propelled flying bomb which was remote controlled by radio.

In summer 1918, Fokker began to experiment with unmanned gliders which would be towed by a specially modified version of the Fokker D.VII fighter aircraft. This towing aircraft had the designation Fokker V.31 and was fitted under its fuselage with a simple winch for the tow line. At the stern of the aircraft, a semicircular ski extended backwards to protect the vulnerable parts of the aircraft from damage by the tow line. Fokker kept these aerial flight trials secret. But we know that just one single V.30 was built. After a successful test, the nose of the V.30 could have been replaced by a warhead.

Independently of this, in 1919 Fokker said in a press interview that in summer 1918 he had received a 'massive' contract for the production of radio-controlled unmanned bombing aircraft. It can be assumed that he was referring to motorised versions of the V.30.

These Fokker aircraft, together with similar developments carried out by Junkers, F.T.V.A. and Merkur, can be considered as the predecessors of the Second World War Argus 'Fernfeuer' and Fieseler Fi-103.

In 1923, Fokker gave a lecture to Dutch officers. In the lecture he stressed the tactical and strategic importance of remote-controlled unmanned missiles.

In considering the concept of 'strategic weapons', it should not be forgotten that in the First World War poison gas was used extensively. It is likely, therefore, that in accordance with the thinking at the time, consideration would have been given to filling all such missiles with mustard gas instead of a conventional explosive, and directing them against foreign countries. It would then only have been a short step to the development of a weapon which could have decided the outcome of the war.

Although the great aircraft manufacturer Fokker was right in his prophetic predictions, he was 20 years ahead of his time. All that he managed to achieve was a few short mentions in some aircraft periodicals of the 1920s.

But the question must seriously be asked whether these German plans from the period 1914 to 1918 for the creation of unmanned guided missiles and glider bombs were not the initial basis for the creation of the German *Vergeltungswaffen* of the Second World War.

In summer 1918, plans were developed to attack New York and the eastern coast of the USA by deploying long-range Zeppelins. These airships, of the types 'L.71 long' and L.100, were capable of flying across the Atlantic to enemy cities at a great height (which would have made them immune to attack by the enemy fighters of the time) and transporting remote-controlled 1000-kilogram flying bombs.

If the war had continued, the deployment of poison gas against cities would have become a reality in 1919. By the end of 1918, the English hoped to have developed their 'Independent Air Force', the predecessor of the later World War Two 'Bomber Command', to the stage where it would be able to carry out bombing raids against Berlin using Handley-Page V/1500 bombers. These 'trial raids' with conventional bombs were then to be followed in the spring of 1919 by heavy raids against the German *Reich* capital using poison gas.[4] This would then certainly have provoked similar German retaliatory measures!

However, conventional long-range bombers with weapons of mass destruction, remote-controlled bombs and intercontinental attacks – all these horrors were something that, by a happy stroke of fate, the world escaped for another quarter of a century!

Only now made public: as early as 1922 there was a German rocket and jet programme - and betrayal

In the winter of 1922, an event occurred that was clearly felt for decades to be so sensitive that, when it was mentioned in 1959 by one of the people who had been present, it immediately vanished again into American secret documents.[5] It was only released into the public domain at the end of 2001.

Shortly after the end of the First World War, in February 1922, three men met in the breakfast room of the Hotel Avalon in Berlin [Author's note: this was likely to have been the Hotel Adlon]. These men were the famous pilot and aerial warfare strategist General Billy Mitchell, Alfred V. Verville and the Air Attaché, Ben Foulois.

Brigadier-General Mitchell had invited Foulois to breakfast, and in their conversation complained that there currently seemed to be no likelihood of any technical progress in the area of aircraft propulsion systems. But then he continued: "You know, Ben, I bet you that at this very moment there's some long-haired German scientist who's working in some hut in a 6 ft by 12 ft laboratory on new propulsion systems for the next war which is going to break out in 15 or 20 years from now", and he said, turning to Foulois, "I'd like you to get out there and find him for me". Foulois replied: "General, I'm sure I don't know what you're talking about, but I'll try anyway". At 11:30am on the same day,

Mitchell and Verville received a call that Foulois had arrived in the hotel lobby with a man. They all then went to another building, which was a wooden hut. A German came out of the hut, and Verville described him as a very formal man dressed in black. He introduced himself as the assistant of another scientist which turned out to be Dr. Oberth, the man who taught von Braun. When Brigadier-General Mitchell outlined his views about the current standstill in the development of aircraft propulsion systems, the man agreed, but said it that the piston engine would be replaced by turbines (in the original English text, it says 'turbeens'), which would run on kerosene (in the original text: 'coal oil'). He said that he was already researching the question, but that none of these propulsion systems had yet been developed. They would, he said, permit the development of a 'rocket bomb'. Dr Oberth then sent his assistant back into the laboratory. The man came out with a container which contained something that looked like CO_2. He emptied the contents into an empty glass - which exploded. The impression was dramatic! The German gave the name of this liquid air and said that, when mixed with alcohol, it would serve as a propellant. The expected range of the propulsion system was, he said, 400 kilometres at speeds of up to 3000 mph. He estimated

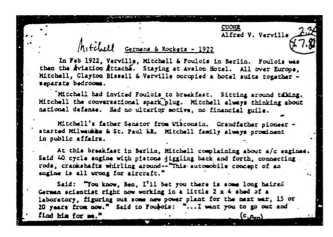

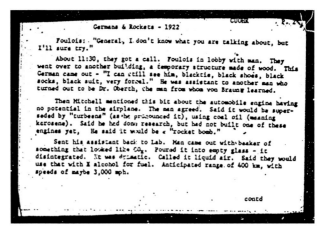

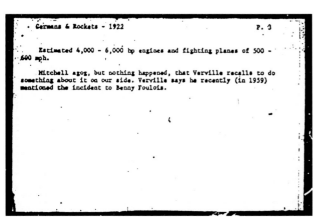

Microfilm extracts only released in 2001 by the US Air Force which report that as early as 1922 research was being conducted into German rockets and jet propulsion systems – and that the later Allies were aware of this even at that time.

that a propulsion system of that kind would generate 4000 to 6000 horsepower and that, using it, a fighter aircraft would be able to reach speeds of up to 1000 kilometres per hour. This information provided by the German scientist back in 1922 describes with amazing accuracy the performance of the later German rockets, missiles and jet fighters of the Second World War.

In 1959, Alfred V. Verville said that Brigadier-General Mitchell was very alarmed at the time at what he had heard, and had demanded that something must urgently be done 'on our side'. But, Verville said, nothing happened!

Mitchell and Foulois were representatives of the victorious powers in the First World War, which in 1922 still had comprehensive monitoring powers in conquered Germany. Thus, they would have had no problem in being able to stop the German jet and rocket project or to use it for their own purposes.

But, at this time, Billy Mitchell had fallen out of favour with the politicians in Washington. The failure to react to his early warning, together with the precise information

(or perhaps, more accurately, betrayal?) from Dr Oberst and his assistant, may have been one of the reasons why the responsible politicians caused the incident reported by Alfred V. Verville to 'disappear' for decades.

But already the element of betrayal was running like a *leitmotif* through all investigation of the new, sensational technologies developed by the Germans.

The futuristic developments in 1922, discovered as the results of a bet between Mitchell, Verville and Foulois, clearly show that the roots of Hitler's rockets and missiles can be traced back to a much earlier period than has previously been assumed.

After the Versailles peace treaty, which not only Germany found to be unjust, the former *Kaiserreich* strove despite the most stringent financial restrictions to find way out of the desperate situation which had been imposed by foreign powers.

But there are indications that even at that time thoughts of revenge were surfacing in addition to purely defensive intentions.

What was Weimar after? The unrecognised roots of the German rocket programme

It is a fact which is often overlooked that worldwide re-armament after the First World War did not only begin after Hitler came to power in 1933, but was already under way at the end of the 1920s. In this process, despite the armaments restrictions imposed on it by the Versailles treaty, the Weimar Republic was no exception.

The Versailles Treaty of 29 July, 1919 had made Germany militarily defenceless. Not only was the Weimar Republic forbidden to possess any kind of weapon important at that time such as tanks, aircraft, submarines, battleships or even (defensive) anti-aircraft guns, even research was banned.

A merciless special committee, the Inter-Allied Military Control Commission (IAMCC), using a system of inspections throughout Germany, saw to it the that the compulsory arms restrictions were being maintained.

But the victorious powers had not included in their list of forbidden weapons a type of weapon which was later to become very important. This oversight very nearly cost the Allies their victory in the Second World War 25 years later. In Versailles, they had forgotten to mention rockets and missiles!

The planners in the Weimar *Reichswehr* had realised that the development of long-range rockets could provide an alternative to heavy artillery, which Germany had been banned from possessing since 1919. Perhaps there was also more to this than simply the development of replacement alternative weapons, because reports were already circulating that an entire city could be destroyed by the impact of one single rocket. The fact was that the military in the Weimar Republic intended to make use of the potential which these new weapons appeared to offer.[6][7]

As early as 1927, the *Verein fur Raumschiffahrt* ('VfR': Space Travel Association) had been founded in Breslau. With various degrees of success, experiments began with liquid-propelled rockets. These experiments took place on a testing ground in Reinickendorf near Berlin, which was called the 'rocket testing ground', and which 'happened' to be located in a military testing zone.

But it would be difficult to see in the VfR a 'military' predecessor, because many pacifists and later opponents of the Nazis were members of the organisation. So, in the *Heereswaffenamt* in Berlin, the then *Oberstleutnant* Karl-Emil Becker pulled together a team of specialists which also included Dr Walter Dornberger and Leo Zanssen. Later, these men were to be the leading lights in the German rocket programme.

But despite the world economic crisis, as early as 1931 *Oberstleutnant* Becker managed to raise enough money to give a research contract to Paul Heylandt, at that time a leading German rocket pioneer.

On 1 October 1932, the 20 year-old Werner von Braun also joined the service of the rocket researchers of Kummersdorf.

In 1932, the Army of the Weimar Republic suddenly closed the 'rocket testing ground' and moved the experiments to the Reichswehr testing ground in Kummersdorf, where it was easier to maintain secrecy.

But as early as 1930, foreign observers had already realised that the apparently harmless 'rocket testing ground' was being used to develop weapons. Fortunately for the German rocket programme, at the time this did not lead to any consequences abroad.

By the end of the Weimar Republic, the rocket team had created the A-1 and was already working on its successor, the A-2. The Third Reich only needed to take up where the Weimar Republic had left off! They didn't even take the trouble to change the designation of the 'aggregates'!

Then, in 1943, General Dr Dornberger himself confirmed the close connection between Weimar and Hitler's later *Vergeltungswaffen*. He published, of his own accord, a memoir in Peenemunde. Its illuminating title was 'Developments in Rocketry carried out by the *Heereswaffenamt, 1930-1943*'.

To date, it is not known whether any researcher has addressed the issue of what might have become of the German rocket programme if Hitler had not come to power in 1933.

The ominous prophecy

As early as 1933, the rocket pioneer Hermann Oberth gave voice to an amazing prediction:[8] "The prospects for a future war are ominous. With one single rocket-borne warhead it will be possible to destroy entire enemy cities, and all our current means of defence will be powerless to stop it. But perhaps the possibility that such dreadful weapons could be developed might at last bring mankind to its senses".

Was the content of this statement a motive force for Hitler's rocket armaments programme? It can be assumed with relative certainty that Hitler was acquainted with Oberth's prediction.

Who was the first to use remote-controlled airborne weapons?

Germany was not the first belligerent power to deploy remote-controlled weapons for in the Second World War. The Russians and the Italians had already taken the step towards push-button warfare.[9] [10] [11] [12]

As early as September 1941, the Soviets, because of the high casualties they suffered in bomber units equipped with the conventional TB-3, began to search for alternatives. Thus, they hit upon the idea of using remote control to keep the crews out of enemy fire. To do this, under the direction of A. G. Federov, Tupolev TB-3 bombers were converted into flying bombs. The cockpits were converted, radio receivers and servos fitted to the flight controls and superfluous parts removed. The explosive charge was to be installed in the fuselage. For this purpose, Professor N. I. Gelperin and his staff developed a special bomb weighing 6500 kilograms, with a length of six metres and a diameter of about one metre. This gigantic explosive charge was manufactured in six individual cylindrical components, which were only assembled into one unit in the aircraft fuselage using screw bolts.

Conventional medium-range bombers of the types SB and TB-3 were to serve as control aircraft, in which remote control transmitters were installed. When in operation, the control aircraft flew slightly higher than, and at a distance of about 50 to 200 metres behind the converted four-engined heavy bombers. This shows that the range of the remote control equipment at the time must have been really short! The crew members of the TB-3, who were needed to start the aircraft, bailed out by parachute when the operational height was reached.

On the first operational trial with a remote-controlled TB-3, the aircraft was lost, probably because the remote control antennae became iced up, after the pilot had bailed out. The first successful deployment of the weapon then took place on 15 October, 1942 against an unknown target. The next attack using the flying bombs, a few days later, against an Artillery depot at Wjasma, failed due to the poor weather conditions. It is not known if further operations were carried out using remote-controlled TB-3s.

Even before the Russians, in summer 1940, the Italians, under the direction of General Ferdinando Raffaelli, had begun the development of remote-controlled large bombs. For this purpose, they used the tried and tested three-engined Savoia SM.79 bomber. This special version was called the S.79 A.R.P. (Aereo Radio Pilotato) and was converted by the Centro Sperimentale di Guidonia. Here, too, improved flight and remote control systems were installed in the bomber, so that, after the manual take-off by a pilot, the rest of the flight could be controlled by a control aircraft are using remote control.

In 1942, the Italians considered that their system was sufficiently well developed to be able to deploy it in action.

During the famous air and sea battle of Mezzagosto, on 12 August, 1942 one S.79 A.R.P. took off, with two 1500-kilogram explosive charges installed under its fuselage. After a successful take-off, the pilot bailed out using his parachute, with the radio control of the flight been taken over by a Cant.-Z.-007-Bis mother aircraft. As a result of the failure of a single duct in the control system in the mother aircraft, however, the remote control failed and the SM.79 flying bomb hurtled, not, as had been planned, straight into a large English battleship, but into a mountain in the Atlas Mountains in Algeria, where it exploded. This failed operation almost created a diplomatic incident, because the Italians wanted to prevent the Vichy French who at the time were in control of Algeria from discovering the secret behind this great explosion.

After they had calmed down the French, the Italian

Armistice Commission climbed to the crash site on the slopes of the Klenchela mountains on 14 August, 1942. There they found a crater which was still smoking – and that was two days after the crash! What destruction could have been wreaked on a battleship or aircraft-carrier if the remote control of the control aircraft had been working properly? The well-known English military writer Peter C. Smith, in his reference work *Pedestal*, said of the SM.79 A.R.P. flying bombs: "It was a great stroke of luck for the Fleet at the time that the Italian intentions once again proved abortive".

The Italians learned from this failure, and made their flying bomb system less susceptible to failure by building in various safeguards and using fighter aircraft of the type Macchi C.202 instead of the difficult three-engined Z.1007.

At the beginning of September 1943, combat-ready SM.79 A.R.P. flying bombs and C.202 control aircraft were standing by on the airfield at Guidonia to strike against the Allied invasion fleet at Salerno. But the armistice of 8 September 1943 prevented this second operational deployment of Italy's flying bombs. A small series of the single-engined Ambrosini-A.R. flying bomb, which had been constructed for the same purpose, and which bore a certain similarity to the German Argus 'Fernfeuer' project, had been stationed on the same airfield and was ready for operational deployment. But these aircraft to waited in vain for the orders to go into action. In this instance, the about-face of the Badoglio government had possibly prevented decisive attacks on the Allied invasion fleet.

The deployment of these remote-controlled weapons were to remain largely unnoticed by the general public throughout the world. Thus the stage was set for the entrance of Hitler's robot bombs and long-range rockets.[13]

PART II

The Secret of Peenemünde and the Real Purpose of Hitler's Rocket and Missile Programme

Introduction

"At that time in Peenemünde" – The world's first technology centre and the end of a legend

On 1 May 1937, the first 'rocket station' in the world was opened in Peenemünde. When the research establishments located there fell into Russian hands on 5 May 1945, it was the end of an experiment, until that time unprecedented, which involved links between scientists, the military, and industry.[1][2]

The Peenemünde research complex was to a certain extent a predecessor of today's technology centres, such as, for example, 'Silicon Valley' in California.

Peenemünde-Ost, the Army experimental establishment, dealt not only with the A–4 rocket and its derivatives, but also with a large number of other projects, proposals and ideas. These ranged from new types of artillery and nuclear research to space travel.

Just next door, in Peenemünde-West, was the Luftwaffe's testing establishment, in which many revolutionary designs and projects were also developed. These included aircraft with unconventional propulsion systems and also new weapons technologies, manned, rocket-powered long-range aircraft and new high-energy propellants.

Occasionally, there was a combination of activities between Peenemünde-Ost and Peenemünde-West.

In equipping the experimental establishmentent, the most modern technology available at the time was used, regardless of cost.

Thus, two specialised TV transmission stations transmitted images of the take-off of rockets from the test pads by broadband cable to the control room which was located two kilometres away. In this way, even at that time, the scientists and technicians could watch the dangerous tests on the TV monitor at a safe distance. Even prominent political figures of the time are said to have often stood observing via the TV monitors.[3]

As early as 1938, the first binary computer in the world – Konrad Zuse's Z–1 – had been invented. In 1944, the enhanced model Z–3 was used for ballistic calculations for the V–2. Indeed, to do this, the first programming language – called 'Plankalkül' – had been developed.

Even at that time, SS General Dr Hans Kammler had computer data stored on so-called 'Magnetophon' devices. This was the first audio/videoband recorder, of which there are verifiable photos dating from 1942.[4]

By the time Peenemünde was evacuated in the spring of 1945, it had been possible to develop an organisational network which allowed a reasonably effective interplay between about 40,000 staff and 5,000 to 6,000 institutes, administrative authorities, companies and also scientists, administrative staff and politicians. This led to the creation of a state, industry and scientific pool, until then unprecedented in the history of business and technology, in which interdisciplinary boundaries could be easily bridged. The first technology centre in the world had been created!

The military-industrial Peenemünde complex very nearly included other continents! If Germany had not been driven out of Africa in May 1943, a rocket testing station could have been created in the Libyan desert. *General* Dr Dornberger and *Oberst* Thoma were staying in Tripoli as early as July 1942 to look for a suitable area.[5][6][7] The advantages of such a location would have been obvious. Even the French carried out rocket and atomic tests in North Africa in the post-war period. German preparations for an African firing range were apparently already far advanced when it the military situation put an end to these plans. This would also explain the presence in Peenemünde of two unusual diesel locomotives in the 'African' paint scheme, and the unusual buff-painted (RAL 8000) rocket launching pads from 1942. This colour of paint 'happened' to be the base colour of Rommel's Afrika Korps! It should also not be forgotten that the last British doubts about the existence of the German rockets evaporated when in the spring of 1943

1941. Hollerith computer: The information secret weapon of Himmler's SS. Gen. Kammler promote his creation for war's production resources improvement.

Konrad Zuse's Z1, world's first binary computer.1938. In 1944, the Z-3 was used in "Dora" factory for V-2's ballistic trajectory calculations. The "Plankalkül", the first programming language was developed for that.

German computer technology: Picture top left: Hollerith computer (1941). Picture top right: Konrad Zuse's Z1, the world's first binary computer from 1938. In 1944 the later z3 model was used in Mittelbau-Dora to calculate ballistic trajectories. Centre picture: The 'Magnetophon' device for data recording (1942). Picture bottom left: The Z–4 computer console. The Z–4, and Zuse's company, were entirely financed by the German *Reichspost* (Arthur Wheeler)

Nazi "Magnetophon"-The world's first audio/video tape recorder. Also used by SS Gen. Kammler for computer data recording. Original photo 1942

Zuse's Z-4 working in 1943, 3 years before ENIAC.

Z-4 general purpose computer console. Zuse's company was totally financed by Ohnesorge's Reichspost in 43-45.

senior generals of the Afrika Korps gave concrete accounts of the German rocket project when they were prisoners of war.

On 22 March 1943, in a conversation which was secretly recorded by the British, the two generals Cruewell and von Thoma expressed their astonishment that London was not yet in ruins as a result of bombardment by German rockets. General von Thoma, who from time to time was deputy to Field Marshal Rommel in Africa, also mentioned in this conversation that he had visited a rocket testing area in Germany.[8]

While only a little is known about plans for testing establishments on Fuertaventura, later on, firing ranges in Poland (Blizna and Tucheler Heide) were set up and remained in operation until they were overrun by the Russians.

Of course, in the post-war period, it was difficult to substantiate the diversity of the activities carried out on

Peenemünde. Thus, in a lecture he gave at the end of December 1962 at a symposium of the American Association for the Advancement of Science, Dr Dornberger said that the large number of diverse projects had been necessary to justify the existence of his rocket group and the existence of Peenemünde. In addition, he continued in this lecture which was intended for American ears, it would have been folly to believe that the Germans had at any time had any concrete ideas about what would develop as a result of their work. Yes, the original small group had dreamed of long-range rockets and space ships. But, he said, at no time in the period between 1932 and 1935 had they received any written specific requests for a weapons system from their military superiors or from anyone else.

Thus, in this lecture and in many similar articles and post-war books, the 'legend of Peenemünde' was created. This was a legend about brilliant, idealistic scientists who were thinking about civilian applications and future space travel destinations and who only by chance had to contribute to the armaments system of the Third Reich, because their proposals were misused for warlike purposes. Of course, in the post-war period, these kinds of explanations fell on fruitful soil, because they resolved any possible problem in justifying the vitally important employment of the German scientists by the victorious powers. In this connection, it is striking that in the USA the first serious criticisms of former Peenemünde scientists for using slave labour in the rocket armaments programme during the Third Reich were only voiced after the Americans had successfully landed on the Moon. Was it not really the case that the protective hand was withdrawn once the scientists were not needed any more? But perhaps we all want to believe in coincidences!

Even the unexplained arrest of Wernher von Braun and the engineers Riedel and Gröttrup by the Gestapo on 15 March 1944 was very likely exploited for the purpose of creating the post-war legend of 'what it was really like in Peenemünde'. It is a fact that von Braun and the two engineers mentioned had to spend one or two weeks in a prison in Stettin without receiving any indication whatsoever from the authorities why they had been arrested. Nothing ever came to light about any questioning that was carried out there – that is, if it took place at all. Afterwards, the three men who had been arrested were suddenly released again. So much for the facts.

After the war, Dr Dornberger wrote that *Feldmarschall* Keitel had told him that the men had been arrested because, in a social gathering in Zinnowitz, the three had said that it had never been their intention to make a weapon of the rocket. They had carried out the whole development programme just to get money for their experiments and to verify their ideas. They said that the their aim was and had always been space travel. After this story had been reported to the Gestapo by a female agent, it had been used as a pretext to arrest the men on a charge of sabotage. Dr Dornberger claimed, together with Armaments Minister Speer, to have managed to get Himmler to release the scientists. However, their release was only for a period of three months and had been regularly reviewed. According to Otto Skorzeny, the affair was somewhat different. He states that at the beginning of 1944, Wernher von Braun had made statements which appeared to come from the fantastic novels in the style of Jules Verne. These, said Skorzeny, had appeared in a German newspaper and had contained drawings which gave an idea of the construction of the rockets. These articles, he said, had been immediately taken up by the press in neutral countries. For this reason, he said, Himmler, still reeling from the large-scale Allied air raid on Peenemünde, had had von Braun arrested and interrogated. Hitler himself, Skorzeny said, had got to know about this and had put an end to this paradoxical situation. The whole affair, he said, had not lasted much longer than a week. Skorzeny's version is very different to Dr Dornberger's account. Which of the two gentlemen gave an accurate account of the events of March 1944?[9][10] It is certainly true that important scientists in Peenemünde were also thinking of later civilian applications of their inventions. Armaments operations in all countries have often thought during wartime of later civilian applications of their products during the post-war period. When in the spring of 1945 Germany's intercontinental America Bomber was being designed, the planners of the Junkers EF-140 - and these were no less than a joint committee of the entire German aerospace industry - had included in their plans the capability for civilian applications of their EF-140 in the post-war period.

It should not meanwhile be forgotten that Peenemünde was a Wehrmacht military establishment, and that the scientists transferred there had already worked under the auspices of the *Reichswehr* at the Kummersdorf military training ground near Berlin. While in the course of daily work at Peenemünde, civilian scientists also carried out management tasks, all important decisions were made by the military members of the Wehrmacht, Luftwaffe and SS. In this process, Wernher von Braun played a sort of hybrid role. While in published pictures he is always to be seen in a civilian suit, according to to an account by Julius Mader, which appeared in the GDR in 1967, as early as 1 November 1933, he was an applicant for the SS. There is a definite proof that he joined Heinrich Himmler's organisation on 1 May 1940. Long before the SS took formal control in Peenemünde, the former Technical Director of EMW Peenemünde had already been at least an honorary member of this military Party organisation. In order not to further endanger the legend of civilian space travel research, it seems that at the end of the war all photographs which showed *SS-Sturmbannführer* von Braun in his 'smart black uniform' were placed under lock and key. Even Otto Skorzeny, who dealt with secret weapons development on behalf of the SS, writes in his memoirs that he had the closest contact with and complete confidence in Wernher von Braun, and that General Dr Dornberger was a great fellow and an outstanding officer. Does this all sound only as if people are talking about civilian 'dreamers'?

Dr Dornberger is said to have got Bernhard Tessmann, another leading Peenemünde scientist, to promise at the end of the war that he would never speak about what they had really been working on.

Possibly, keeping quiet in this way was a matter of survival for the Peenemünde scientists. Because for a while, in the British intended, instead of the 'vanished' Dr Kammler, to bring his subordinate Dr Dornberger to trial at the Nuremberg War Crimes Tribunal, because he had been the person responsible for the V-weapons bombardment of London and Antwerp. But after a few months in prison, the British suddenly released Dr Dornberger. What caused this change of heart, after the British, in the course of his inter-rogation, had been irritated by Dr Dornberger's alleged nationalist views and his prophecy of the danger of a Third World War? Probably his specialist knowledge of the German rocket programme was more important for the Allies than the political triumph a which would have been achieved if one of the top brains of the V-weapons programme had been put into the dock before the Tribunal. Did he have to do some special 'deal' before he was released? Even if at the moment there is no definitive answer to this question, it is nevertheless a fact that Dr Dornberger, like the other leading Peenemünde experts, was able to begin a new, brilliant professional career with the victorious powers.

But what would have happened if the general public had known what the men at Germany's leading technology centre were really working on at the end of the war?

If this had been the case, at the very least the Western Allies could not have employed such former Nazi scientists in their service, even if they had wanted to on military grounds. It does not need much imagination to think what would have happened if the press had got wind of something like this. Thus, both the former German scientists and the victorious Allies in both East and West had a common interest in maintaining and promoting the legend of the 'dreamers'. The paradox of this situation can be expressed very well in the following sentence: 'With his rockets, Wernher von Braun was always aiming at the stars … but, as things turned out, he always hit London'.

Logically, somewhere along the line the question arises as to whether German rocket development really only centred around the A-4, and what it was meant to serve, or whether there was something completely different going on. What did all the many Peenemünde specialists and scientists do after the A-4 had gone into production from 1943? Admittedly, they continued to be problems with this new rocket which had to be solved, but are these concerned only individual, narrowly defined areas of its development. If we take this fact to its logical conclusion, the Peenemünde designers must, within only a few months, have become almost 'out of work'. And, in the light of the war situation, this is scarcely credible!.

Why has so little significance been attributed to this question, even up to today? Perhaps because in looking for an answer, the fact would have emerged that, after the normal process of development of the A-4 had been completed, work was going on on quite different things?! After mass production of the A-4 began, the Peenemünde organisation was not reduced in size but, on the contrary, steadily enlarged. A contradiction? Not really, if we consider the alternative question as to whether there were not more important projects for the top people at Peenemünde to work on.

Why has it until now struck nobody as remarkable that in the experimental establishment there is verifiable evidence that propulsion system tests stands existed which were intended for the A-9/A-10, A-11 and A-12 inter-continental rockets and/or satellite carrier systems?[11]

We should recall here the question addressed in the first volume in this series, namely to what extent Peenemünde was active in the field of nuclear research. What happened to Luftwaffe *Generalmajor* Wolfgang von Chamier-Glyczynski who was killed in the Allied air raid on Peenemünde on 17/18 August 1943? Although at the time he was one of the top military personnel at Peenemünde, it seems today as if he had never existed.

Arnold Kramisch, one of the physicists on the 'Manhattan Project' for creation of the American atomic bomb, and also a successful historian and author, thus wrote on 7 August 1994 in a letter to Philip Henshall: "You are right when you say that the whole story about the German rocket and atomic programme has not yet been told. As time goes on, it will probably never be told". But can we not see to it that the true story is in fact told, and the truth thus helped to emerge?[12]

What needs to be done is or to separate the carefully created post-war Peenemünde legend as far as possible from what really went on on the Usedom Peninsula. During the war, Peenemünde was the most advanced weapons development centre in the world, the most important results and products of whose research (at least some of them!) were later able to be used to benefit mankind.

The legend of 'what it was really like at that time in Peenemünde' is nothing other than a protective statement born of the post-war cant of coming to terms with the past and Cold War. As with so many lies and self-deceptions, it was all too comfortable to maintain this particular one even after the end of the Cold War. People were afraid of the questions which would inevitably emerge.

But, looking at the matter rationally, we should not be afraid of the truth. This is shown, for example, in the dictum of American General Schriever, who in the 1950s was in charge of American medium-range and inter-continental rocket development. This well informed American expert even came to the defence of Wernher von

Braun many years after his death in 1977, when he said: 'It didn't worry me, because I understood that a war was going on, and that the military and the scientists over there were doing the same as we were - they were trying to win the war'.[13]

The SS 'Rocket Tsar' takes control

Something that is all too often overlooked is what a great influence the SS had on the production and deployment of the V-weapons.[14] [15]

Very closely connected with this is the legendary rise of *Diplom-Ingenieur* Dr Hans Kammler from Luftwaffe construction functionary to *SS-Obergruppenführer*, and eventually to being the third most powerful man in the Third Reich.

His intelligence, his brutality, and his talent for organisation made him appear in the eyes of Hitler and Himmler to be the right man to be able to make up for lost time and to deploy the decisive weapons at the eleventh hour. Dr Kammler's attention was therefore first turned to Peenemünde and the rocket and missile programme.

Almost all of these ground-to-ground long-range weapons, with the exception of the V-1, were originally developed by the Army under the control of the *Heereswaffenamt* (HWA), which for a long time appeared to be almost all-powerful. Thus, the Army experimental establishment at Peenemünde-Ost was also an Army establishment.

Later, the Luftwaffe experimental establishment Peenemünde-West was added. It carried out work on the V-1 flying bomb and similar projects.

While Reich Armaments Minister Speer tried to gain influence over the HWA through his control of raw materials distribution, by summer 1944 the Army again succeeded in gaining the upper hand.

But the results of the assassination attempt of 20 July 1944 on Adolf Hitler were quickly to bring about radical changes. During the war, the HWA was under the command of the Head of Army Armaments, who was also the Supreme Commander of the Reserve Army. After the assassination attempt of 20 July 1944, the authority came under the control of the *Reichsführer-SS* Heinrich Himmler after he had been nominated by Hitler as the new Supreme Commander of the Reserve Army.

This allowed Himmler without any problem to unload the technical control of Peenemünde-Ost onto his then *Gruppenführer*, Dr Kammler. A short time later, in September 1944, he also obtained tactical command of the two Army rocket groups 'Gruppe Nord' and 'Gruppe Süd'. Dr Kammler now had control over all the rocket projects on Peenemünde, from the future planning of futuristic space developments to the details of the deployment of V-2s against London and Antwerp. He carried out this control with incredible precision, which also brought under his spell those who initially doubted him or were in competition with him, such as Dr Dornberger.

Kammler replaced the influence of Speer (with whom his relations were nevertheless friendly) in many areas by means of a parallel organisation and an administrative system that was almost completely computerised. The 'Hollerith' computer, Germany's IT secret weapon, was one of Kammler's hobby-horses!

Certainly, Kammler did not make the mistake of depriving of their power the irreplaceable old experts of the other Wehrmacht units, but allowed most of them to continue working under his direction.

But there were still many decisive weapons which were outside the control of the men of Hitler's 'Black Order' - and this was now changed.

At the beginning of 1945, the Luftwaffe also had to hand over control of the Fifth Flak Division, and hence control of the V-1, to Dr Kammler.

This development led to some paradoxical situations, such as in Spring 1945, when Army units were launching 'Luftwaffe V-1s' under SS control.

After *Reichsmarschall* Goering had handed over the management of the other rocket programmes of the Third Reich to Dr Kammler on 26 January 1945, Kammler received from Hitler new plenipotentiary powers which, in addition to all anti-aircraft weapons, included control over all long-range weapons (heavy bombers, jet bombers, rockets).

On 13 February 1945, Kammler was nominated for a leading position in the influential 'Board of Trustees for High Frequency Research' in the *Reichspost* Research Establishment, and only a few days previously he had been given control of a weapon which, according to received historical wisdom, did not exist at the time. On 31 January 1945, Hitler had the enterprising 'Rocket Tsar' of the SS appointed as the 'Führer's General Plenipotentiary for *Strahlenwaffen*' (see the following volume 3).

Mind you, this appointment had nothing at all to do with the jet aircraft! The Luftwaffe was still able to retain control of the 'Strahlenflugzeuge' for a while, but here too, the pendulum swung inexorably in favour of the SS. On 27 March 1945, on the basis of an order from the Führer, Kammler also took over this element of war weapons production. He became the General Plenipotentiary for *Strahlenflugzeuge* - the SS had managed to achieve its aim here as well!

In this way, shortly before the end of the war, Himmler's people gained control over all important modern secret weapons in the German armaments programme (perhaps with the exception of some naval weapons) - including the victory weapons.

Even after this happened, Kammler was directly responsible only to Hitler. All the powers assigned within the field of the Armaments Ministry were transferred directly to him. From now on he was able to take advantage of all the command authorities, administrative authorities, Wehrmacht establishments and the apparatus of the NSDAP, which all had to follow his instructions without question.

As late as 3 April 1945, as the Americans were poised to capture Ohrdruf and Nordhausen, Kammler and Hitler had had a conference in Berlin, at the end of which – according to Dr Goebbels – the overwhelming conviction was that Germany's miracle weapons could still win the war. Now, all the hopes of the Führer of the Third Reich rested on Kammler! Amazingly, in almost all reference works about the Third Reich today, the name of Kammler is missing. At the end of the war he disappeared without trace!

Section 1: Hitler's "Push-Button" Warfare: Development and Overview of the German use of *Vergeltungswaffen* against England and the Continent

"Star Wars 1947-style"

What strategic ideas did Hitler and his planners have at the end of 1943? After the initiative had been lost on the Eastern Front, Italy had defected, and the German U-boats had been beaten in the Battle of the Atlantic, the signs that there had been a crucial turning point in the war blazed like the fiery letters of a biblical warning on the wall for all to see. As early as 1941, Hitler had believed that it was no longer possible to win the war by conventional means, and that it was thus necessary to completely re-think strategic planning, because with their demands for an unconditional surrender, the Allies had put an end to any hopes of a negotiated settlement.

The first strategy was for the SS, with the help of foreign volunteers and the newly created SS Panzer and Panzer-grenadier divisions, to hold the enemy as far as possible away from the borders of Germany during the period from 1944 to 1946. Meanwhile, it was planned to push forward mass-production of the new miracle weapons. This included new jet aircraft and rockets which would be far more effective than the later V-1 and V-2 *Vergeltungswaffen*.

These new weapons systems would – so it was hoped – put Germany in the position of being able to begin a new, decisive offensive in 1947.[16] [17]

"All dreamers and visionaries" – weapons deployment plans before deployment of V-weapons began

It is not least partially as a result of Dr Goebbels' war propaganda that the impression persists today that it was the aim and the great hope of the Führer of the Third Reich to bring Britain to its knees in a hail of fire from V-weapons, and thus claw back the fortunes of war which he had lost. Even after the war, these plans were being put forward as fact. But, in actual fact, was this what was being planned in the conditions of 1944?

As Commanding General of LXV *Armeekorps*, *General der Artillerie* Erich Heinemann was responsible for the actual deployment planning for the new *Vergeltungswaffen*. On 6 January 1944, he prepared a long report, only five copies of which were circulated, which set out a precise outline of the planned deployment of V-weapons in 1944.[18]

In this report, among other things, Heinemann writes that 'without taking into account the heavy air raids being carried out by the Allies, it was expected with some degree of certainty that all special projects (*Author's note*: Fi-103, HDP) would be completed by the middle of April 1944. At this point, the greatest average number of the weapons which could be launched per day would be: A-4: about 18 rockets, FZG 76 (Fi-103): about 130 missiles, *Tausendfüssler* (*Author's note*: HDP): about 120 projectiles. This makes a total of 268 missiles, rockets and projectiles being launched every day against the principal target.

In addition, Heinemann said, during the initial period, approximately 100 projectiles could be fired by long range artillery at secondary targets (the county of Kent).

According to the figures at the time, this meant, in the case of the A-4 (payload at the time 750 kilograms) 13.5 tonnes, in the case of the Fi-103 (payload at the time at 830 kilograms) 107.9 tonnes, and in the case of the HDP (payload 30 kilograms) 3.6 tonnes. This gives a maximum figure of 125 tonnes of explosive per day.

What a huge discrepancy between the massive expenditure which had gone on for years and this pitiful result! With hindsight, even these conservative predictions would prove to be too optimistic.

Thus, even before any weapons were deployed, it was already clear that bringing about victory by means of a hail of V-weapons was outside the scope of German capabilities.

General Heinemann's depressing report was not repudiated by any of the political or military leadership of the Third Reich. On the contrary, it has been proved that, even after Heinemann made his situation report, huge reserves of personnel and material continued to be poured in to V-weapons production. There must have been cogent reasons for this!

How long will people try to talk us into believing that the German leadership had really believed that it would be possible to force the Allies to abandon the war by daily launching a maximum of 125 tonnes of explosive?

Nevertheless, even the most sober person observing the effect of the normal V-weapons on the course of the war may be surprised at them actually being deployed - after many delays - from June 1944, although probably more people lost their lives in connection with their development and production, and in preparing them for active deployment than ever there did as a result of being on the receiving end of V-weapons bombardment.

Did treachery and incompetence prevent the weapons being deployed earlier?

Many clues suggest that it would have been possible to deploy the V-1 and the V-2 considerably earlier.

On 1 November 1943, *General* Korten, Chief of the Luftwaffe General Staff, had informed *Generalleutnant* von Axthelm that the A-4 would be ready for combat deployment at the end of 1943, and von Axthelm replied that people had a similar date in mind for the Fi-103 by way of a 'New Year's present'. Then, on 23 December, 1943, a telegram issued by the Wehrmacht Command Staff gave orders to prepare for the first deployment of the weapons against London in the first half of January.

While the weapons launch batteries had been being brought up into France since the autumn of 1943, as a result of an almost incredible sequence of delays, it was not possible to produce the necessary missiles and rockets, although mass-production of both weapons had been under way for a long time. Thus, at the end of November 1943, 2000 Fi-103s in the Volkswagen factory were summarily scrapped as a result of a fault in their aerofoil, and the whole production process was once again brought to a halt. It seems incomprehensible today why, instead of doing this, a programme for repairing the faulty component had not been instituted.

In the case of the A-4, there was similar disarray and confusion. Although an announcement had been made in summer 1943 that it was ready for production, there were repeated alterations to the construction drawings which were justified on the grounds that they had been necessary as a result of observations during tests and in order to rationalise production. This way of going about things made it not only impossible to achieve a high rate of production of the rockets, but also meant that large quantities of components for the A-4 had to be altered or scrapped. Inevitably, this flood of requests for alterations was bound to result in delays.

Thus it was that, on 25 December 1943, *Generaloberst* Jodl wrote bitterly in his diary: "A-4 and FZG-76 : More dragging of heels!" (FZG-76 was one designation for the V-1).[19]

At last it was hoped to be able to launch the fire of retribution at least by the beginning of 1944. In accordance with an order issued by Adolf Hitler, the bombardment of Britain with V-1s was to begin on 15 February 1944 with attacks on London. But this was not to be. When it became clear that it was not possible to meet the new deadline, *General* Milch passed this on news to Hitler in the last days of January. Hitler was furious: "When I was at Rechlin you blew a lot of blue smoke in my eyes, and you're doing it again now!"

In saying this, Hitler showed that - as had happened in previous instances - he felt himself to have been betrayed and led up the garden path concerning weapons development significant enough to have decided the course of the war. What he said referred to the demonstration which is said to have taken place in Rechlin on 3 July 1939, shortly before the outbreak of the war. Hitler's expectation, which had been falsely raised by the Luftwaffe leadership and industry, that the new types of weapons which had been presented to him at Rechlin were already very nearly ready for deployment (many of them never got to be ready even by the end of the war) may have misled him into enforcing his ultimatum to Poland. Staff on the test site later called the 'weapons theatre' at Rechlin by the nickname '*Hermannschlacht*'.

In the second half of 1943, construction had begun on the launch ramps for the Fi-103s on the Channel coast, and from December 1943, Germany was gradually moving up to the Channel coast launching sites the V-1 units which were ready for combat deployment

Agents among foreign workers immediately saw to it that the Allies obtained a relatively precise idea of what the Germans were trying to do, and the responded with a rolling programme of air raids by the RAF and USAAF.

But continuing problems with the mass-production of the Fi-103 were the real reason why the the first attack was deferred until after the beginning of the Allied invasion on 6 June 1944. By then it had been possible to assemble all four Fi-103 flak units in combat readiness in France and Belgium, with about 6000 V-1s standing by to be deployed.

Apart from the time-consuming transport from the interior of Germany, because of the destruction caused to transport routes by air raids, air raids on the Fieseler aircraft works in Kassel prevented the necessary numbers of missiles being ready in the right place to be able to mount devastating attacks on the invasion area. In this case, too, treachery had seen to it that the Allies knew exactly that at this particular time it was mainly the Fieseler works where the Fi-103s were being produced. The scheme, proposed in August 1943, for production of the flying bombs to be moved underground, was only just getting up to speed in the spring of 1944.

The fact remains that, if there had been no treachery, from a tactical and organisational point of view, it would have been possible to deploy the Fi-103 months before the beginning of the Allied invasion, because the EMW A-4, the fundamental design principles of which had already been perfected in 1939, was not yet suitable for active deployment because of continuing (unneccessary?) alterations.

Sabotage may also have played a part in a considerable number of the failures. Dipl. -Ing. Gerhard Frank, at that time *Kommandant* of a V-1 launch ramp, later gave this account of what he discovered: "The thin pneumatic tubes for the compass and rudder installations were punctured in inaccessible places. This caused our projectiles to fall to the ground too early, often in our own lines, or caused them to go in circles or turn back on themselves, which caused severe casualties in our own territory."

General Ernst Remer, to whom we owe this account, asked the question why this widespread 'fault' in the V-1 had not previously been noted during the handover process, which was carried out by German officials, in contrast to the production process which involved inmates of concentration camps.

Were these handover checks only carried out negligently or was it a case of sabotage by political 'opponents' among the officials concerned? In Spring 1945 there were still problems with V-1s dropping too soon, going in circles or turning back on themselves.[20]

German negligence and the business acumen of the government of a neutral country were additional reasons which ensured that the senior circles of the Allies very soon had a good overall idea of Hitler's new weapons. Thus, the essential technical data of the German *Vergeltungswaffen* were known to the British long before the weapons were first deployed. Because the route of the Fi-103 test flights along the Pomeranian coast was always the same, the British relatively quickly managed to listen in on, and decode,[21] [22] the evaluation results transmitted by radio from the German radar observation stations to Peenemünde. Thus, the Allies very soon knew the most important characteristics of the later V-1, such as duration of flight, range and speed.

The parameters of the A-4 had also fallen into Allied hands before the weapons were actually deployed. When, on 13 July 1944, an A-4 test rocket launched from Peenemünde accidentally came down in neutral Sweden, parts of the rocket were immediately sent on to Britain. Previously, the Swedes had actually offered the German secret weapon for sale to the British, a proposal to which Churchill's people were only too willing to agree (German secret agents - with a hearse and dressed as a grave digging team - are said, before this happened, to have vainly attempted to gain access into the restricted area and to recover the components of the rocket). As a result of this clear breach of neutrality, the British obtained basic knowledge concerning the second secret weapon which until then had largely been a mystery to them.

Did the V-weapons do more harm than good to the Third Reich?

Why did the German armaments programme, increasingly suffering during the war from disastrous shortages of raw materials and workforce, expend such gigantic quantities of resources on getting their rockets and missiles to a state of combat readiness? It is a post-war legend that the use of these most valuable resources was primarily to serve to bring about the dreams of some brilliant scientists from Peenemünde. Did these people really succeed in enlisting for their purposes and hoodwinking all the important people from Speer right up to Hitler?

Certainly, the German rocket and missile programme was the most expensive armaments project in history up to that time.[23] [24] [25] Created during the Weimar Republic as a German response to the Versailles *Diktat*, in terms of cost it far exceeded even the American Manhattan Project to produce the American atomic bomb.

According to American calculations, German expenditure on the V-1 project amounted to 200 million dollars. The V-2 project cost even more, at 2,000 million dollars. If you add to this all the costs for personnel, transport and supplies, and all the construction projects in France, you will arrive at a total cost of 3 billion dollars for the two weapons programmes. On the basis of these assumed overall costs and taking into account that 20,000 V-1s and

3,000 V-2s were actually launched, every successful V-1 launch cost 50,000 dollars and every successful V-2 launch cost 500,000 dollars.

The only thing which this expenditure succeeded in achieving by the end of the war was in delivering somewhat more than 20,000 tonnes of conventional explosive on enemy targets. Seen in itself, this is beyond all doubt a miserable result! Therefore, unavoidably, it raises questions about what the real purpose of this programme was.

Which brings us to another series of puzzles: Why did Reich Armaments Minister Albert Speer use more than half the largest underground factory in Germany at Nordhausen for rocket production, when the Army, the Luftwaffe and the Navy were desperately crying out for petrol and oil, and the Allied bombers were hammering production of German fighters, electric motors, rubber and nitrogen by day and night? In these areas of production there were supply bottlenecks which, if they were not overcome, would sooner or later cause the German war economy to collapse.

Even at first glance it is notable that the V-1 programme, which was much more interesting from a war economy point of view, only received a fraction of the resources allocated to rocket development. And the V-1 would have been a weapon which it would have been possible to put into mass production, in contrast to the V-2.

The production of each V-1 cost 3,500 *Reichsmarks* as opposed to an expenditure of 240,000 *Reichsmarks* for a V-2. In terms of man-hours, production of a V-1 took 350 hours as against 60,000 man-hours for a V-2.

From 1943, everything had to serve the rocket project! It was only when the construction of the Raketenbau-Mittelwerk GmbH in Nordhausen was completed that work began on tooling up a jet engine factory and building an underground refinery in the same complex of tunnels. Why had the Germans, usually so hard headed when it came to calculations, turned the logical order of urgency completely on its head in this way?

Other important weapons programmes of the Third Reich also suffered as a result of the insatiable hunger of the V-1 programme, and above all the V-2 programme, for special materials, specialists and production capacity.

Thus, there are many indications that the German V-2 rocket project in particular very considerably affected Luftwaffe aircraft production. It is estimated that 20 fighter aircraft could have been built with the resources it took to build only one V-2. But would there have been enough fuel for these additional aircraft - quite apart from the necessary pilots? Very probably not, because from 1944 the Luftwaffe already did not have enough trained pilots and fuel for the aircraft it actually had.

It is also repeatedly insisted that the V-weapons had delayed Germany's jet fighters. But today, no one contests the extent to which the jet aircraft programme of the Luftwaffe, which could have decided the course of the war, suffered through competition with the V-weapons. It is the greatest tragedy in the history of German aviation that here a combination of different influences created an unnecessary delay of several years. The result of this was that the Me-262 jet fighter, the basic design of which was completed in 1939, only gradually began to come into service from summer 1944. A lost opportunity! But the V-weapons were not the cause of this delay, which is still the subject of protracted discussion today. The Me-262 and Ar-234 jet aircraft were given greater priority than the V-weapons!

Other modern developments in German armaments technology, however, did suffer as a result of the com-petition from Peenemünde. Military technology at the time needed above all electrical equipment. From summer 1943, the shortage of this equipment caused by the rocket programme did seriously hinder the necessary programmes for equipping submarines and radar installations.

It was not only the construction and equipment of the V-weapons which were pushed through at the expense of other developments, but it was also only with great difficulty that enough 'fuel' could be produced for them. Here this figures speak in favour of the V-1. To achieve the same range, the Fieseler works required 435 kilograms of fuel for a V-1, as opposed to 10,300 kilograms for a V-2.

The fact that the rockets' oxygen consumption would create an insuperable shortage in terms of production and supply was a fact of which all those responsible were well aware even before the weapons were first used.

But the massive fuel requirements of the V-1 and V-2 also created a bottleneck in supplying this material. Other projects which suffered as a result included the Me-163 rocket fighter and the new Walther U-boats. As a result of priority in fuel deliveries being assigned to the Fi-103, many Me-163s had to remain unused on the ground of their airfields, while the Walther turbine-powered U-Boats might have gone into operational service if there had been no V-1s and V-2s!

Even foodstuffs production had to make sacrifices, because a large proportion of the potato harvest was required for the production of alcohol, one of the second fuel elements of Wernher von Braun's A-4.

It will therefore be clear that principally the rocket pro-gramme, and to a lesser extent the V-1 programme, repre-sented a considerable burden on German armaments.

When Allied interrogation officers asked Albert Speer in May 1945 whether he thought that the V-weapons pro-gramme had done more damage to the British economy or to the German economy, he is said to have replied: "It did more damage to the German economy". He said that the V-weapons programme was the greatest mistake made during his period in office!

In recent years, therefore, evidently as a result of consid-erations like these, the opinion has been expressed that the V-weapons had hastened Germany's defeat as a result of this ill-advised expenditure of valuable resources. But is this actually true?

V for Vergeltung: The propaganda value of the missiles and rocket weapons

Did the V-weapons save the Third Reich from the collapse of German morale in summer 1944?

By the middle of 1944 it was finally clear to the German soldiers of all ranks, and also to the civilians on the home front, that the 'Total War', with all that it involved, had turned against the Third Reich, and that Germany was in the process of losing the war. A secret situation report pre-pared by the SD stated in March 1944 that German war morale had sunk to its lowest level since the war began.[26]

The much-promised miracle and victory weapons had indeed repeatedly been announced by the leading politi-cians in the Third Reich, but had never materialised. This dilemma of lack of credibility was now to be resolved by the V-1 and V-2. After the first V-1 had been launched against London on 16 June 1944, and when, on 8 September 1944, the V-2 was also launched, the vague indication that more victory weapons were to follow was enough to keep the German public hard at it until the end of the war.

All the media tricks available at the time were employed in the service of moral rearmament. Thus, the whole world stood witness when the war reporter Dr Karl Holzamer transmitted on the radio the thundering and rattling of the Argus exhausts of the Fi-103 as it took off against London. Dr Holzamer had travelled with his radio transmission van directly to the launch ramps in France to capture a realistic idea of the atmosphere which prevailed in the nightly operations against 'Target 42', and to record them on tape.[27]

The influence of the rockets and missiles on German morale and general determination to stick it out cannot be overestimated.

But this last-minute 'gift from heaven' for propaganda was at first not recognised as such by the Reich Propaganda Minister, Dr Goebbels.[28][29] Goebbels wanted to have Otto Kriegk, a reporter on the *Berliner Nachtausgabe*, shot, because on 21 June 1944 he had prematurely published over-optimistic reports about the effects and the deployment of the Fi-103 against Britain. He had begun the leading article for his newspaper with the sentence: "The day for which 80 million Germans have been desperately longing is here". Some people made bets that the war would be over in three, or four, or eight days. Goebbels was furious because he knew that the actual victory weapons had not yet been deployed.

But the report about the deployment of the flying bomb acquired, among the German public, a momentum of its own which could not be stopped. Goebbels now suddenly recognised the propaganda value of the new weapon. What was needed was to find a suitable framework in which to publicise the stories. On the suggestion of the then chief commentator Schwarz van Berk, the name which was currently used for the Fi-103 - *Höllenhund* (Hell Hound) - was discarded in favour of the designation of V-weapon. This served the purpose of transforming the wild optimism which had been created by the launch of the Fi-103 into an active will to resist and to stick it out. This feeling could then be built on - thus, on 24 July 1944, Goebbels issued an official communique in which he created the concept for 'Vergeltungswaffe 1', at the same time giving the impression that other weapons would follow.

This political effect then still retained its force when the conventional V-1 and V-2 - initially thought by the general public to be victory weapons - proved not to be.

The leaders of the Third Reich had a very different agenda. Thus, in the periodical *Das Reich* of 5th December, 1943, Schwarz van Berk wrote: "With our concept of *Vergeltung*, we are not thinking of a triumph of arms, and not even of a criminal court, for which today our whole *Volk* is longing. What we are trying to do is to bring to an end this unbridled mass murder by one extreme, very drastic blow. Mankind is now not far from the point in which they will be able to blow half the earth to smithereens".

This introduces the concept of the victory weapon. The later conventional V-1 and V-2 attacks were clearly not what the article was talking about here.

It was not only on the German public that the new weapons made an impression. Among the countries at war with Germany and in the neutral states as well, a completely new dimension of terror was created, and a sense of powerlessness, of not being able to do anything to stop the weapons despite considerable material superiority.

Thus, on 24 September 1944, Goebbels wrote enthusiastically in his diary about the results of his propaganda campaign: "Our rocket bombs have become the object of sensational reporting and wild rumours throughout the world." Every attempt was made to reinforce these effects, with the *SS-Standarte Kurt Eggers* firing off at Britain V-1s containing thousands of airmail letters and postcards from British prisoners of war. These were carried in capsules in the fuselage of the bomb, and when it exploded were scattered on the ground over a wide radius.

And so, on Christmas Eve 1944, there came about what is probably the most remarkable Christmas post operation there has ever been.[30] On that day, 28 Heinkel He-111 bombers of KG53 had launched 31 V-1s against Manchester. Some of the flying bombs were also carrying special airmail. These carried the inscription v-1 POW Post, and were printed field postcards written by wounded British prisoners of war whose homes were in the region of Manchester. In their Christmas greetings, they said that they were being treated well as prisoners, and that, at heart, the Germans were 'nice people'. The British authorities gave orders that the population had to hand over to the police all the letters that were found.

The few remaining letters and airmail from the SS Christmas post operation and other flying bomb operations which are still in the possession of individuals today fetch very high prices at auctions as 'V-1 post'.

Did the conventional V-1s and V-2s have any effect on the course of the war?

After *Heeresgruppe* Afrika had capitulated, and the last German offensive had been stopped at Kursk in July 1943, the armies of the Third Reich were everywhere in retreat. The overwhelming Allied superiority on land, at sea, and in the air made any further German attempt at resistance meaningless. When, from 6 June 1944, the Allied invasion of Normandy had also been successful, the end of the Third Reich seemed to be near. The Allies calculated in all seriousness that the war would be over by Christmas 1944.[31] Senior German military personnel who were in contact with the 20 July resistance group shared this opinion, and said that the war would be 'all up' in September.[32] But then it happened! Eight days after the beginning of the invasion, the first four V-1s exploded in the British capital. After a three-day pause, the bombardment began in earnest. 300 flying robot bombs were launched within 24 hours. The attacks which now followed using flying bombs of the Fieseler Fi-103 type, and, after September 1944, also ballistic rockets of the V-2 type, had an almost unbelievable effect on the further operations and war plans of the Allies, although even today this is something which is not readily mentioned publicly! Instead of that, the serious assertion is made that the V-1s and V-2s had only been of incidental significance.

The use of the Fi-103s and A-4s made the costly air raids by propeller-driven German bomber aircraft against heavily defended targets such as London superfluous. In this way, the lives of many young and inexperienced air-crew were saved. Thus, for example, before the V-weapons were brought into operation, on 18/19 April 1944, 125 German aircraft took off for night bombing raids on London. 13 aircraft were shot down by the British. The unmanned missiles and rockets brought these senseless sacrifices to an end.

There is no dispute that by 29 March, 1945, 10,492 Fi-103s had been launched against targets in southern Britain and London. Over 3,000 crashed immediately after take-off because of technical failure. Of the remaining 7,488, 1,847 were shot down by British fighter aircraft, 1,878 by anti-aircraft fire, and 232 were brought down by barrage balloons. 2,419 fell on London, the rest on southern Britain. From the end of 1944, V-1s were also being fired against the cities of Antwerp (8,696) and Liege (3,141).

Between 8 September 1944 and 27 March 1945, according to the accepted view today, 1,403 rockets were launched against London and southern Britain, of which 1,054 hit their targets. But it is very likely that for decades V-2 impacts in Britain were glossed over, because, according to the publication of new secret reports, in actual fact 1,190 rockets from Peenemünde hit targets in Britain. 2,050 A-4s were launched against Antwerp, Brussels and Liege. One out of five of the rockets was lost because of technical failure or sabotage.

Until now it had been assumed that the total casualties inflicted on the British population by V-weapons were 8,938 dead and 24,234 injured. In Belgium, 6,448 people were killed and 22,524 injured.

These figures for casualties caused by V-weapons, which have been put forward for decades, must now be brought into question after new papers and documents have emerged! Thus, on 17 January 1994, the British newspaper *The Times* reported the discovery of an unpublished manuscript by the author H. E. Bates which had been the victim of censorship for 50 years, because Bates had insisted in telling the truth about the extent of civilian casualties.

The latest sources also set the actual casualties caused by V-1s in Britain as 10,000 dead and 1.1 million houses destroyed, and 2,724 dead and 6,000 injured by V-2 impacts.[33]

Thus, the macabre 'tally of success' of the entire V-weapons campaign amounted to as many casualties in Britain as the Western allies achieved in one single larger night bombing raid in 1944 against the German Reich.[34] But since none of these raids could affect the outcome of the war, the counter-question is also automatically raised as to whether the V-weapons had any tangible effect anyway.

Thus, the opinion most expressed today is that the German *Vergeltungswaffen*, although they killed and injured thousands of civilians and soldiers, had no effect on the course of the war.

But this effect began even before the V-weapons were used. The increasing threat that new German *Vergeltungswaffen* might be used against Britain was in itself enough to cause the British finally to abandon and scrap two new planned battleships, the *Lion* and the *Temeraire*, the construction of which had been temporarily suspended since 1941. The steel from the ships was instead be used to build 100,000 new air-raid shelters.

Between December 1943 and June 1944 the American and British air forces had flown 25,150 missions against suspected V-1 positions and support bases, dropping 36,200 tons of bombs. This was the greatest bomb load which had ever been dropped on a single enemy target up to that time. However, it is doubtful whether these planned air raids, which also had to be carried out at the cost of heavy casualties, delayed the V-1 bombardments by more than just a few days. Although the results had to be regarded as unsatisfactory, the bombardment of the suspected launch ramps was continued with increased vigour. If, in June 1944, the Royal Air Force dropped 28 per cent of its total bombload on German V-weapons bases, in July this percentage was 42 per cent. In total, in June, July and August, more than 100,000 tons of bombs were dropped by British and American aircraft on V-weapons positions. Eventually, they absorbed up to half of the total quantity of Allied bombs dropped, and in this way relieved the load on the German soldiers at the front and the civilians in the severely tested towns and cities in the Reich. The British had even tried their new 'Tallboy' bombs, weighing 5500 kilograms, against the rocket bunkers, and the Americans launched remote-controlled B17 bombers, filled with 9000 kilograms of explosive, against the launch ramps.

The total effect of all these gigantic efforts, which went under the codename 'Crossbow', was that the number of flying bombs falling on Britain reduced from 3004 to 2667 per month.

Adolf Hitler had assigned London as the single target of the summer 1944 V-weapons offensive. Fortunately for the Allied troops, apart from one single brief episode, the embarkation ports for Allied troops on the British coast remained untouched by flying bombs.

Thus London had to bear the full weight of the German V-weapons offensive. Within the first two weeks of the offensive, 200,000 houses had been damaged and 1,600 people killed. On 16 June Winston Churchill called together his War Cabinet to a very serious meeting. At this meeting it was decided not to abandon the battle in Normandy. It was agreed that London had to bear its own fate, while all efforts were to be made to overcome this danger.[35] Does this mean that because of the V-1, at least some consideration was given to halting the invasion?

During the V-1 offensive, the morale of Londoners steadily deteriorated. The robot-like nature of the flying bomb and the completely unpredictable way in which it could strike at any time, by day or night, and in any weather, without anything being able to stop it, wore down their nerves. The V-1 affected everyone - right up to the Allied Supreme Commander Dwight D Eisenhower. Thus, for example, on 21 June 1944 he wrote to his wife that he had not even been able to write two long letters because he and his stenographers had had to take refuge in the air-raid shelter 19 times that day. By the middle of August, 1.45 million people had left London to escape the V-1 bombs. This was a greater number of people than in the German air raids of the 'Blitz' in 1940. Of these people, however, only 275,000 had been officially evacuated. This mass flight gave the British authorities great cause for concern. There was the threat that public order would break down, and cases of looting became more and more frequent. The productivity of the city fell by 25 per cent. By September, for example, in all the city buses there was not one single window glass left intact.

The morale of the soldiers on the Normandy front was also affected by the bombardment at home.[36] [37] [38] [39]

Evidently, the deployment of the robot-like Fi-103 had succeeded in spreading panic and terror among the British civilian population. The air raids carried out by the German Luftwaffe or in 1940/41 had not even remotely come near to achieving this! Thus, on 26 June 1944, the British Home Secretary Herbert Morrison stated that up to that time 691,000 houses had been affected by German V-weapons. He stated that there was every indication of a threat of mass panic. He continued: "I am afraid that as with continued bombing the areas which have been totally destroyed increase, the anger of the public is also growing. Whether this anger is directed entirely against the enemy seems questionable, after we have failed to prevent this destruction even with our air superiority and military strength".

Would there have been a threat of public disorder and insurrection in Britain if the Germans had succeeded in continuing the bombardment with conventional V-1 flying bombs at a similar rate? Such a scenario had to be prevented at any price. Were people prepared even to prolong the war in order to achieve this?

In any event, the Allied efforts to stop the German V-weapons were overwhelming. Finally, in summer 1944, up to 50 per cent of the total Allied tonnage of bombs was being dropped almost without effect on suspected V-weapons positions. All British fighter aircraft, apart from the Second Tactical Command, were withdrawn from the Continent and transferred back to the home front in order to assist in defence against the V-1s.

A gigantic aerial defence belt, the so-called Diver Belt, was set up. Eventually, it comprised up to 1500 anti-aircraft guns and 200 radar positions which were manned by 250,000 men and women.

Eventually, the progress of the battles in Normandy came to the assistance of the British. Shortly after the Fi-103 was first deployed, with the beginning of the invasion, a large part of the Channel coast had fallen into Allied hands. Thus it was only possible to launch the V-1s from a narrow sector which still remained in German hands. And so the British aerial defences could concentrate their anti-aircraft guns and barrage balloons within a narrow approach route. This made anti-aircraft defences considerably easier! But it was nevertheless not possible to provide effective defence for the British capital against the devastation caused by the Fi-103, because at least some of the robot aircraft, which attacked at all times of the day and night and in all kinds of weather, always got through to their target.

On 23 August 1944, a V-1 struck East Barnet, a northerly suburb of London, causing the highest number of casualties which had been sustained up to that date, with 211 dead and several hundred injured.

In their despair at not being able to do anything against this weapon, the British were so bitter that as early as 6 July 1944, Churchill gave orders to prepare to use poison gas against German cities by way of retaliation. 32,000 tonnes of phosgene and mustard gas were to be dropped by the RAF and USAAF over the Reich and 2500 square kilometres laid waste. German agents informed their spymasters in the RSHA (*Reichssicherheitshauptamt*) of these British plans, but they were only 'officially released' into the public domain in 1986.

Later in Autumn 1944, the plans for using poison gas were withdrawn after objections by British and American military personnel (see relevant chapter in Volume 1). And in any event, in the meantime, after the German launch bases in France had been lost, the main phase of the V-1 attacks had already come to an end.

The V-1 bombardment of London had thus only by a whisker missed unleashing a new dimension of terror and counter terror - general gas warfare in Europe.

The Allies also considered other responses to the German V-weapons offensive. Thus the Allied plan 'Vengeance' (literal counterpart to the German *Vergeltung*) was developed as a counterpart to the German V-weapons offensive. It comprised various different plans.[40] [41]

As early as summer 1944, Churchill had considered ordering Bomber Command to reduce to ashes 100 German small towns by way of retaliation.

This then developed into the plan named 'Thunderclap'. Four alternatives were considered. Variant 1 involved terrorising the whole of Germany for days on end by the use of all available fighter aircraft, fighter-bombers and bomber aircraft to cripple any rail or road traffic. Variant 2 proposed ceaseless attacks on all civilian targets including hospitals and kindergartens, while Variant 3 took up Churchill's plan to annihilate a few dozen small German towns. A fourth variant was proposed, which involved once again turning heavily-bombed Berlin into a landscape of ruins in a four days' round-the-clock bombardment, or concentrating the entire bomber force on a single target which until then had not been hit by air raids.

After such annihilation raids, the German population were to be informed by leaflets that these attacks were being carried out expressly as retaliation for the bombardment by V-weapons. After initially agreeing to such punitive actions, however, the American members of the 'Crossbow' committee, on the instructions of General Eisenhower, vetoed all British plans for 'Thunderclap'. Did people want to avoid a direct connection being made between the V-weapons attacks and Allied vengeance? Were they afraid that even worse German vengeance weapons might be used?

Nevertheless, tragically, one later indirect result of the V-weapons offensive was that Allied air warfare against Germany intensified. Instead of Allied 'vengeance raids', now 'annihilation raids' were being carried out:

The first plan from summer 1944, an offensive against the German transport system, was carried out in February 1945 ('Operation Clarion') and made a significant contribution to the later German collapse.

Fortunately, the second plan, an unrelenting attack on hospitals and kindergartens, was not implemented, but the plan to annihilate a few dozen German small towns by air raids was actually carried out just before the end of the war.

It is true that plans for four days of round-the-clock annihilation bombing against Berlin were not implemented, but the plan to concentrate the entire strength of the American and British bomber forces on one single target which had not yet been bombed, was carried out scandalously in February 1945 when the baroque city of Dresden in Saxony was devastated in a firestorm.

This terror raid would have just missed by a whisker unleashing the use of gas just before the end of the war, this time, it is true, by the Germans. And this action then would probably have involved for the first time striking targets on the other side of the Atlantic (see following volume).

Many of the former Thunderclap measures were, remarkably, only implemented in the spring of 1945, when the V-weapons bombardment, and thus any possibility of German retaliation against Britain, had already been considerably reduced. However, the question must be asked whether this intensification of Allied aerial warfare could have been avoided if, in summer 1944, the Fi-103 had not been principally used as a terror weapon against London. Might there not, instead of this malicious use of the weapon, have been the opportunity to use the flying bombs exclusively against military targets?

The Allies found with relief that almost no V-1 missiles had been launched against their invasion ports. Was this clear evidence that the supply ports had been spared one of the arguments for pressing on with the Normandy invasion at the meeting of the War Cabinet in London on 16 June 1944? The fact that such considerations had been deliberated on the German side was reported by the Japanese naval attaché in Berlin. In this report, picked up by Ultra, the opinion was expressed that if the flying bombs were not deployed against the Allied invasion ports, the Normandy invasion could not be repulsed. On 5 July, the Japanese Ambassador in occupied France reported in another message picked up by Ultra, that Otto Abetz, the military commander of France, had admitted that the flying bombs would have no effect on the military situation on the Normandy front. On 22 July 1944 came the final relief, when the Japanese naval attaché reported to his government in another report that members of the Luftwaffe had told him that it was not possible to use V-1 against the Allied landings.

The reason for this could have been that the earlier versions of the V-1 still only had a very short operational range. And so they could only have reached the main Allied ports if they had been a launched from the Cotentin peninsula in Normandy. But the launch bases which had been built there were already for the most part in the immediate area of the front. Attempts carried out almost secretly by *Oberst* Wachtel, commanding the V-1 launch units, to mount 'chance' strikes with V-1s against the Allied port of Southampton, against Hitler's orders, were expressly forbidden.

Was a great opportunity missed here? Yes – and this is confirmed by the then Supreme Commander of the Allied invasion forces, General Dwight D Eisenhower, who, as a specialist, might be expected to have a considered judgment about the use of the V-weapons. In his memoirs, *Crusade in Europe*, which were published after the war, he writes: "It can be assumed that our invasion in Europe might have proved to be extremely difficult, and perhaps even impossible, if the Germans had succeeded in producing these new weapons six months earlier. I am convinced that Operation 'Overlord' would have failed if the enemy had succeeded in using these weapons over a period of six months. Particularly if they had made the area of Portsmouth and Southampton one of their principal targets".

Eisenhower, who, in putting forward these opinions, was no doubt able to refer to the post-war evaluations of the results of the later German V-1 and V-2 offensive against the main Allied port of Antwerp, thus stated unequivocally that the the Normandy invasion could only have been saved if the deployment of the weapons had been delayed by six months and if – once the weapons were used – they had then not been directed at the wrong target.

Did other influences also play a part? When from August 1944 the Arado Ar-234 jet reconnaissance aircraft, which was almost invulnerable to the aerial defence measures of the period, came into service over the Western Front, *Luftflotte 3* tried, under threat of court-martial, to prevent the Ar-234 carrying out photo-reconnaissance flights over

London. As a result of this ban, which remained in force until the beginning of September, there was not only a lack of any means of correcting accuracy by monitoring impacts in the target area, but also Hitler and the Wehrmacht Staff were kept in the dark about the failure of the V-1 offensive to 'take out' London. If this had not been the case, in view of the increasingly desperate defensive fighting on the invasion front, would the target of the V-1s have been changed to the Allied bridgehead in France and the invasion ports, as Marshals von Rundstedt and Rommel had been vigorously demanding since June?

On 8 September 1944, the first V-2 hit London!

Significant Allied sources also considered that the later use of V-2 rockets could have had a potentially decisive effect on the course of the war. The post-war 'United States Strategic Bombing Survey' contains the following statement: "If the Germans had succeeded in carrying out their offensive with the V-2 one year earlier and with 10 times as many projectiles, events could have taken a very different course".

In heavily built-up areas of London, a single V-2 rocket could destroy or damage 600 houses. In doing so, it was not the blast or the effect of the explosive which was the decisive factor, but the massive shaking of the earth. The impact momentum of a V-2 was the same as if 50 locomotives each weighing 100 tons had struck each other simultaneously at a speed of 100 kilometres per hour. And because it was not possible to give any warning of the V-2, their impacts led to great indirect economic losses in the form of lost working hours and of workers not turning up at their places of work. According to British reports, these effects involving interruptions to production and adverse effects on working discipline in London were more serious than the destructive effect of the explosive charge in Hitler's second V-weapon.

And it was precisely this weapon which was to have a diabolical effect on the further course of the Second World War.

On 7 September 1944, the first phase of the 'battle of London' had come to an end with the loss of the German V-1 launch bases in France to the advancing Allied troops. Only one day later, however, a new chapter in the history of Hitler's 'push-button warfare' began with the launch of the V-2 rockets against London from Dutch bases in the vicinity of the Hague.

Witnesses to the rocket impacts in Britain described "an explosion which sounded like a clap of thunder, which was immediately followed by the sound of a heavy body rushing through the air". The inhabitants of London could not explain these explosions, because neither German aircraft nor V-1s had been seen beforehand. But remarkably, neither the British Government nor the leadership of the Third Reich gave any explanation in the subsequent two months as to the cause of these explosions which increasingly shook southern Britain.

While the motives for German silence on this count appear puzzling (why had Goebbels' Propaganda Ministry missed this chance?), the British reasons for keeping quiet were obvious. The authorities were afraid that the population of the industrial cities within range of the V-2s would be gripped by panic. The British had only just succeeded, with the reduction in the number of V-1 launches since the beginning of September, in halting the flight of the population from London, which until then had been uncontrollable. What kind of reactions might be expected if now a weapon was being used which hit the target completely by surprise before any warning whatsoever could be given?

The British Government therefore decided to pass off the V-2 impacts as 'explosions of gas mains'.

There was no defence whatever against the V-2 weapon! In bitterness at this fact, it was even proposed that General Eisenhower should make a report in person to the British Parliament about what measures were planned for defence against the V-2.

Although initially it was only possible to launch individual V-2 rockets on London, these few rockets had an effect on the course of the war which bore no relation to their military significance or to the casualties which they caused. Shortly after the first two rockets had exploded in London, the deputy chief of the British General Staff sent a delegation to Field-Marshal Montgomery's headquarters. This delegation urged Montgomery to capture as quickly as possible the launch sites of these rockets in the Antwerp-Utrecht-Rotterdam area.

At that time, the military situation on the Western Front was such that supplies did not allow the Allied troops to advance on a broad front, but were only sufficient to allow for one wing of their armies to advance. Field Marshal Montgomery originally wanted to capture a bridge over the Rhine and from there to advance across the North German plain into the area of the Ruhr.

To enable him to carry out this advance, Montgomery had received the lion's share of Allied supplies, and most of the leading German commanders confirmed after the war that at the time an advance of this kind would have led to the military collapse of the Third Reich, because it allowed the Germans no time to construct a strong defensive position. But Montgomery had to abandon this uniquely favourable opportunity.[42]

Under political pressure because of the V-2 rockets, he had to change his plan to such an extent that he chose the - for him - unfavourable route through Arnhem. Nevertheless, on 17 September, the Allies began Operation 'Market Garden'. In conjunction with a massive land offensive, a gigantic airborne operation involving 35,000 men was to decide the course of the war and bring an end to the V-2 attacks.

Thus, on 17 September 1944, there began the famous battle for the bridge at Arnhem, a battle which failed because of bad weather, insufficient planning, poor equipment, shortage of aircraft, and above all because of the stubborn German resistance. The parachutists had disastrously been dropped right in the midst of two SS Panzer divisions!

After this battle, the Allied airborne troops had lost as many men as the German parachutists had after their costly operation to take Crete in Spring 1941. After Arnhem, Allied airborne landings became impossible until the spring of 1945.

But the development which Hitler had originally expected at the end of June 1944 had not yet occurred. The Allies had not been diverted into undertaking a 'second invasion' in the Dieppe area to stop the flying bomb offensive. Such an operation was impossible for them at the time!

But in September 1944, when - in contrast to June 1944 - the military resources were available for a further offensive advance on the part of the Allies, the desire to take out the V-weapons bases was the basis for a mistaken choice of target, and necessarily led to the offensive force being defeated.

The German defensive victory at Arnhem led to a stabilisation of the Western Front which persisted until February 1945, and which was itself an indirect consequence of the deployment of V-2s. Only on 17 April 1945 were the Allies finally to take Arnhem.

The direct effects of the battle for Arnhem on the V-2 offensive were only slight. On the very first day of the battle, the German V-2 batteries were very hastily withdrawn so as not to be cut off by the Allied airborne troops.

Thus, Kammler's rocket troops could for a few days still reach the cities of Ipswich and Norwich with V-2s launched from south-western Frisia.

When, soon after this, the front at Arnhem had stabilised, the rocket units moved back on the morning of 25 September 1944 to their old positions near Wassenaar. On the same afternoon, Dr Kammler's people resumed their V-2 launches against London.

But now something was to come to the assistance of the inhabitants of southern Britain which would free them from a great part of their 'rocket problem'. The Germans suddenly abandoned their previous policy of concentrating their use of V-weapons on the annihilation of London, and began to launch more and more of their rockets (and missiles) at targets in Belgium.

The problem of extended supply lines was continuing to produce bottlenecks in the supply of ammunition and fuel, which caused a certain bitterness between the Allies. One staff officer of the First US Army complained, for example, that the dash through France had been hampered because the British had got all of the fuel to enable them to be in a position to capture the V-1 bases. Here, too, the deployment of V-weapons had a detrimental effect on the Allied advance in the West.

The great port of Antwerp in Belgium was the solution to all the Allied concerns about supplies. Antwerp was captured as early as 14 September 1944, but was only able to become operational as a port on 26 November 1944. On 7 November 1944, the first V-2 hit the city, followed by the first V-1 on 11 November. This occurred 10 days before Hitler gave orders for the official offensive against the port.

From then onwards until March 1945, the Germans kept Antwerp under constant bombardment by V-weapons. It has been established that the greater Antwerp area was hit by 4248 V-1s and 1712 V-2s. The port was severely tested by this bombardment!

Because of the shorter range and as a result of the increased use of beam directional guidance systems, the accuracy of the V-2s targeted on Antwerp was considerably greater than that of the rockets launched against London.

On 9 January 1945, a single V-2 hit the Rex cinema in Antwerp and caused a terrifying death toll. The devastating direct hit left 567 people dead and 291 severely injured, among them 490 British soldiers. Material damage caused by the weapons was also severe. Thus, on 19 January 1945, a V-weapon scored a direct hit on a fuel depot in the port of Antwerp. Despite desperate attempts to extinguish the blaze, 3,557 tons of fuel were lost in the fire. By the end of the war, 90 percent of the glass in all windows around the port was shattered, and 150 ships in the harbour had been sunk or damaged.

Eventually the city was known to the American soldiers only as 'the city of sudden death'. By means of the bombardment by V-weapons, the Germans finally succeeded in reducing the unloading capacity of Antwerp to less than 25 per cent of its total capacity.

In addition, railway and river traffic were severely impeded, because railway lines, bridges and railway wagons were destroyed by rockets and flying bombs. In Antwerp, too, the civilian population fled *en masse* from the city, as had happened in London during the summer of 1944.

US Air Force General Spaatz then also said after the war that as a result of the rocket bombardment, Antwerp had become so worthless to the Allies that other solutions had to be sought.[43]

A later V-weapons target was the city of Liege, which was an important supply, railway and communications centre for the US Army. By bombarding Liege, Kammler was trying to relieve the fighting front because of the winter battle in the Ardennes. Here, too, the damage was as extensive as it was in Antwerp. Thus, on 10 January 1945, a V-2 scored a direct hit on a fuel depot in Liege, causing 1,500 tons of fuel to be lost in the fire.

From December 1944 to March 1945, practically every Allied 90-millimetre anti-aircraft gun was sent to Antwerp to assist in defence against the V-1s. In the Mediterranean and in the Pacific an acute shortage of anti-aircraft ammunition was created because such great quantities had to be diverted to Antwerp.

As before, there continued to be no defence against the V-2!

On the other hand, the third long-range rocket of the 'Rheinbote' type had no measurable military success.[44] But this was not the fault of the weapon itself. Between 24 December 1944 and 15 January 1945, around 220 of these four-stage rockets were launched from Nunspeed in Holland at Antwerp. Despite technically successful launches, not a single rocket hit the planned target area!

What was the reason for this? Although even before the 'Rheinbote' rocket was first used, 'Testing Station Z' had reported that its range (at 65 degrees elevation) was 230km, HAA(mot) 709 had only been informed of this after it had been launching the weapon against Antwerp. Their incorrect firing tables were still based on a range of 160km! As a result, all 'Rheinbote' long-range rockets landed ineffectually on open terrain in the region of Ghent. Were carelessness and chaos to blame, or did sabotage play its part in this case, too?

The German V-weapons offensive can be divided into roughly two phases:

The first phase was the *Vergeltungseinsatz* (retaliation/ vengeance operation), as terror weapons were fired on London. This lasted from June 1944 to September 1944 when, because of the Allied airborne landings at Arnhem, the V-2 batteries had to temporarily discontinue their bombardment of Britain.

Meanwhile, there were apparently also seemingly pointless individual launches of V-2s against many French and Belgian towns and cities.

The second phase involved a combination of rocket and flying bomb launches against Allied supply locations on the Continent and also against various cities in Britain.

Although, in terms of numbers, the bombardment of London was no longer comparable to that of summer 1944, it continued to be dangerous. Thus, on 25 November 1944, the impact of a single V-2 on a Woolworths shop in Deptford near London killed 160 people. In view of the reduction of the threat in numerical terms, and the fact that the dreaded third V-weapon with even greater destructive effect had not materialised, in the last months of the war the people in London and south-eastern Britain displayed a strange mixture of hope resulting from the advance of the Allied troops on all fronts and fear of the dreaded rocket with which, however, they had become familiar in the meantime.

The V-weapons had lost the 'battle for the morale' of the British population. But it was clear to the Allies that the suffering of Britain and Belgium would not be over until their armed forces on the ground had captured all the launch sites. Until the very end, the RAF had tried to destroy the launching sites in Holland by means of carpet bombing and targeted fighter-bomber attacks. But, as had happened previously in France, instead of the V-weapons batteries, the main casualties of the air raids were the surrounding houses and cities, and the attacks on the Dutch transport system, which had never caused any great interruption to supplies for the V-weapons, were, in the spring of 1945, mainly to blame for the developing risk of famine among the Dutch civilian population.

Until the end, Germany's V-weapons units were able, seemingly unhindered and with full supplies of ammunition, to launch their missiles and rockets against Allied targets. The conclusion can be drawn from this that the V-1, V-2 and 'Rheinbote' were not hit while they were in action. Their operational deployment only came to an end at the end of March 1945, when *SS-Obergruppenführer* Dr Kammler had to withdraw his units because of the Allied breakthrough on the Rhine front.

Therefore, the question remains as to what, in this first attempt at 'push-button warfare', the V-1s and the V-2s had actually achieved.

The deployment, late in the day, of the V-1s and V-2s had caused the senior Allied commanders no longer to be led by exclusively military requirements, but had made it necessary for them to react to the political demands for an ending to the the V-weapons bombardment, with all the negative consequences which this entailed for the further conduct of the war. Without the V-weapons, would the war have been over in December 1944 with an Anglo-American march into Berlin?

It can therefore be concluded with certainty that the conventional V-1 and V-2 had a great influence on the course of the last stages of the Second World War. Of course, they were not able to win the war for Germany, but they were able to delay defeat and thus perhaps gain the time which Hitler might have still needed to prepare his real victory weapons.

Thus, in addition to the undisputed political and moral effect of the V-weapons, a clear military effect had been created which bore no relation to the relatively small tonnage of explosive which had been launched at Western Allied targets.

Seen in hindsight, did not this consideration alone justify the expense which Germany had incurred in developing its V-weapons?

The conventional V-1s and V-2s had been produced in far too small numbers, and came far too late, to bring about a change in the course of the war. Even to achieve Hitler's aim of 'taking out' London would have required many more V-1s and V-2s than were actually available. But the German war economy was not only not in a position to manufacture the necessary numbers of the weapons, but from summer 1944 there were more and more shortages of basic materials all over the place which prevented the war being waged effectively. Thus, the successful V-weapons bombardment of Antwerp and Liege could also be no replacement for the shortages of fuel for German armour during the Ardennes offensive.

Could Hitler's attempt to change the course of the war using ultra-modern 'push-button weapons' – which from our contemporary perspective seems to have been futile – be seen as a measure to deploy a few V-1s and V-2s with conventional 1000kg explosive warheads in order to offset the material inferiority of the Third Reich which was evident in all areas?

If this was really Hitler's intention - and we shall discuss this question later - then from the outset the first 'push-button warfare' in history, even if the V-weapons had been used with maximum effectiveness, could only have had a negative result.

In this context, it should not be forgotten that throughout the period that the German rockets and missiles were in operational use, work was continually under way to resolve their technical shortcomings. These were completely new weapons which were being introduced into front-line service without any sufficient operational trials.

Is it in fact the truth that their deployment in 1944/45 was itself their operational trial?

Certainly, during the short time in which these predecessors of 'Star Wars' were in front-line service, they gave ample demonstration what could have been achieved with these revolutionary carrier systems in more favourable circumstances.

The after-effects of the deployment of the V-1 and V-2 in 1944/45 extend right up to the present day. Today, tactical and strategic rockets and missiles are part of the weapons arsenals of almost any self-respecting armed forces.

Could even more have been achieved?: Negligence, treachery and false hopes among the leadership of the Third Reich

Only rarely in the history of warfare did the inferior power have such a clear technological advance over its victorious opponents as the Third Reich had in the field of rockets and flying bombs. At the end of the war, there were decades of difference between the state of development on both sides. But all the German resources which had been expended to achieve this end were nevertheless to prove futile.

Even if Germany's flying bombs and rockets were the largest official armaments programme of the Third Reich, neither the conventional V-1 nor the V-2 could win the war for Germany. They came too late, and had been built in insufficient numbers. In addition, they were too widely dispersed to able to hit any given targets precisely, and the effect of their conventional warheads was not sufficient to turn the course of the war.

Could things have turned out differently?

Hitler, who had shown a lively interest in rocket research since the 1920s, and who as early as 1936 had ordered the *Heereswaffenamt* to set up an establishment on Peenemünde to manufacture rockets, nevertheless, until October 1942, showed an ambiguous attitude towards the Peenemünde projects. Although, for example, on 4 September 1939 he sent 3,500 technically qualified troops to reinforce the scientists already at Peenemünde, only two days later he reduced the priority of all the projects which were under way there.[45] Henry Picker explains this by pointing out that Hitler had for many years suspected that the scientists at Peenemünde would neglect their actual task of building weapons and instead of this would carry out all sorts of other research which had little to do with Germany's war effort. Therefore, Hitler is said to have tried by various methods (restriction of financial resources, restriction of deliveries of raw materials etc.) to force them to concentrate on the task which they had been assigned.[46]

But even worse things were to come!

When the war was scarcely a few months old, the leadership of the Third Reich made a fateful mistake. This made a significant contribution to Germany robbing itself of the opportunity to turn its massive superiority in the field of high technology into weapons capable of operational deployment.

The conventional German system of armaments had, even at the outbreak of the war, proved to be unsatisfactory. Germany's opponents had managed the transition from a peacetime to a wartime economy a lot more quickly and purposefully.[47] As early as 1940, the British and the French had twice as many tanks as the Wehrmacht. To produce effective quantities of armaments it would have been necessary for Germany, as in the other belligerent countries, to set up a total war economy. But the Führer of the Third Reich wanted to avoid this. So, therefore, an apparently comfortable compromise was arrived at - to mobilise existing armaments production reserves at the expense of the expensive research and development of 'uncertain' futuristic projects which tied down production capacity. The rocket project also became a victim of the famous (and notorious) order issued in 1940 to stop all weapons developments which could not be brought into operational use within one year.[48] General Dornberger tried to circumvent the effects of this fateful decision by having individual components such as the rocket engine developed separately, and by using the A-5 rockets which had been in existence since 1937 to obtain the data required for the A-4 programme.

The reasons for the problems Penemünde experienced during the first years of the war may be that, in all its pre-war planning, the Third Reich was preparing not for a *Blitzkrieg* in 1939, but for a longer-lasting, larger-scale conflict in the mid-1940s, which Germany would carry out as an economic and military superpower.[49] But when the Second World War, which Hitler had not expected, broke out 'prematurely' in 1939, this also had consequences for the projects at the Peenemünde Army research establishment. Thus, at the end of November 1939, it was estimated that it would take about four years to develop the 'devices' (as the rockets were called), and the Army Supreme Commander gave orders to make the best use of this long period to set up a production capacity for 500 per annum per shift.[50] To carry out this order, at the beginning of 1939, *Gruppe* VI was set up within *Wa Prüf* 11.

As was the case with so many other German weapons projects, in September 1939, development of the A-4 rocket - the basic features of which had already been designed - had not yet reached a state of operational readiness, but for the large-scale conflict in the mid-1940s which was expected by the Third Reich leadership, Peenemünde's ballistic rockets would have been ready 'according to plan'.

The rapid Blitzkrieg victories in the years 1939-41, which were unexpected by the German leadership, then led the Third Reich to (as it later turned out) a suicidal mixture of self-satisfaction and incompetence. Not even the futile aerial battle for Britain in autumn 1940 was recognised as a serious warning sign that Germany's conventional armaments were too weak for a longer lasting conflict. Added to this was the fact that leading individuals such as *Reichsmarschall* Hermann Goring intentionally withheld the real production figures from Hitler in order to be able better to conceal from him to the actual weakness of the German position.

Thus, during the Blitzkrieg, the Third Reich continued to remain within a war economy which resembled that of peacetime instead of mobilising all forces for armaments as the seriousness of the situation demanded, and as its enemies were doing.

Only in autumn 1941, with the first reverses in Africa and on the Eastern Front, and with the threat of America entering the war, was fresh thought given to mobilising the German economy for a longer lasting conflict. This change of approach can also be seen in the further development of Peenemünde. Thus, on 15 September 1941, Hitler suddenly assigned to rocket construction degree of extreme urgency, and immediately after the first successful test flight of the V-2 in October 1941, the highest level of urgency was assigned to the rocket project. Thus it received the same degree of urgency as to the production of tanks. This was a clear sign that the situation was now considered to be so serious that it was necessary again to push for the urgent development of futuristic weapons-no matter what the cost!

On 7 July, 1943, Hitler also admitted to Dornberger and von Braun that he had not given them sufficient credence in 1939. As early as October 1939, however, they had succeeded in installing all important components of the A-4, with the exception of the warhead and the rocket engine, into the rocket!

According to Dornberger, after 7 July 1943, at last men and material poured ceaselessly and almost without limit into the programme. Now, they were achieving in weeks what would otherwise have taken months or years.

The race against time had begun! But now were these high-technology weapons, which until then had been carelessly overlooked, still able to compensate for Germany's mistakes in conventional armaments against enemies which were growing ever more powerful?

In the case of the V-2, the consequences of all this were that it was only after the loss of the French Channel coast in September 1944 that it was possible to deploy them, whereas under the plans of 1938 it had been intended that they should be ready for deployment as early as 1942.

There were also equally grotesque delays in the case of the Fi-103. The basic design of the later V-1 had been sketched out as early as 1934! At that time, the engineer Paul Schmidt tried to interest the Reich Aviation Ministry in a flying bomb equipped with his new Schmidt jet propulsion system. But the idea for the missile which would attain a speed of 800 kilometres per hour was rejected at the time as 'uninteresting' (!).

Only several years later, in August 1939, were new proposals submitted to the Luftwaffe under the code name 'Fernfeuer'. But the idea for the missile, now equipped with a piston-engine propulsion system, was again rejected on 31 May 1940.

In the meantime, on 7 February 1940, Goering had issued the famous, and catastrophic, order to stop production. This decision was even confirmed in September 1941. It was only with difficulty that it was possible later to make up for the time lost in the production of the flying bomb.

But then, between February and April 1942, the brilliant engineer Robert Lusser managed, in only two months, to develop the project Erfurt E35 - the later Fieseler Fi-103. Although the Luftwaffe Fi-103 project made rapid progress, there was now a clear lack of collaboration between the Luftwaffe (Fi-103) and the Army (A-4). Thus, many of the problems which had occurred in the long-range A-4 weapon, which in the meantime had been successfully resolved, had to be dealt with again in the case of the Fi-103. This was also the case, for instance, with the auto-pilot and the guidance system for the Fi-103, which were markedly inferior or to those of the A-4. This was why the standard Fi-103 had a markedly inferior accuracy than the A-4. It was only later, and in piecemeal fashion, that it was possible to make improvements with additional guidance and steering systems.

According to Allied information during the post-war period, if the V-1 had been ready in time, it could have had a decisive effect on the war by impeding the Allied Normandy invasion through continuous bombardment of the embarkation ports. Fear of bombardment by the Fi-103 during critical moments in the planned landing on the Continent caused the Allies to consider transferring preparations for invasion to the western areas of Great Britain, which were outside the range of the German flying bomb. They need not have worried, and only needed to rely on the customary confusion of the Luftwaffe! In this case, too, it was only when the Allies had already formed bridgeheads on the coast of France that the bombardment began in earnest.

Added to this was another factor which is often denied - treachery!

Thus, the attention of the British was only drawn to Peenemünde after numerous items of information from German sources were passed to the Allies concerning the secret rocket developments which were taking place there. This process had begun immediately after the outbreak of war, when, in the so-called 'Oslo Report', Peenemünde was mentioned as a location where rocket research was being carried out. Fortunately for the rocket and missile project, it was a long time before the British reacted to these numerous warnings. Only when the photo-reconnaissance flights which they had carried out by chance on the Usedom Peninsula had demonstrated the accuracy of the information did the RAF strike the Peenemünde installations hard in a large air raid on 17/18 August 1943.

The British were eventually convinced by the treachery of Dr Otto John. During the war, John was not a soldier, but an official with Lufthansa, and during this time was able to travel freely abroad, because he possessed one of the travel passes issued by admiral Canaris' *Abwehr*. As is proved by political interrogations of his brother Hans, he was not only a participant in the resistance of 20 July 1944, but also a member of the Soviet espionage organisation *Rote Kappelle*. As far as is known at the present time, Dr John began his work as an agent in Madrid in March 1942, when the recommendation of Prince Luis Ferdinand of Prussia gave him access to the British and American businessmen. His specific information, which at the time he had received direct from the General Beck, General Oster and General von Hammerstein, did not fail to have an effect.

After Dr John's eventual defection to the Allies after the failed assassination attempt on Hitler on 20th July 1944, the British Colonel Daniel Shapiro was John's minder. Colonel Shapiro stated on 8 August, 1954 in Stern magazine: "I was simply not prepared to to be suddenly sitting opposite the man who had told us all about Peenemünde with its new experimental station for miracle weapons. This was a great coup, up to that time perhaps the greatest success achieved by our intelligence services. I remember quite precisely. The report came from Berlin from well-informed circles within the Luftwaffe. It had come to us through Spain, and immediately afterwards the RAF first sent Mosquito reconnaissance aircraft to Peenemünde and then soon after that 600 bombers, and the man to whom we owed all that was now sitting in my office with badly dyed hair."

But this was not all, because in autumn 1943 Dr John was able to report to his Allied contacts in Madrid that the production of a German atomic bomb was ready on paper, but that for technical reasons for it was not yet possible to manufacture it. At the same time he was also able to report what the current situation with regard to the V-1 and V-2 weapons projects in Peenemünde actually was!!

The comprehensive information which Dr John was able to pass on demonstrates the close contacts which must have existed between various groups of the military and scientists are associated with the German resistance.

What later became of Dr John also speaks volumes. On 24 July 1944 he was able to leave Berlin by aircraft completely unscathed after the failure of the assassination attempt on Hitler, although he had been recognised by Gestapo officials.

Later in 1944 he officially entered service with the British and after the war rose to the position of head of the *Amt fur Verfassungsschütz* of the newly founded Federal Republic of Germany. But his sympathies were with a very different system – in 1953 he defected to the East!

Dr John's activities had a great impact on Peenemünde in 1943. 600 RAF bombers saw to it that extensive sections of the plant, which up to that time had swallowed up 500 million *Reichsmarks*, burned like a torch.

Over 700 scientists, engineers, technicians and workers were left behind under the rubble.

Inexplicably, 14 days before the large British air raid, which went by the name of Operation Hydra, the heavy 8.8 centimetre and 10.5 centimetre flak batteries were withdrawn from Peenemünde. This left the secret rocket research establishment with only light flak installations and thus left it effectively unprotected against any large-scale bombing raids. Did this happen as a result of stupidity, or was sabotage behind it, bearing in mind the imminent British operation intended to destroy the installations?[51]

The flak batteries were also not reinstated when the Army research establishment at Peenemünde was warned by the Reich Aviation Ministry, only a few days before 'Operation Hydra', that an air raid was imminent, and despite the fact that the British reconnaissance aircraft which were constantly overflying the installations gave ample warning for anyone with any sense that an action was imminent.

The air raid of 17/18 August 1943 was one of the largest air raids which the British had until then mounted during the Second World War. But it came too late to stop the project.

Besides hundreds of dead and a six-week delay in the programme, the only consequences of 'Operation Hydra' were that the SS was finally able get its foot in the door of the V-weapons programme. Until then, the programme had been exclusively controlled by the Luftwaffe and the Army.

Despite the increasing influence of the SS on everything to do with *Vergeltungswaffen* – an influence which continued to grow until the end of the war – Germany's V-weapons programme continued to suffer as the result of treachery, espionage and sabotage.

The results of ground-breaking contemporary modern research are indicating more and more clearly that within that the leadership of the Third Reich and there was a widespread culture of high treason, which extended into the highest positions within the Wehrmacht, the SS, and the NSDAP. Thus, from a contemporary perspective, it seems that, by the end of the war, almost everyone except Hitler had been engaged in some kind of conspiracy.[52] It goes without saying that such action had a very negative effect on the development and the possible deployment of of the victory weapons.

Thus, as early as 1943, Martin Bormann, Hitler's radical

'grey eminence', prevented early mobilisation of the German war economy. This, too, is no surprise, because it could well have been Martin Bormann who, as Stalin's master spy 'Werther', had passed crucial German plans to the Soviets even before they could reach Hitler's commanders in the field.

Who would then be surprised that, according to contemporary accounts, the rocket gliders, which had been ready since October 1944, were never used in action? It is said that that a direct line ran from their depot to the Fuhrer Headquarters in Berlin - direct to Martin Bormann.

In the desperate efforts to limit the ever-present threat of treason, in the first years of the war Dornberger was given orders that all documents from Peenemünde, even design plans themselves, had to be recalled and destroyed, apart from three copies. But this measure also had no effect – apart from wasting further time.

How poorly the SS and Gestapo came to grips with the security problem at Peenemünde is indicated by the statement of the American Colonel Keck, who at the end of the war was chief of the intelligence service for enemy technology in the European theatre of war. Colonel Keck indicated that that there was a regular traffic in espionage 'into and out of Germany', and that it had been no problem for the Allies to obtain an almost daily view of the current state of the developments at Peenemünde.

The Third Reich proved to be incapable of protecting its most vital weapons secrets. If this was not the case, how can it be explained that, in the same state which was quite ruthless in punishing the slightest misdemeanours of its citizens, the secret weapons spy Paul Rosbaud was able to carry on his activities quite freely and quite unscathed until the end of the war, although there were grave suspicions held about him?!

It was precisely in the area of the V-weapons that false hopes, delays and treason played their sinister role. This was the case not only in relation to the fact that the weapons could have possibly been deployed earlier, but also applied to the production of larger numbers of weapons and to the question of improving their accuracy.

It is possible that another major opportunity was missed – yet again.

Section 2: "The aim": Was Wernher von Braun really only reaching for the stars?

When Hitler gave orders that the V-weapons offensive to take out London was to begin on 15 February 1944, Generaloberst Jodl wrote in his diary: "Watchword for the project: THIS IS ONLY THE BEGINNING".

" ... Cannot be deployed in unlimited numbers"

The planners in the Third Reich had realised relatively early on that the initially planned mass deployment of rockets and missiles could not change the course of the war.[53][54]

The first plans for the mass production of the Peenemünde A-4 rocket had been developed as early as autumn 1941, and, after, the first successful launch of an A-4 had been carried out on 3 October 1942, in mid-October Adolf Hitler ordered the immediate deployment of 5000 rockets. But it was soon to become clear that it would be impossible to launch such a quantity of rockets, if only for the reason that it was not possible to store sufficient quantities of liquid oxygen.

Added to this was the fact that as early as the end of July 1943, Speer had received a report, which he himself had commissioned, from Prof. Dr Carl Krauch. Professor Krauch, who at the time was the Chairman of the Board of IG Farben Industrie AG, stated that the long-range A4 rocket project was not suitable for conventional deployment in large numbers. He pointed out that 'the missile represents an extremely complicated and expensive mechanism, particularly its electrical components, and can therefore only be deployed in limited numbers to achieve aims which are crucially important for the course of the war'. He also dismissed as illusory the thought that Britain could be brought to its knees by retribution attacks using V-weapons.

In the early days of December, even the Wehrmacht command staff stated that, according to their calculations, the A-4 rocket could never achieve the effect of a heavy daylight raid carried out by conventional bombers. No mention was made initially of the Fi-103.

Thus, long before these weapons were first deployed, it was clear to all those responsible that deploying them in a conventional manner alone would have no decisive effect on the course of the war.

For a long time, Hitler vacillated in assigning priorities between the types of V-weapons which had hitherto proved to be justified. It was only after the late beginning of the V-1 offensive against London, an offensive which had already been postponed several times already, that Hitler first gave this weapon priority over the A-4, only to give priority again to the A-4 rocket after the loss of the V-1 launch bases in France, at the expense of the V-1.

In autumn 1944, after overcoming all delays and setbacks, Germany was in a position to deploy both V-weapons. But from the known production figures, and from the fact that it was only possible to increase production to a small amount, it was now clear that any success achieved by the deployment of these weapons would only be limited. Since this was precisely what responsible German authorities had been expecting since 1943, it remains an open question as to why the leaders of the Third Reich were so optimistic that they could nevertheless effect a decisive change in the course of the war by using these weapons.

Why were there plans to use secure locations, bunkers and tunnels

None of the many contemporary witnesses at Peenemünde or people who have written books about it has provided a plausible explanation why in the Third Reich such great expense was directed to the construction of rocket bunkers and improvised protective positions (for example railway tunnels). On the contrary, it was precisely the people who must have known the real facts who tried to play down these gigantic projects which were implemented with great efficiency from 1943.

At this point, by way of investigating the real reasons, it will be helpful to have a look at the rocket technology of the early 1950s, which at that time was still almost exclusively based on previous German work.

On 21 June 1956, the Russians brought into service the first specially developed atomic rocket of the type R-5M. These rockets were further developments are based on the V-2 Design. In the launch trials, it transpired at that it took 30 hours to prepare the rocket with its explosive warhead for launch. By contrast, in 1944/45, all the preparations for launch of a mobile conventional V-2 took only 90 minutes from arrival to launch. It can therefore be assumed that in the 1940s the time required to prepare for the launch of nuclear rockets could similarly have been no less than the 30 hours required to prepare the more advanced R-5M from 1956. Preferably, this important work would have to be carried out in quiet conditions, undisturbed, and, if possible, protected by concrete or underground.

It was also important that the launch should, if possible, follow immediately after the launch preparations, because, since the alcohol and oxygen tanks of the rocket were now filled, the rocket itself was not 'capable of being stored'. It would have been dangerous to transport a fully loaded and armed nuclear rocket after the preparatory work for launch had been completed. Special warheads, such as chemical, radiological and other sensitive or experimental charges, would have required special measures to be taken before the rocket was launched. Thus it was customary, until well into the 1950s, for the rocket warheads to be transported separately and only to be mounted on their carrier systems immediately before the launch. An operation which would have been dangerous in 1944/45 as a result of the necessity for the launches to be carried out only at night or in twilight and within the shortest period of time, because of the complete Allied air superiority.

This therefore raises the question as to whether the German efforts to create harder and more protected launch bases must not be seen as being intended to provide undisturbed and safe preparation for deployment for important special weapons.

If this is the case, it is clear why the whole subject is today played down and why the documents relating to the British 'Operation Crossbow' over the German rocket bunkers in northern France are still classified.

The silence of the scientists

Has the truth about the German secret weapons fallen victim to the spirit of the modern age?.

It seemed an obvious idea to look for clues about the real purpose of the German rocket and missile programme in the memoirs and accounts of the former German scientists and technicians, but this research was a largely unproductive.

There are clear indications that 'those in the know' among the German scientists were sworn to silence at the end of the war. In this connection, a statement made by Bernhard Tessman is well known. Tessman, who was one of the leading staff of Wernher von Braun at Peenemünde, is said to have said that he had promised Dornberger that after the war he would tell nobody what they were really working on.

Of whom or of what were the Peenemünde scientists afraid?

To answer this question, we will use Dornberger's own words, which give a hidden clue to the real purpose of the rocket programme:

"The military situation in the middle of 1943 had for a long time been such that a world war of such dimensions could have been brought to an end by launching 900 V-2s armed with a one-tonne warhead every month over a range of 250km. I began to have suspicions ..."

This statement can be interpreted in two ways: either to mean that Dornberger himself considered the war to be lost, or to mean that his suspicions were that ultimately quite different and far more effective warheads were to be carried by the V-2.

Although so many years have now passed since the war came to an end, it seems that today more and more important statements of former German scientists remain classified in the archives of the victorious powers. One of the leading authorities among them, however, broke his silence during the last years of his life. The statements which this man made go far beyond what might have originally been expected on the basis of the research carried out by the present author. The name of this insider, however, must at the moment remain as anonymous as his original materials, which were intended for succeeding generations. Therefore, within this book, his statements and documents are assigned the provisional source designation 'Dr X'.

"Like a scene out of a nightmare"

In the current Peenemünde exhibition on rocket development, in the summer of 2001 an interesting picture was presented to researchers. The picture came - as further research indicated - in an extract from a 'special supplement' edition of the periodica *Signal* dating from 1945, and showed drawings by the well-known war artists Hans Liska and Richard Hennis. This extract concerned the reson why the V-2s were deployed and their possible destructive effect. The report focussed on describing a devastating rocket attack on an (imaginary?) city.

Looking at the picture, the following thoughts present themselves: the four radii of destruction which are shown on the drawing are far too large to have been caused by the conventional warhead of a normal V-2 rocket. But they do amazingly recall the concentric circles of the impact plans of Dr Sänger's Antipodes bomber for a planned attack on New York, which date from August 1944!

The rocket attack described in the publication title as like a scene out of a nightmare impressively shows how the shockwaves created by the impact of the rocket warhead and the formation of the crater radiate out like an earthquake, so that in the first two zones of effectiveness nothing is left standing of conventional housing and other buildings.

The article ominously recalls the radii of destruction of an atomic bomb, and the precision of the sketch raises the question as to how at that time, even before the first American atomic weapon was dropped on the Japanese city of Hiroshima, this effect could have been known and reproduced in detail, without previous experiments having been undertaken. As the source of its information, *Signal*

"... Like a scene out of a nightmare ..." Hypothetical annihilation of a major city (London?) as a result of the impact of a single German rocket (from the periodical *Signal* from 1945). Are the concentric circles of destruction supposed to represent the effect of a nuclear rocket, or is it the effect of some other terrible weapons system which is illustrated here? (*Signal Extra-Beilage* 1945, drawn by Hans Liska and Richard Hennis)

says little other than to refer to the previous experiences of the British with the V-weapons, and also to a speech made by the British Prime Minister Winston Churchill before the House of Commons in November 1944. But these clues do not even begin to explain the detailed representation of the radii of destruction on the drawing, because on the drawing very different effects are shown. The only thing which is clear is that this level of destruction could never by any stretch of the imagination be connected with the explosive effect of an normal A-4, as we know it. So something entirely different must have been involved.

The drawing made available to the public in Peenemünde was done by the war artists Hans Liska and Richard Hennis, who were both well known at the time, and it appeared, as I have already indicated, as part of a so-called 'extra supplement' for the German Wehrmacht illustrated periodical *Signal* in 1945, in which the second German V-weapon was presented to the public.

As stated, it remains a mystery what actually was intended to be shown on the accompanying drawing. Certainly, the impact of conventional explosives and their effects are not the right answer.

What was the real purpose of Hitler's missile and rocket programme?

"There would have been no war if the rockets had been ready in 1939! With these weapons, mankind will not be able to withstand a war". When Hitler said these words on 7 July 1943 to Walther Dornberger, he clearly indicated that he considered the rockets from Peenemünde to be the weapons which would decide the outcome of the war![55]

But how could such expensive projectiles, which could only carry 850 to 1000 kilograms of explosive, have prevented a war taking place? Even at the beginning of the war, normal medium-range bombers such as the Do17, Ju 88 and He111 carried a payload of more than 1000 kilograms of bombs. This detail would never have escaped Hitler's famous, and notorious, detailed knowledge of Germany's weapons programme!

From a technical point of view, as early as 1939 German expenditure bore no relation to the possible payload of the rockets. But this factor did not appear to deter the Germans from carrying on with this technically risky project. Quite the contrary! As far as we know, eventually, in Germany alone, over 200,000 people were working on the various rocket programmes. But by the end of the war, not even 6000 A-4s had been produced, of which only 3000 were actually used. But was this really the full story, or was it the real truth that something entirely different was being planned?

It appears that as early as 1936, when the Army research establishment at Peenemünde was being planned, there were plans for building test beds for rocket propulsion systems of 200t. These would have been far too large for the V-2, but would have corresponded with the performance requirements for the propulsion systems on the later A-10 America rocket. Was this 'foresight' merely a coincidence?

Fortunately there are many statements made by experts during the war and after the war which give a clear picture of the real German plans.

In May 1945, after the German surrender, the senior German naval officer Kay Nieschling was taken prisoner by the Americans when they intercepted the U234 secret weapons transport. When he was interrogated he repeatedly stated to his interrogators that he doubted whether the United States had fully comprehended what 'dreadful and unimaginable possibilities' were contained in the already existing V-2 and the planned V3 with its unlimited range and its boundless potential.[56]

Certainly, in mentioning these 'dreadful and unimaginable possibilities', Nieschling is not speaking of the conventional one ton explosive warheads which were launched in their thousands against London and Antwerp.

Even in the euphoria which followed the first deployment of these weapons, a telegram sent by the National Socialist command staff at OKW to the German soldiers in France on 17 June 1944 indicated relatively clearly that the V-weapons were eventually to be armed with very different armaments than normal explosives. 'Although the most powerful explosives had not yet been used, the retribution had worked not only as a threat before they were deployed'.[57] At that time, the term 'the most powerful explosives' could only have referred to the expected nuclear bombs.

What was eventually planned for the V-2 is illuminated by a series of statements such as those of Gunter Wruck, who had been trained in Peenemünde to survey the rocket launch pads, and who is quoted in Jungbluth's book.[58] Wruck was present when at the beginning of 1944 on the Usedom Peninsula Wernher von Braun said in a lecture that the Germans were in a position, with this rocket, to decide the outcome of the war, because it would have the power to launch, in one second, a weight of hundreds of thousand of tonnes kilometres into the air. This was far more than could be achieved by the propulsion system of the normal V-2. It must therefore have been something entirely different which was powerful enough to wrest eventual victory from the Allies. According to the calculations made by Professor Fuckert, such power could only have meant atomic power. Were the people at Peenemünde working towards the eventual development of nuclear rockets and missiles?

Any remaining doubts about the purpose of these massive German efforts may be removed if we consider Adolf Hitler's position with relation to the German missile and rocket developments.[59]

It is repeatedly asserted that Adolf Hitler showed interest in rocket development far too late. But this is demonstrably false. Hitler owed his knowledge of rockets to his old Munich acquaintance Max Valier. This inventor of practical solid fuel and liquid fuel rockets, who was born in the southern Tyrol, tested his designs himself by means of rocket sledges, rocket cars and rocket aircraft and lost his life in 1930 in a test drive on the autobahn in Berlin/Britz. Hitler had been watching and encouraging his research activities since 1927. He also supported them by publishing, in the *Illustrierte Beobachter* in 1929, several articles about Valier's work, and urged that the necessary financial resources should be made available. He repeatedly emphasised his admiration for Professor Hermann Oberth, born in 1894, who with his scientific knowledge and calculations had made the liquid fuel rocket and later space rocket possible. It was also Hitler who gave orders to the *Heereswaffenamt* in 1936 to set up a rocket construction establishment. This was then created in Peenemünde.

But in contrast to the enthusiastic support given by Minister Speer and a whole series of important generals in the *Heereswaffenamt*, Hitler showed great reserve towards the Peenemünde researchers (see section entitled 'Could more have been achieved?'). This attitude only officially changed on 7 July 1943. At Hitler's request, Speer invited Dornberger and von Braun to visit the Fuhrer Headquarters, where they were to make a presentation to Hitler of everything that had been achieved to date in the rocket programme. This presentation was a complete success for the people from Peenemünde - so much so that, even until today, that date is regarded as the day when Hitler was finally convinced by the A-4 rocket. But it was not only the A-4 which secured official approval on 7 July 1943. When, at the end of his lecture, Dornberger once again (!) mentioned that the A-4 was only an intermediate stage on the way to the A-10, Hitler immediately demanded that the larger rocket should also be built.

This means nothing other than that on that 7 July 1943, an 'official' commission was given to build the A-10 America rocket at the same time as the A-4, even if, in the books he published after the war, Dornberger tried to play this down.

In actual fact, it was as early as 22 November 1942 that Hitler had decided, after a lecture given by Albert Speer, to assign the highest priority to the rocket programme. The search for suitable launch bunkers in France had begun immediately afterwards in December 1942! These large bunkers were intended to be suitable for launching the A-4 against London and also for launching the A-10 against New York.

Hitler had demonstrably been convinced since November 1942 that the rocket would become the decisive weapon of the war. It must have been clear to him that this could not be achieved with the normal one-ton explosive warhead. When, for instance, Hitler asked Dr Dornberger in June 1943 whether he could not increase the payload to 10 tonnes and the monthly production of rockets to 2000, Dornberger explained that it was impossible to meet both requests. Whereupon Hitler is said to have screamed: 'But I

want mass destructive effects!' In response to this, Dornberger said "You can do no more with a ton of explosives than that ton of explosives will in itself produce. When we began this development programme, we had not thought of effects of mass destruction". Hitler interrupted him. "You! Of course you haven't - *you* weren't planning such effects, but I am!"

In the book he published after the war, Dornberger then continued: "To achieve this we needed other destructive agents, other sources of energy, atomic energy? Never thought of it!" This immediate denial that they might even have given a thought to atomic energy runs so noticeably like a leitmotif through the memoirs of the other leading people from EMW Peenemünde. Even their choice of words is remarkably similar when they are talking about this subject. Is this coincidence, or had they agreed between themselves beforehand what to say?

The dilemma of the German scientists in the post-war period was that they found it difficult to justify the expenditure of personnel and material during the period of the Third Reich on the basis of the A-4 and Fi-103 alone. Thus they had to put forward the 'noble' reason that in actual fact what they were interested in was civilian space travel, and that they had provided the leadership of the Third Reich with rocket developments which 'unfortunately' it was also possible to use in a military capacity. All this was perhaps a noble legend created to enable them to be able to continue to work professionally with the victorious powers after Germany had surrendered. But in no way does it correspond to the historical truth about the German rocket and missile programme!

Many reports from Allied agents indicated during the war that it was the aim of the German leadership to mount uranium warheads on their rockets. Even if this information provided by agents was to prove to be inaccurate in respect of minor details, it nevertheless repeatedly pointed to the same factual evidence.[60]

In summer 1943, just as the Germans were about to start mass production of the A-4, British agents reported that the weapon was ready for deployment on 1 September 1943. Afterwards, they said, the Germans had developed a missile with a theoretical range of 800 kilometres and a practical range of possibly 500 kilometres. The first third of the weapon, the agents reported, was explosive and contained explosive materials of 'a fissile atomic type'.

Another report from Peenemünde which arrived in Britain on 1 September 1943 stated that in Peenemünde a weapon was being developed with a range of some 500 to 600 kilometres and which would kill everything living within a radius of 700 metres of the explosion.

The third agents' report, dating from as early as June 1943, had described a rocket weapon with a range of 200 to 300 kilometres which carried a five-ton explosive warhead and had a fatal effect on everything within a radius of 500 metres. The report stated that this weapon had already been the subject of successful trials in the Baltic area.

Why did all the reports of agents from Peenemünde agree that the planned explosive charge within the new secret weapon was to be of 'a quite special kind'?

On 11 August, 1944, even senior American generals were discussing the fact that they would soon have to deal with the deployment of a new German rocket with a destructive effect which was significantly greater than that of the V-1.[61]

In the minutes of the conference of 17/18 July 1943, a further indication can be found of plans for later use of the rockets as victory weapons: "The Fuhrer once again confirms that development of the A-4 is to be pursued with the utmost urgency - he considers that this weapon, which can be produced with relatively little resources, is a measure which could decide the outcome of the war and relieve the homeland".

Another indication is found in a question which *Generaloberst* Jodl asked at a meeting of the Wehrmacht command staff on 26 October 1943. Jodl raised this question: "One question concerning the deployment of the A-4 - should it be announced, should we talk about it or not? I am asking because various press announcements, and also questions from Budapest, are turning up on the basis of a speech made by Robert Ley, in which he has announced that within six weeks a new weapon will be deployed which can raze entire cities in Britain to the ground. Should we speak about this openly?" Hitler and Jodl then agreed not to do this in order to avoid disappointment among the German people, in the event that the deadline which had been announced could not be met.

Did these nuclear plans also apply to the Fi-103 flying bomb?

On 13 November 1943, at a discussion with Keitel, Milch, Jodl and Speer, Hitler had given to understand that the main purpose of the Fi-103 was not to deploy it as a mass weapon to defend against invasion. On the same day, Generals Korten and von Axthelm were about to announce to the OKW that with the resources which were available to date, it would not be possible to mount any defence against enemy invasion. Even before it was made, the lecture aroused great interest, because Hitler had said that he himself would be present. On 8 November 1943, in his speech to commemorate the anniversary of the 1923 'March to the *Feldherrnhalle*' at the time of the Munich *putsch*, Hitler had announced: "Even if at the moment we can't reach America, at least, thank God, one country is close enough for us to reach! We will see to it that this remains the case". At the conference on 13 November 1944, *General* von Axthelm stated that the planned flying bomb offensive would not only be directed against London, but also against the invasion ports on the South Coast. But in order to enable such an offensive to take place, he said that he would need German industry to produce at least 30,000 bombs per month. Then, when von Axthelm criticised the current German production programme and stated that it a represented only a tenth of what was necessary to strike

at Allied invasion preparations, he was angrily interrupted by Hitler. "Don't worry about defending against the invasion, and concentrate on the theme of retribution!" Then, when a General von Axthelm continued to point to the urgency of the situation, Hitler concluded his response with the words: "Just get the rockets across to the targets, and then you'll get whatever munitions you need!"

With this, Hitler made it clear that the flying bomb offensive against Britain was not to be (or could not be?) a programme of mass deployment to defend against the threatened invasion fleet, nor was it intended to completely annihilate London. Rather, he saw the programme as being a large-scale military exercise which would be later followed by provision of the required munitions (which would decide the outcome of the war). Because the target of 30,000 bombs a month demanded by General von Axthelm was outside the capacity of German production facilities, then this remark could logically only have referred to a qualitatively new type of munition for the V-1.

Then, in March 1944, Hitler then made an unequivocal statement about the real purpose of his V-weapons programme. Oberst Hans-Ulrich Rudel gives an account of this in his book *Trotzdem*.[62] Hitler had a high regard for the young Luftwaffe officer and placed special confidence in him. He was even able, later, to present Rudel as a suitable candidate to succeed him.[63]

On 29 March 1944, at the Oberberghof in Berchtesgaden, Rudel received from Hitler and the distinguished military decoration of the Knight's Cross with Diamonds. Rudel then describes what happened after he received the decoration. "We were drinking tea together and talking for another two hours. Innovations in weapons technology, the war situation and history are the main topics of conversation. He made particular mention to me of the V-weapons, which we have just begun to deploy. People should not overestimate the effect of these weapons at the present time, said Hitler, because the accuracy of the missiles was still very poor. But, he went on, this would not always be the case, because at the moment all he wanted was to have rockets which were able to fly without any problem. Later, Hitler said, there would be an explosive which was like no normal explosive such as we know at the moment, but something entirely different, which would be powerful enough to effect a positive outcome to the war. He said that the development of this explosive was far advanced, and that it would soon go into production. For me, all this is completely new territory, and I can't imagine what he is talking about. Later, I hear that the explosive power of the new rocket will be based on atomic power".[64] [65]

This means that, in Hitler's own words, the V-1 was to be armed with nuclear warheads as well as the V-2.

In comparison with normal bombers, the unmanned missiles and rockets had the disadvantage that they could only carry a payload between 850 and 1000 kilograms.

On the other hand, Goering's four-ton bombers were

able to carry bombs of the heavy Hiroshima type without any problem. But first they either had to be redesigned, or they were improvisations of old aircraft types and conventional technology which were susceptible to Allied counter-measures (see first volume). As result of this, in an accompanying document to Führer order 219 of October 1944, the Fi-103 and the A-4 were designated as the preferred carrier systems for the nuclear weapons, production of which was to be accelerated.

This is also confirmed by Russian documents of the post-war period:[66]

On 6 June 1946, the head of the Soviet secret service in the Soviet zone of occupation, General Serov, received some alarming information. On the search for former German rocket specialists, the engineer Horst Kirfes had been tracked down among the German inmates of the GULAG-type 'Spetslager 7' in Sachsenhausen. Kirfes was familiar with the development of the V-1 and V-2, and knew the former Director of the *Mittelwerke*. The latter, who had died in the meantime, had told him how the V-weapons were produced and said that they were to be equipped with atomic bombs.

According to what was said in a Soviet document which was only released in at 2001, the Planning and Operations Director, engineer Albin Sawatzki, who later committed suicide in US captivity, confirmed what Kirfes had said with regard to the German intention to ultimately deploy the V-1 and V-2 as atomic weapons carriers. Sawatzki knew what he was talking about! Since Hitler had given orders for the mass production of V-weapons in July 1943, engineer Sawatzki was intimately familiar with the A-4 and later also with the Fi-103. As the creator and organiser of the underground system of mass production of both V-weapons in the *Mittelwerke*, no essential detail of these weapons is likely to have been unknown to him. This must certainly have included plans to arm them with atomic weapons!

When General Serov received this information, Albert Sawatzki was beyond reach. Perhaps his suicide was not only connected with the war crimes which he had been alleged to have committed.

Unfortunately, there is no record of what happened to engineer Kirfes after his statement to the NKVD about the German atomic weapons plans.

Sometimes during the post-war period, important German scientists were also not quite able to conceal their pride regarding their earlier achievements.

Thus, in 1952, the Italian journalist Luici Romersa gave an account in the magazine *Il Tempo* of a conversation which he had had a few months previously with the German scientists Helmut Hoeppner and Prof. Dr. Herbert Wagner. As executive member of the board of directors of the Junkers aircraft firm, Prof. Dr. Wagner was significantly involved in the production of armaments and the development of jet propulsion systems. After the war began, he worked at the Henschel factory in Berlin-Schönefeld on the development of remote-controlled weapons (HS-293) But as part of this work he was also involved in the use of nuclear technology and the first computers (in collaboration with Konrad Zuse) for remote-controlled weapons. After the war, he continued to work in the same field in the USA for the US Navy. Prof. Dr. Wagner said to Romersa, with a note of pride in his voice: "... the American B.61 'Matador' missile is to carry atomic charges. We were also planning to do the same thing with the V-2, the A-9, and the B-2 (the 65-ton rocket which was designed to be fired at America)." During the conversation, Helmut Hoeppner had listened quite quietly while his colleague was speaking, but sometimes he interrupted, and confirmed what Wagner was saying by nodding in clear agreement.

As is outlined below, the 'Rheinbote' rocket and a new 'mobile missile' in Norway are also associated with German nuclear plans!

Thus, the first great goal of the German missile and rocket programme is clear – to carry nuclear payloads by means of new types of carrier systems, against which it is impossible to mount any defence.

But Hitler did not only want to use his atomic rockets and missiles against Britain. Thus, he is known to have made secret statements that the America rocket was to carry a uranium bomb. In this way he wanted to bomb America until America sued for peace.

The leaders of the Third Reich expected nothing other than the end of the war to result from the use of these weapons. This is clear from a discussion which Mussolini's confidant Luigi Romersa had with Dr Josef Goebbels at the end of October 1944. In the conversation, the Minister also began to speak of the rockets: "... we have a dozen remote controlled rockets with amazing power and accuracy. When the enemy see a rain of A-4 and A-9 rockets with atomic warheads dropping on them, they will have to reconsider whether it is worth continuing the war". In his book *Rechenschaft abgelegt*, the former President of the *Reichsbank*, Dr Hjalmar Schacht, wrote that at the Nuremberg war crimes trial, the man in the cell next to him, the *Reichsminister* for Armaments, Albert Speer, had warned him in his concluding statement before the end of the trial that in the future it would be possible, using a small complement of only 10 men, without warning, and by night or day, to launch a rocket equipped with a nuclear warhead which could fly faster than the speed of sound, and in this way annihilate one million people in a few seconds in the heart of New York. Speer's knowledge about the future threat posed by nuclear intercontinental rockets must have been based on his knowledge of of the German A-9/10 war project.

Certainly, in Nuremberg he is said to have prophesied that it would only be five or ten years before military technology made it possible to do that. Was Speer keeping quiet about something at the time, against his better judgement, or was the pressure upon him so great that he had to shift this period so far into the future?

Certainly, when Romersa was speaking with Dr Goebbels in October 1944, Germany was not so far advanced! Goebbels indicated that a maximum of six or seven months would be needed to achieve what he had been talking about. The only problem was whether Germany would be able to hold out for so long. Could the victory weapons be brought into service more quickly than the Allied troops on the ground were advancing?

How this the decisive race against time was to be run, and the exciting, but ultimately vain attempt to maintain its momentum while struggling against massive enemy superiority, will give the reader pause for thought!

Section 3: Unconventional carrier systems and secret payloads

The standard versions of the Fi-103, A-4 and 'Rheinbote' are generally well known. But what were the weapons with which Hitler planned to achieve final victory actually to look like? In the first instance, the main basis of these victory weapons plans was to be provided by special versions of the V-1 and V-2. On land, sea, and in the air, however, additional carrier weapons were planned, development of which was at various stages when the war came to an end. Some of these weapons had already been developed to such a stage that they were ready for front-line service.

At the same time the question poses itself as to whether, in any event, there were really any suitable payloads for these revolutionary carrier systems. Was all this simply wishful thinking on the part of a German leadership who had lost their senses, and had long since lost any contact with reality?

The following pages will attempt to provide an overview of what was planned, and how far advanced those plans were.

I) Ground-to-ground rockets and missiles

1) Fieseler FI-103 'V-1' - special versions and their further development

For attacking large, medium-range targets, the uncomplicated flying bomb, because of its simplicity, economy and effectiveness, was without equal.
From a British analysis of the V-1

A) Further developments of the basic Fi-103 model

The V-1 'high-speed cell' and further developments
As early as the spring of 1944, in the strained situation before 6 June 1944, the commanders of the invasion armada were waiting tensely night after night for V-1, whose devastating effect on the invasion ports crammed with soldiers and material could have put paid to any chance of the Western Allies succeeding with the invasion.

In January 1945, the V-1 appeared to have largely lost its terror. Although, in comparison with the V-2, it still represented more economical alternative, even Adolf Hitler admitted on 10 January 1945, 'unfortunately, the V-1 is no longer capable of deciding the outcome of the war'.[67]

What had happened? In the intervening period, by means of a dense radar controlled anti-aircraft net, shells with proximity fuses, and the deployment of fast fighter aircraft with special engines, the Allies had succeeded in shooting down a considerable number of of the flying bombs which had actually been launched. In addition, as a result of the rapid German retreat on all fronts, the most interesting Allied targets were now outside the range of the flying bombs, which still, for the most part, had to be launched from fixed launch ramps.

As regards Hitler's intention of using the V-1s with nuclear warheads, if it was to be achieved under the more critical conditions of 1945 with any prospect of success, clear improvements to the flying bomb needed to be made with regard to speed, accuracy and range.

The opinion which is repeatedly put forward, namely that by the end of the war no significant improvements or further developments had been made to the V-1, is demonstrably false.

In addition to the development of higher-performance propulsion systems, significant improvements were also carried out on the cell of the flying bombs to meet the new requirements.

The aerodynamic limitations on the performance of the conventional F-103 had, from Spring 1944, been the subject of discussions and led to demands for the development of a high-speed cell. To achieve this, the top aircraft engineer Friedrich Graf von Saurma and his brother, Hans Harald von Saurma, developed a significantly refined cell.[68] [69] As early as 1943, they had developed a high performance laminar wing for the Fi-103, which, in addition or to a wooden structure, was significantly thinner and weighed less. It is true that the thinner wings also required a higher launch speed at the launch catapults. To solve this problem required yet more time.

In conjunction with improved fuel regulators, changes in the area of the ailerons and the shape of the fuselage, a top speed of 830 kilometres per hour was measured over a range of 350 kilometres. The target was to develop a version with a range of 500 kilometres and a speed of 900 kilometres per hour.

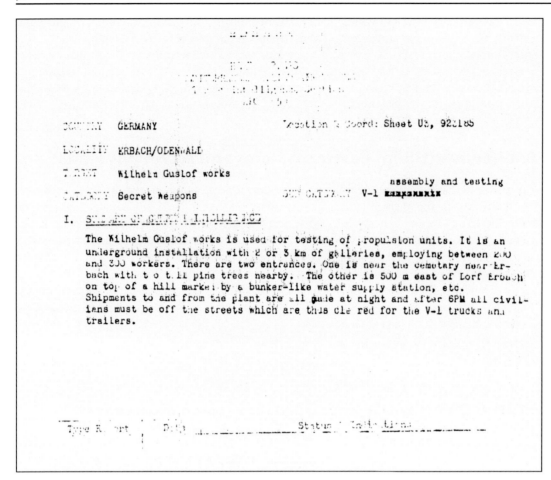

The American document reporting on the underground installation in Erbach/Odenwald belonging to the Wilhelm-Gustloff-Werke.

There are indications are that there were various high-speed versions. One report even speaks of a delta wing V-1.[70]

American microfilm documents, only recently discovered,[71] give further clues which couldpoint to secret activities in connection with the V-1 or its further developments. Thus, in Erbach/Odenwald, an underground installation, two or three kilometres long, belonging to the Wilhelm-Gustloff Werke, was in operation. In this small underground factory, which only employed between 200 and 300 workers, something very special must have been going on. Rumour has it that it was also used to test propulsion systems for the V-1. It is said that all transports to and from the underground factory in Erbach had to take place at night. It is also said that these transports were so secret that civilians were not allowed to be on the streets after 6pm so that they would not see the lorries carrying the V-1s and the accompanying convoy. This suggests that unusual activities must have been involved which departed from the activities associated with the normal V-1. Mention is also made of several production sites connected with V-1s and V-3s in the area of Gossel (Thuringia), so it can be assumed that here, too, there were production sites for further developments of the V-1, but that these were more likely to have had the status of experimental workshops.

At least ten high-speed cells were fired in trials from the Zempin troop exercise area. It is also said that these achieved improvements in target accuracy.

But there was no longer sufficient time to incorporate these improvements in the regular mass production of the conventional V-1.

This does not exclude the possibility that Flak Regiment 155 (W) or a research unit nevertheless tested one or another high-speed cell in military exercises.

As possible photographic proof of this, there exists a photograph,[72] which shows an Fi-103 on its way to Antwerp, but which clearly indicates that this is no standard Fi-103. As far as can be judged from the quality of the photograph, this 'improved' V-1 had a fuselage with truncated tip. The shape of its wings resembled the wings of the FW-190-D or Ta-152 fighter aircraft. Here, too, an Argus tube on the back of the fuselage served as propulsion system.

At the end of the war, work was under way in Königshofen on developing a radar-absorbent coating for flying bombs. The tensile strength of this material is said to have been as great as that of aluminium.

Such materials with – as we say today – 'Stealth' characteristics would have made the improved flying bombs much harder to attack. Because it is in the nature of a flying bomb to end its flight by impact on an enemy target, there was of course the risk that the secret of these radar-absorbent coatings would sooner or later fall into enemy hands. It can therefore be assumed that the use of such top-secret materials would have been restricted to those flying bombs which were intended for a decisive special purpose - to carry victory weapons.

FVt 3

Among the victory weapons developments which continue to present a mystery is also a project with the name of FVt 3.

This weapon is mentioned in an official German document seized by the Allies and dating from 1945.[73] This is interesting because in the document a number of weapons are mentioned which appear in no other documents which have hitherto been published.

According to this list, the FVt 3 is said to have been an improved V-1, but instead of the normal high explosive warhead, it carried a multiple incendiary warhead. Unfortunately, although in the meantime more than 20 years have passed since this document was released, it has not been possible to find any documents giving further information on the FVt 3. Nevertheless, it is possible to give a more detailed description of this weapon. Mention of the concept of an improved V-1 can only mean that the FVt 3 was to be created on the basis of the Fi-103 high-speed cell (see relevant chapter). This was able, at a top speed of 850 kilometres per hour, to achieve a range of 500 kilometres.[74]

The incendiary warheads could not have been any kind of normal incendiary charge, because Adolf Hitler had decided against using such charges at the beginning of the war.

The multiple incendiary warheads must have been a completely new type of design, and to have been filled with the new *N-Stoff* (N-material). We know that Hitler's proposal to incorporate *N-Stoff* warheads in the weapons was not carried out by the Wehrmacht, as a result of which Hitler handed over the entire project for the development of *N-Stoff* to the SS. After one single 15-centimetre *N-Stoff* shell, in test conditions, burnt the earth over a radius of 800 to 1000 metres after it exploded, it might perhaps be imagined how serious the damage would have been if the Fi-103 with a total payload of one tonne of incendiary fluid had been used, because the total weight of one 15-centimetre shell (including casing and propellant) was only about 43 kilograms.

According to an allied CIOS report, the V-3 was an enlarged V-1 with an incendiary warhead instead of a normal high explosive charge, but there is very little known about the control system of the V-3. So, the FVt 3 was developed into the V-3, without plans of this version having turned up to date.

It is to be wondered whether we will ever know the whole truth about the FVt 3?

B) Improving V-1 performance by means of better propulsion systems

The Argus As-014 jet engine, also called the Schmidt engine, served as the standard propulsion unit for the Fi-103. This was a so-called pulse propulsion system. In contrast to the liquid-fuel V-2 rocket, the Schmidt engine drew in the oxygen necessary for combustion direct from the air.

Engineer Paul Schmidt developed this amazingly simple propulsion system, which was recognisable by the process of repeated explosion and propulsion which itself was dependent on the resonance speed of the jet tube. The result was the typical 'stutter' of the flying bombs.

Once it was started, the engine worked by self-ignition. But because of the characteristics of the propulsion system, it could only fly at a height of between 300 metres and 2,500 metres.[75]

The Argus As-014 gave the Fi-103 a speed of some 650 kilometres per hour close to the ground, and 575 kilometres per hour at 2,500 metres.

At these speeds and heights, under suitable conditions, the fastest Allied fighter aircraft such as the Mustang, Spitfire, Tempest, Mosquito and Meteor could overtake and shoot down the Fi-103. The required operational height imposed by the propulsion system also forced the Fi-103 to fly precisely in the area where Allied anti-aircraft defence was most effective.

Therefore, proposals were developed with some urgency to improve the performance of the Fi-103 by more efficient and better developed propulsion processes. Thus, on the drawing boards of the Porsche factory, the material saving Type 300 turbojet engine was born. Itself weighing 325 kilograms, its purpose was to enable the flying bomb to achieve a speed of 800 kilometres per hour and a range of 500 kilometres. At the end of the development process, the designers of the V-1 were about to deliver a range of 700 kilometres at a top speed of 900 kilometres per hour. The flying bombs equipped in this way would then be able to reach targets at the same distances as those reached by the 'winged rockets' of the A-4 series, but they would have been faster than the first jet fighters of the period.[76 77]

Whether or any test flight of the Type 300 took place is unknown.

But by the end of the war, this new kind of jet propulsion system under the alternative designation of Porsche 109/005 was not ready for operational service.

In Wetzlar, the inventor of the high-pressure pump, the brilliant weapons designer August Coenders, was similarly developing an alternative V-1 propulsion system. To do this, he developed a stern mounted aircraft engine of simple design. This propeller apparatus, concerning the performance of which nothing is still known, is said to have been designed in such a simple way that it could have been produced by any small assembly shop. And but here, too, the engine never came to be produced.

British sources also report an unknown new 'ramjet' system which similarly was intended to provide considerable improvements to the performance of the Fieseler missile.[78]

What became of the miniature high-performance engine and the ramjet after the Allies captured them?

During the last months of the war, work was also going

on with great speed on a further development of the Argus engine under the designation As-044, which was to be a a higher performance version of the As-014 with a maximum thrust of 500 k p. The new pulse propulsion system, however, at a length of 6.92 metres, was almost twice as long as the previous engine, which measured 3.66 metres in length.

By the end of the war it had even been possible to substantially increase the performance of the original As-014. By means of a series of refinements and by using nitrous oxide injection, by August 1944 it had been possible to improve the combustion system and thus to increase the speed of the V-1, first to 645 kilometres per hour, and finally to 765 kilometres per hour. On 2 February 1945, using an improved As-014, for the first time a speed of 800 kilometres per hour was achieved.

To what extent individual Fi-103s with 'souped-up' As-014s came into front line service is uncertain. But in 1945, British fighter pilots confirmed that the Fi-103s had become considerably faster

Thus, by the end of the war, as far as propulsion systems were concerned, all the conditions had been fulfilled to increase the performance of the Fi-103s to such an extent that they could not be intercepted even by the jet fighters of the period.

C) How were the 'V-1 Victory Weapons' to be actually used?

Improved launch ramps for the V-1

For a long time, one of the main disadvantages of the Fi-103 was that it depended upon being launched from fixed launch ramps. Thus, the concrete launch ramps in France, which could be seen from a long way away, were one of the preferred targets of the Allied air forces. Therefore, several different V-1 launch positions were developed which were increasingly simpler to erect and easier to repair.

Then, in autumn 1944, a semi-mobile launch ramp was ready for service. This was developed by the von Saurma brothers and no longer needed any kind of concrete works. All that was needed was a firm infrastructure. The new simplified launch ramp was rammed into the floor using strong iron ropes and blocks, or simply fixed to the surrounding trees.

One example of this was the V-1 launch bases in the Eifel which came into service from 20 October 1944. The majority of these launch ramps were located in evergreen coniferous forests, which even in winter provided cover against being spotted from the air.

In Spring 1945, V-1s were also launched directly from built-up areas. To achieve this, the simplified launch ramps of the von Saurma brothers were once again used. These could be hidden among large buildings.

Thus, in Rotterdam, the V-1 launch ramps were located in a large storage warehouse by the docks and in a sugar

factory. All that was needed to carry out launches and was to open the large doors of the building. However, it is not difficult to imagine how bad the conditions must have been under which the launch cruise had to work, in the largely enclosed spaces, with all the noise, the exhaust gases of the catapults and the engines.[79]

Shortly before the end of the war, there were plans to launch V-1s from U-boat bunkers or munitions bunkers in northern Germany.[80]

Kammler's intention to make the Fi-103 launch ramps fully mobile using two motor vehicles with caterpillar tracks based on the Panther tank as a it would have been possible to set up completely mobile V-1 batteries.

Later, during the post-war period, the Soviets carried out successful tests, based on this procedure, to launch their Type '10X' Fi-103 derivatives from converted T-34 tanks.

'Special operation'! The V-1 bunkers in France

As with the V-2s, it was planned to launch the V-1s from large bunkers at England. For this purpose, from 1943, huge concreted launch bunkers were built in Siracourt, Lottinghen, Courville, Tamerville and Brécourt, which were for the storage, maintenamce and launch of the Fi-103.

Like the later built simple bunker positions on the Normandy Peninsula, Brécourt was also intended for the combined launch of V-1, V-2 and 'Rheinbote' rockets.

Looking at the installations planned in Brécourt for use by the V-1s, the striking feature which catches the attention is the thick protective walls for the Fi-103 launch ramp - some 4 metres thick. The other V-1 positions in Brécourt are of such a scale that the whole installation can only be explained by assuming that special preparation and monitoring requirements were needed before the flying bombs were launched. This also indicates that it was planned to launch something different than standard warheads from there. The fact that something special was planned in Brecourt is also clear from the fact that a special operations group of V2 rockets, was to be accommodated there for 'special operations'.

As is also the case with the V-2 installations, the notable thing about the large bunkers planned for the V-1 is that they seem to be far too large for the simple launch and maintenance of the Fi-103s.[81] [82]

The heavy Allied bombing raids of Spring 1944 and the rapid collapse of the Normandy front in August 1944 prevented these V-1 bunkers being completed and brought into operation.

Aerial launch: launch using carrier aircraft

As already mentioned, one of the great disadvantages of the Fi-103 was that it depended upon fixed launch ramps. Was it also planned to launch Fi-103 victory weapons from carrier aircraft?

It is known that during the Second World War normal Fi-103 missiles were launched at Britain in increasing numbers from carrier aircraft. After preliminary trials had been carried out using the aircraft types FW-200, Do-215 and Do-217, from a summer 1944, Heinkel He-111s, H-16s, H-20s and H-22s launched 1,250 V-1s against Britain. In the night between 1 and 2 September 1944, 23 V-1s were also launched from a He-111 at Paris.

Moreover, the opportunities which aerial launches offered of splitting the enemy defence capabilities by frequent changes of target, were only used on one occasion. On 24 December 1944, 50 flying bombs from carrier aircraft from KG 53 attacked the industrial city of Manchester in the north of Britain, but heavily defended London remained the main target of the Heinkel/V-1 combination.

According to British accounts, only a very few flying bombs reached their intended target. Although they presented Allied ground and aerial defence with a difficult task, probably only 65 of the bombs were launched from the air reached the London region and only another 150 V-1s struck other British targets. The rest were either shot down by the British air defence, or simply malfunctioned.[83]

But more recent British publications have revealed that the effect of the V-1 offensive from the air was somewhat greater than had hitherto been assumed.

At least 17 He-111 mother aircraft fell victim to British night fighters during these operations. Even more Heinkels exploded at the dangerous moment when the V-1 was launched in the air, or crashed in accidents.

The main disadvantage of aerial launching was the poor accuracy of the V-1s which were used, and the fact that their Heinkel He-111 carrier aircraft were completely out of date.

To resolve these difficulties, between September and November 1944, many further aerial launch trials were carried out using He-111s to improve accuracy.

By the end of December 1944, it had also been possible to launch 32 Fi-103s of the new types G-1 and H-1. These further developments of the weapon were improved performance versions with an increased volume of propellant. To date, it is not known what these improved Fi-103 missiles, launched from the air, actually looked like. In any event, they were never used in action.

This raises the question, therefore, whether these missiles were perhaps not prototypes for later victory weapons. This would explain the remarkable silence which was maintained about these versions!

Trials using remote control of the missiles from the air were also undertaken as early as 1943. This procedure was also used at the end of 1944 over Antwerp, using He-111 control aircraft.

At the beginning of January 1945, the Allies took very seriously the dangers posed by the conventional aerial launch of the V-1.[84] But at that time, because of shortage of fuel, the V-1 launches by Heinkel He-111 squadrons were coming to an end. In as secret study carried out by the American Strategic Air Forces regarding German potential in 1945, it was firmly expected that soon up to 450 flying bombs per month would be launched from the air against Britain. The only limiting factor, the report said, was the small number of the He-111 mother aircraft which were still available.

What the Allies are obviously did not know was that by the end of the war of, in addition to the old Heinkel He-111, other considerably more modern types of aircraft were available suitable to launch V-1s. These were aircraft of the type Junkers Ju-88, Ju-188 and Ju-388. These had been tested already for suitability as launch aircraft and could have been used without any problems to launch missiles.

According to a modern American account, some Ju 88s with a Fi-103 suspended beneath them were used against Britain. Unfortunately, it is not known whether these were converted aircraft of the Ju-88-A, G or S versions.

The new Arado Ar-234 jet bomber was also to be used as a carrier aircraft for the Fi-103, and would carry the aircraft as part of a *Mistel* arrangement with the help of a starting sledge. Test flights of this combination are said to have been made. How far had these advanced by the time the war came to an end?

Another plan intended to use the single-engined Focke-Wulf Fw-190 fighter as the launch aircraft for the V-1. To support the overloaded aircraft assembly, a three-wheeled starting sledge was to be used. In this way, it would be possible to avoid using multi-engined bombers to launch V-1s, since these are bombers could no longer be operated during the last months of the war because of shortage of fuel. In addition, this DFS *Mistel* project had the advantage that the single-engined fighter could have more easily detached itself after the launch of the V-1. The Fw-190/Fi-103 project had the project designation of F 59 'Brummer', and by the end of the war had got as far as a test launch.

Aerial launching was at the end of the war an effective alternative to the ground launch of the Fi-103 missiles. Improved missiles with greater range and greater accuracy could have been carried by fast carrier aircraft against any target within range. But despite this, from mid-January 1945, fuel shortages meant that no more operations were flown with conventional Fi-103s.

2) EMW A-4 'V-2' - Special versions and their further development

The only thing I know with absolute clarity is that two
words tellingly describe the plans for deployment of the A-4:
Too late!
General Dr. Walter Dornberger, 1952

Were special versions under construction?

Did former leading Peenemünde scientists leave hidden clues in their published material?

The former Peenemünde rocket technologists Dieter Huzel wrote in his postwar memoirs what happened when the first rockets produced in Nordhausen arrived in Peenemünde: to camouflage the armour and protect them against the weather they were covered, when the first vehicles were pushed into the great hall, the entire test-bed crew gathered to watch them being uncovered. But the excitement quickly diminished when the covers were removed to and nothing else appeared but the 'gherkins' which were so well known to them. Huzel went on to say that the expression 'gherkin' came from the fact that the V-2 rockets were painted in a dull olive green colour and had the familiar long shape.[85]

Dieter Huzel, who was one of the leading specialists, had a comprehensive knowledge about what went on in Peenemünde. According to him, other rockets than the normal standard V-2s were under construction away from Peenemünde, and their arrival for checking and launching was eagerly awaited. Huzel places this event in Spring 1944 when the first rockets arrived from Nordhausen on the Usedom Peninsula. But at the same time he writes that these rockets, like the other rockets tested at Peenemünde, were camouflaged in an olive green. But the single-coloured olive green camouflage paint (green gherkin) was not introduced in Spring 1944, but only in 1945. This change of colour from three-coloured camouflage to a single coat of olive green camouflage cannot have been unknown to specialist Huzel. Did he want to give us a clue here that special variants of the rockets were under construction, whose arrival was awaited in Peenemünde in 1945?

Further developments of the EMW A-4
Whether the A-4 was decades in advance of its time or not, Hitler's rocket experts did not rest on their laurels.

Immediately after the A-4 development programme was completed in 1942/43, further research work on the basic A-4 model at the Army research establishment at Peene-münde split into two different directions.

On the one hand, work went on with increasing the range by alterations and improvements to the rocket. This produced the so-called range A-4, but also winged rockets and multi-stage versions.

On the other hand, work went on with developing rocket propulsion systems which would either enable performance to be further increased or which would not create such a great bottleneck for the heavily pressed German war industry as the previous models had done.

This was because the A-4 or suffered from the fact that production of its fuel of alcohol and liquid oxygen could not so easily be increased as would be necessary to make the weapons available for mass deployment.

Therefore, a commission for a fundamental investigation of new types of propulsion system was issued as early as 15 October 1942 to the German *Reichspost* Research Establishment, and had the same high degree of urgency as the rest of the A-4 programme.

Another plan, caused by the war situation, was to look to replacements by alternative materials (for example, replacing steel by aluminium) for the construction series B. The A-4 V-15 was to serve as the trial prototype. How many of the originally planned 450 Series B A-4 rockets were finally built is unknown.

A) Improvements to the A-4 basic model

'Reichweite (Long-range)' A-4
The constant withdrawal of the fronts in 1944 soon made it necessary to increase the range of the A-4. By small improvements in the standard design of the rocket, such as, for example, increasing combustion pressure, discarding the electrical apparatus which had become superfluous as a result of the integration apparatus, and by slightly increasing fuel tank quantities, it was possible to increase the range of the operational A-4 to 320 kilometres.

In trial launches at Peenemünde, individual trial missiles with enlarged fuel containers achieved a range of 480 kilometres. But the larger tanks could only be accommodated at the expense of reducing the payloads.[86]The use of non-conventional devices, such as, for example, radiological charges, Zippermayr explosive and small uranium bombs would have a certainly overcome this disadvantage. Whether a small production run of these long-range A-4s were ever manufactured for field trials is unknown.

A-4 with extended fuselage
The extended fuselage was achieved by incorporating an additional section for enlarged fuel tanks and a 'Visol' propulsion system (with only two ventilation openings at the end of the fuselage).

The overall length of this rocket was 15,030 mm as against 14,030 mm in the case of the normal A-4.[87] What stage of development this design had reached at the end of the war remains unknown. The A-4 with extended fuselage was the later pattern for the Russian post-war R-2 project.

A-4 'Dora' - railway-artillery combination
The 'Dora' project involved the largest gun which had ever been used in the world until that time.

In the context of his planned retribution measures

against Britain, Adolf Hitler personally proposed using a combination of *Aggregat-4* (A-4) and the 'Dora' railway-mounted gun. This hybrid consisting of rocket and artillery was to fire special shells loaded with at least 1000 kilograms of explosive at London from appropriately built gigantic bunkers located, for instance, on Cap Gris Nez. To test out this idea, shells were even constructed with three rocket stages which would ignite one after the other after they had been fired.

There was no further development of the A4 'Dora' idea.[88]

B) Alternative types of rocket propulsion system

EMW propulsion system variants: A-6 to A-8

EMW A-6 (*Aggregat 6*): This rocket, sometimes called *Aggregat 6*, was based on the A-4, but had a propulsion system powered by 'Salbei' (sulphurated salpetric acid) and 'Visol' (a mixture of petrol and benzole). This propulsion system was designed to provide 30 t of thrust. But it only remained at initial study stage. According to other information sources, the designation A-6 was later used for a rocket aircraft (see Volume 3).

The 'Visol' rockets were easy to differentiate from the normally-powered A4 (alcohol plus oxygen), because at the end of the fuselage they had only two ventilation openings. The standard version had four ventilation openings which were clearly visible between the tail fins.

EMW A-7 (*Aggregat 7*): see below.

EMW A-8 (*Aggregat 8*): The designation *Aggregat 8* comprised a whole series of designs, some of which differed markedly from each other. It was originally planned that the A-8 would have a great significance for the German rocket project.

In November 1941, Dr Dornberger had ordered Wernher von Braun to throw the main weight of research behind the search for a successor to the A-4 by concentrating on the A-8 instead of the A-9. He considered that the new propulsion system in the A-8 had a better chance of being implemented than the A-9 glider rocket. French work after the war on an A-8 derivative, called the 'Super V2', later demonstrated that his arguments were correct.

The following versions of the A-8 were to be created:

EMW A-8/1: This rocket design was about the same size as the A-5, but, like the A-6, was to be powered by 'Salbei' and 'Visol'. The project never came to be implemented.

EMW A-8/high-pressure rocket: This rocket was to be the same size as the A-4. It was intended that its fuel complement of 8330 kg of 'Salbei' and 1670 kg of 'Visol' would achieve 50,000 kp of thrust. This propulsion performance was to enable the rocket to carry a 2-ton warhead over a distance of 300 kilometres. This represented twice the payload that the A-4 could carry over the same range. The project was not implemented.

EMW A-8/3: This rocket design was developed as early as 5 February 1943 in collaboration with the BMW factory in Berlin/Spandau. The rocket propulsion system was conceived by Dr. Thiel and Helmut von Zbrowski as a hypergolic and non-cryogenic system. Although the thrust of 35,000 kp was to be less than that of the high-pressure rocket, it was hoped that a longer combustion period of about 100 seconds would enable extremely high speeds to be achieved. The rocket would in this way be able to carry a 2.5 ton payload over a distance of 450 kilometres. The external shape of the A-8/3 would have been similar to that of the A-4. Its launch weight was to be 22.37 tons. The project was abandoned again in mid-1942 for unknown reasons.

It was never clearly established why these potentially very successful variants of propulsion systems were not pursued with more urgency. Possibly the death of the brilliant propulsion specialist Dr Thiel in the British air raid on Peenemünde on 18 August 1943 (Operation 'Hydra') represented a loss which it was difficult to replace. Post-war evaluations also took the view that the death of Dr Thiel in itself had made the entire RAF air raid on Peenemünde 'worthwhile'.[89] [90] [91] [92]

Hydrogen technology: the A-4 'America Rocket'

After the United States of America entered the war in December 1941, consideration was given to producing, with the greatest possible urgency, a long-range rocket which could cross the Atlantic, and thought was given to making appropriate modifications to the A-4.[93]

One possibility which suggested itself was to use liquid hydrogen as a propellant. Using hydrogen in this way in conjunction with liquid oxygen as an oxidator would have produced an exhaust velocity of 3,100 metres per second. It was calculated that this 'America A-4' would achieve the desired range whilst maintaining the payload.

Liquid hydrogen represented the ideal rocket propellant in the minds of all leading rocket visionaries. But it had great disadvantages. First of these was that it was very expensive, although in wartime this consideration was less important than it might otherwise have been. More important were its high level of cryogenicity and its low density. The latter made it necessary to provide large fuel tanks if it was planned to achieve appropriate ranges.

During the post-war period, Dr Dornberger wrote that the whole idea had been put on hold until the hydrogen question had been resolved. But this does not mean that solving the hydrogen question was not tackled! It remains unknown even today to what extent the question of hydrogen powered propulsion systems for rockets in Peenemünde was pursued by Germany's experts in propulsion systems and propellants. Perhaps we should expect a surprise here, too, although it is certain that at the time it must have been extremely difficult to solve this problem with the ersatz materials available in wartime.

Only in the mid-1950s did the former Peenemünde scientist Krafft von Ehricke succeed in getting to grips with the technology of hydrogen propulsion in the United

States. In the 1960s, the upper stages of the 'Saturn' rockets were powered with the help of this propellant. A hydrogen propulsion system is even used today in the Space Shuttle. This, too, is a direct consequence of the work of Krafft von Ehricke and Professor Eugen Sänger, the effects of which are still apparent today.

Nuclear-powered rocket propulsion systems

It is a fact that in the Third Reich research was going on into developing a nuclear propulsion system for rockets. With such a propulsion system, it would have been possible to solve the important 'range problem' and to achieve unheard-of speeds.

Dr Dornberger wrote[94] [95] that after 1943 the Peenemünde scientists had linked up with Professor Heisenberg to investigate practical possibilities of this. Dornberger continues: 'We were dreaming of atomic energy, which ultimately would give us the propulsion system which was needed to enable flights to be made into the infinity of space and to the farthest stars'.

In his British hearing, Wernher von Braun pointed out[96] that this was only a private and not very intensive contact with the Kaiser Wilhelm Institute in Berlin-Dahlem and to the researchers Heisenberg, von Weiszäcker and von Ardenne. Certainly an illustrious band of scientists for a purely private contact!

According to von Braun, the project was abandoned because the researchers lacked the necessary raw materials. But in actual fact, as early as 15 October 1942, a wartime commission was given by the *Oberkommando des Heeres* to *Postrat* Kubicki at the German *Reichspost* Research Establishment in Berlin-Tempelhof. The commission was issued by *Abteilung XI* of the *Heereswaffenamt's Amtsgruppe*

für Entwicklung und Prüfwesen (development and testing authority) and was given the highest level of priority – SS (*Sonderstufe*: special priority). This gave it the same level of priority as the A-4 rocket programme itself! This shows the seriousness and urgency of this 'A-planning'! Certainly, in this light, there can no longer be any question of a purely 'private contact'!

The commission consisted of two parts. Firstly, it required 'fundamental research into increasing the performance of various liquid fuel propulsion systems for rockets by the use of propellant mixes with the highest energy content'. This may well have referred to the hydrogen propulsion system which was only ready for operational use in the 1950s.

The second element of consisted of just one brief sentence: 'Investigation of the possibility of using atomic decay and the chain reaction as the basis of a rocket propulsion system'.

The authors who have mentioned this document in the past are agreed that it was about the development of nuclear rocket propulsion technology. But on closer observation, the second element conceals two different development tasks. In referring to the planned use of atomic decay, it was clearly not referring to a type of propulsion, because of the impossibility of changing the atomic decay rate of uranium radioisotopes. Probably this element was nothing other than a covert commission to develop radiological weapons to be used in conjunction with the A-4 (see chapter concerning radiological armament).[97]

A precondition for using the chain reaction as a rocket propulsion system was the use of a specially designed reactor, and, although the OKH commission was only issued on 15 October 1942, long before this, on 31 August

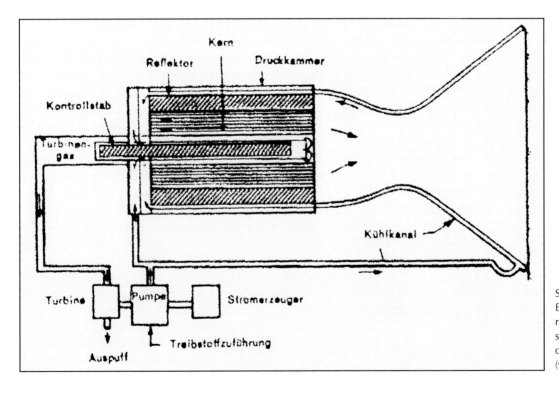

Sketch by Krafft von Ehricke of a nuclear rocket propulsion system with 45 tons of thrust at launch (www.jonastal.com).

1941, contacts on this issue had taken place between the brilliant Peenemünde propulsion specialist Dr Thiel and the representative of the *Uran-Verein* (Uranium Association), Professor Schumann. Later development work was also carried out by the Peenemünde expert Krafft von Ehricke in collaboration with Professor Heisenberg. Then, in the 1950s, in the USA, von Ehricke put forward the design of a nuclear rocket propulsion system providing 45 tons of thrust at launch which was a development of former German wartime plans.

Dr Sänger, too, wanted to incorporate an atomic propulsion system in a version of his Antipodes bomber.

In addition to the German *Reichspost* research establishment under Manfred von Ardenne, the so-called Kammler complex at Skoda in Prague was also involved in the development of nuclear propulsion systems. In these propulsion systems, the heat of a nuclear reactor was to serve to heat a propellant (nitrogen or oxygen). In the reactor chamber it was very likely that enriched uranium U-235 metal dust embedded in graphite would serve as the combustible material.

This project also received a serious setback with the death of Dr Thiel in the Allied air raid on Peenemünde on 17/18 August 1943.

Further work on the development of nuclear rocket propulsion systems may later have also been carried out in Object 'Quarz' near Melk. The underground secret factory there has already been connected with research on atomic propulsion systems for aircraft (see Volume 1). In the tunnels there, mounting assemblies for propulsion systems for the A-4 were found.

According to research carried out by the Austrian researcher Schmitzberger, a concealed bunker test-bed was also included in another tunnel. This remarkable tunnel-based test-bed is amazingly similar to the typical A-4 propulsion test beds.

In the meantime, things have gone remarkably quiet about atomic propulsion systems for rockets.

Too quiet? - Things were very different at the end of the 1950s.[98] [99] [100] [101] At that time both the Americans and the Russians were planning multi-stage rockets with atomic propulsion systems. This type of propulsion was considered to be the perfect solution of almost all propulsion problems. Thus, in 1955, Project 'Rover' was created as a joint programme of the US Atomic Energy Commission and the US Air Force with the purpose of creating a nuclear rocket propulsion system. In the event, some nuclear rockets were built and successfully tested in the Nevada desert. But further information about the success of the Rover project still appear to be classified. Is this another case where the plans and ideas were based on the former German wartime projects carried out by von Heisenberg, RPF, and Skoda?

It is already known of the early Russian designs that they, like the German designs, 'happened' to use nitrogen and oxygen as the propellant which would be heated in an atomic reactor.

Unfortunately, without the Allied secret archives being opened, it is not possible to make a judgment as to whether the German researchers did actually succeed in solving the technical problems of nuclear propulsion for rockets.

But it is certain that such propulsion systems, even if they had been developed at some time in the Third Reich, would have ideally been available as individual prototypes. Therefore it is not likely that there would be any question of them being used in a normal A-4 rockets with conventional Amatol explosive.

But it would have been a very different matter if they were to be incorporated in the reusable Sanger Antipodes bomber in a rocket with a nuclear warhead which could potentially have decided the outcome of the war.

V-2 with nuclear explosive material

A British report dating from 1947, concerning secret hiding places in which Wernher von Braun securely concealed the most up-to-date rocket plans from the Allies before the war ended, mentions a nuclear-powered V-2 which was to be constructed of so-called nuclear exposive materials. This must have referred to materials such as nipolite, which were also to be used in producing other weapons such as missiles and bombs (S A 4000). The raw explosive material used for this purpose could, because of its mechanical strength, be used instead of metal for the outer shell of the V-2. The British report continues that it would not need a great deal of imagination to conceive the effectiveness of a V-2 powered by a nuclear propulsion system and entirely or partly constructed of nuclear explosive materials, with this nuclear material shell acting as additional explosive on impact.

Unfortunately, the report does not describe whether it was hoped to achieve the critical mass of a nuclear explosion when the rocket impacted, or whether it was intended that the conventional explosion would spread the radioactive material over the impact area and its surroundings.

The idea of producing a rocket composed of explosive nuclear materials combined with a nuclear propulsion system promised not only to achieve long (intercontinental?) range, but also the possibility of creating great devastation in the target area. But the weapon would have required special preparations at launch. This raises the question as to whether the planning of V-2 launch bunkers in Ebensee in December 1944 were meant to be used in connection with this weapon.

Evidently the nuclear explosive materials V-2 project is one of those German designs which were to be kept secret after capitulation to the Allies. Until today, no such rocket has ever been developed.

Long-range ramjet rockets based on the A-4

a) V -2 with Trommsdorff propulsion system

As a further project for increasing the range of rockets, in December 1944 research was carried out into the possibility of achieving an increase in range by increasing the final velocity. To achieve this it was planned to combine the A-4 rocket with a large Trommsdorff propulsion system in a second stage. It was hoped that this rocket could carry a 250 kilogram payload.[102] [103] With a smaller supply of fuel, it was planned to accelerate the rocket to a speed of 560 metres per second, before the Trommsdorff propulsion system in the second stage became operational at a height of some 20 kilometres.

In this way it was hoped to achieve a final velocity of 1,980 metres per second and a range of 400 kilometres. The missile itself was to be stabilised by means of additional ailerons. It was planned that a guidance system for the second stage would be operated via the 'Tonne' television camera. Apparently, the calculations were not continued after January 1945, because it was believed that it would be possible to achieve a longer ranges for less expense using the A-4-B rocket.

b) Two-stage rocket with wing assembly

During his time as an American prisoner in Garmisch-Partenkirchen, Wernher von Braun once again began working on the design of a two-stage V-2, and on 11 January 1946, in Fort Bliss, Texas, he presented to US Major-General Barnes the design for his 'two-stage V-2 with ramjet propulsion system'. Here, too, six small ramjet propulsion systems with rectangular air inlet openings in the stump wings were to be incorporated in the second stage.

At the beginning of 1944, the Americans also adopted this former Second World War idea in their own planning. This led to 'Hermes II'. The first rocket, called 'Missile 0', and equipped with a wing assembly, was launched on 29 May 1947. It was the notorious and well-publicised rocket which became known as a result of the accident it caused when it crashed in Juarez in Mexico. At the time, however, it was referred to everywhere as a V-2 and not as 'Hermes II'.

In November 1950, the Americans abandoned the idea of developing a tactical rocket with warhead on the basis of the 'Hermes II', and instead used the Hermes II for purely research purposes. In the meantime, however, successful tests had been carried out with the ramjet propulsion systems in the Californian High Sierra mountains. Finally, in 1953, all work on the 'Hermes II' was brought to an end. The aim was now to develop a three-stage rocket called 'Hermes C' on the basis of the V-2. This rocket was to have a range of up to 500 miles. This design eventually became Wernher von Braun's famous 'Redstone' rocket - the USA's first tactical nuclear rocket.

c) Two-stage rockets with ramjet propulsion systems

In 1944, in the process of developing two-stage rockets, it had become the view of German scientists such as Wernher von Braun that a ramjet missile with speeds of up to Mach 3 was the technically superior solution to pure rocket propulsion systems.[104] [105]

The Peenemünde scientists therefore planned to produce a V-2 which would have a second stage with a wing assembly and provided with a ramjet propulsion system. It was hoped with this rocket to be able to achieve a range of 2,500 kilometres in a flight time of 70 minutes. In comparison to the normal V2 (flight time: five minutes) and the A 9/A 10 (45 minutes' flight time), this was a considerably longer duration of flight. The purpose of this design was not to achieve the greatest possible maximum height, as was the case with the ballistic missile, but to achieve the greatest possible rate of acceleration in order to guarantee optimal functioning of the ramjet system. Only by rapid ignition velocity could the maximum range be used.

What did these Peenemünde developments look like? We know that work was carried out on an A-9 with duck-wing configuration, and that during the post-war period Polish soldiers gave accounts of the testing of a 'V-4' (see section 'V-4'). This 'V-4', the manufacturer of which remains unknown, would have been outstandingly suitable as the second stage of the A-4 and displays great similarity to post-war Soviet designs for two-stage rockets.

There were two possible options for incorporating a ramjet stage in the A-4. The ramjet stage would be attached directly to the A-4 as a second stage, or the ramjet missile could be attached to the side of the A4 in a *Mistel*-style configuration. The second solution promised fewer problems in separating the rocket stages and also required no expensive alterations to be made to the first stage.

Although work was carried on on the 'two-stage version', there are no more details available about the design.

In Peenemünde there was also on a project called '*Ross und Reiter*' (horse and rider), in which a rocket with ramjet propulsion system was to be fixed to the side of an A-4. The ramjet missile would, in this way, be carried like a rider on a horse up to the point at which it would be released.

According to information provided by U S General H A P Arnold from 1946, the Germans also undertook experiments in using the 'piggyback' principle in conjunction with the V-2 rocket.

The official plans of the *Ross und Reiter* project have completely disappeared today in the same way as those of the V-4. Is this a coincidence or is there some connection here? In the post-war period, work was carried on by the Russians and Americans on developing both combinations of ramjet rockets. Now this is scarcely a coincidence, because both East and West forced captured German rocket engineers from Peenemünde to undertake such development work.

In the Soviet Union this led to the design of the R-15 and EKR rocket/ramjet missile by the German aerodynamics engineer Albring. In this project, he planned to create a two-stage rocket similar to that in the former German wartime project. The rocket, flying faster than sound at a height of 13 kilometres, was to carry a nuclear warhead weighing 3,000 kilograms over a range of 2,900 kilometres.

The Americans went the other way, and via a further development of the duck wing A-9 with a ramjet propulsion system (XSSN-A-2), created Project 'Navajo', which was to have been a further development of the former *Ross und Reiter* project. Here, too, there are remarkable similarities between 'Navajo' and the 'V-4/A- 4'.

Nobody has yet been able to ascertain how far advanced these German plans were by the end of the war. However, it could very well be the case that they were linked to the small two-stage long-range rocket for which *SS-Obergruppenführer* Kammler had been ordered by Hitler to create an underground launch base. Where this base was planned and how far it had been possible to develop it remains an open question even today.

C) A-4 'Winged Rockets'

EMW A-4B 'Bastard'

> *Our expectations had been fully met.*
> *General* Dr. Walter Dornberger, 1952

Although coming a long way before the A-9 in the project numerical sequence, the EMW A-4B only came into play a long time afterwards on 10 October 1944 as an improvised makeshift solution.[106] [107] [108]

At the time, the Allied advance in France required urgent solutions for extending the range of the A-4. Unfortunately, the development of its planned successor model, the A-9, proved to be complicated and difficult, so that a temporary solution had to be sought.

As early as the beginning of September 1944, Wernher von Braun had ordered that progress on the A-9 project should be slowed down in order to speed up the development of the 'Bastard'. In this project, normal A-4s would be used which would be fitted with new gliding wings and an enlarged compensating aerial rudder on the tail of the rocket. Because time was pressing, the first test prototypes of the A-4B were to be fitted with the wedge-shaped wings which had already been tested with favourable results in the wind tunnel tests undertaken before 1943. Whether in the meantime further developed wedge-shaped wings were to be used for later 'Bastard' rockets as it was planned to use for the A-9 is unknown, although conceivable.

The greatest problem which had not yet been resolved was initially the creation of the enlarged aerial rudder and suitable servo motors which were able to cope with the greater demands placed on the guidance system.

In the A-4B, an attempt was made to apply the principle of Dr Sänger, in accordance with which a missile, as it returns through the thicker layers of air, carries out a long gliding flight to the target. Once it got to the target, the 'Bastard', like the A-9, was to shed its wings and go into a terminal dive.

It was hoped that the A-4B would replace the A-4 in production and in front line service, before, finally, the improved A-9 with greater increases in range and payload could be brought in to service.

Because of its additional 52-degree wedge shaped wings, the A-4B weighed 1350 kilograms more than the basic design and and was to achieve a range of 450 to 500 kilometres. There were later plans to increase this value still further. The target was a range of 750 to 800 kilometres!

On 24 October 1944, orders were issued for five prototypes to be produced. By the end of the war more than 20 'Bastard' missiles had been produced.

Two versions of the A-4B were known. The differences between them were in the wings and the auxiliary control surfaces. In the later version, the wings were 1.1 metre higher on the fuselage, and this version had triangular auxiliary control surfaces. By contrast, the earlier design had rounded auxiliary control surfaces.

The first test launch took place as early as 27 December 1944 and the second on 8 January 1945, but both of these were failures. But the third test on 24 January 1945 was a success, although in the literature it is still disputed as to whether a range of 750 kilometres was achieved.

The question which remains unresolved to date is thus whether the A-4B's wings which were designed before 1943 would be able to withstand the demands of re-entry and gliding flight.

However, *General* Dr Dornberger said that he was very satisfied with the results which had been achieved. At least six 'Bastard' A-4Bs were brought into semi-official front-line service within the framework of a troop exercise. This is no speculative assertion, but is based on reliable sources! Afterwards, and until the end of March 1945, the increased range V-2 rockets were launched in small numbers from Westphalia, north-west Germany and the Lüneberg Heath at Great Britain.[109]

In addition to being tested at Peenemünde, shortly before the end of the war the 'Bastard' was also to be tested at testing sites in Austria. As early as the summer and autumn of 1944, appropriate investigations had been carried out within the framework of 'Object Salamander/Zement', where there were plans for A-4B production and launch facilities. Nothing more came of these plans because of the war situation.

During the post-war period, the idea of winged rockets was not pursued any further despite the development potential which it contained.

The A-4 B 'Bastard' rocket is until today repeatedly confused with the A-9. Both rockets were said to have no significance in military terms, and Wernher von Braun said that the efforts expended in developing the A-4B 'Bastard' were a trick to deceive the leadership of the Third Reich into thinking that his rocket team were busy. In this way it was hoped to prevent the Peenemünde rocket crew from being dissolved and called up into the Wehrmacht. But can we seriously believe this?

EMW A-9: The second generation of rockets

The first time the A-9 is mentioned is as early as 10 June 1940 on a Peenemünde design as the final stage of the two-stage 'Atlantic rocket'.[110] [111] It was originally planned that this design would replace that of the A-4 which dated back to the 1930s, but because of the rapidly deteriorating war situation the rocket could not be produced in time. The aim with the new rocket was to overcome many of the disadvantages which were associated with the A-4.

In the past, many contradictory and incorrect things have been written on the subject of the A-9. One only needs to recall the repeated assertion that, in order to get Hitler's approval for its development, the designation of the A-9 was changed by the scientists at Peenemünde to A-4B in 1944. In actual fact, Hitler's orders to build this rocket were issued during the now famous conversation between him, Dr Dornberger and von Braun in July 1943.

With the same external fuselage measurements, the A -9 was not simply a winged variant of the A-4, but it was a completely new development with different fuselage structure and propulsion system. With a weight of 18,750 kilograms, it was intended to be capable of transporting up to 2,500 kilograms of explosive.

As already mentioned, the roots of the A-9 go back to shortly after the outbreak of the war, when the winged rockets came on the scene. The idea of the Peenemünde scientists was no longer to allow the rockets, as previously, to impact the target at 800 metres per second, but after the conclusion of the burn to convert this momentum into range by the addition of wings.

As was the case in the Sänger project, the difficulties connected with the wings of the A-9 were that the problem of the speed of sound had first to be resolved. Because it was not until 1945 before German pilots in Messerschmitt Me-262 aircraft successfully went through the sound barrier, for the design of the rocket it was necessary to fall back on comprehensive measurements and tests in the wind tunnel.[112]

By the end of the war it had in this way been possible to produce at least three different versions of wings for the A-9, although it is unclear which of these was planned to be used in the mass production version of the rocket. These included a type of wedge shaped aircraft wings, a delta wing extending only part of the way along the fuselage and an extreme delta wing extending along the entire fuselage.[113]

The first 45-degree wedge shaped wing was based on the results of the wind tunnel tests carried out since 1940 (Zeppelin factory) and later turned up in aircraft developments in the post-war period! But later wind tunnel tests up to Mach 10 showed that problems might be expected with this form of wing in connection with a the load imposed by re-entry as the second stage of the A-10. In the first wing variant also, an additional enlargement of the tail control surfaces proved to be necessary. The same wing combination was used later for the temporary solution A-4B Bastard.

Only a little is known about the second wing. Its shortened delta wing configuration emerges as a main variant in some later designs of the A-9.

The third wing was a successful design for flight at speeds beyond the speed of sound and also at the same time solved the problems which arose in transonic flight. Flight tests, however, showed that in this variant there was a danger of fire. There was also a fourth option for the A-9 on the drawing board, with a duck wing configuration.

Table: Further developments of the A-4 basic model carried out at Peenemünde and postwar developments of the design

German project	Postwar development
Separable warhead (A–4, A–9)	Russians: R–1 (1949)
	Americans: Redstone (1953)
Separable payload capsule for living animals (hamsters, rabbits, dogs) (A–4)	Russians: R–2 (1947)
Single-hull construction (A–9)	Americans: Redstone (1953)
	Russians: R–11 (151)
Duck-wing A–9	Americans: XSSM (1950)
Second stage (*Ross und Reiter*) with ramjet propulsion system (two-stage A–4)	Americans: Hermes II (1947), Navaho (1956)
	Russians: EKR (1953), Burya (1957)

Many tests in 1944/45 had already demonstrated that the German winged rocket configuration was fully controllable in flight both at speeds beyond the speed of sound and below the speed of sound.

The second important and distinguishing characteristic of the A-9 was its lighter fuselage structure,[114] in comparison to the A-4. Possibly this indicated that trials had been carried out with a single-hulled version. In this way, besides saving on material, it would at the same time have been possible to achieve an increase in range. But precise data concerning this lighter structure are no longer available today.

The third difference was in the propulsion system. One of the great disadvantages of the A-4 was that its fuel components of oxygen and alcohol could only be put into the rocket immediately before the launch, so that, once the fuel tanks had been filled, the rocket could not be stored and had to be launched immediately afterwards. Therefore, in the A-9, as was the case with the *Wassefall* flak rocket, Visol and Salbei were used as fuel. Rockets whose fuel tanks were filled with Visol and Salbei could be stored.

Design and construction of the A-9 propulsion system had already been begun in 1941. The initial target was 30 tons of thrust. It was finally possible to reach exit velocities of 2,100 metres per second (the exit velocity for the A-4 was 1,700 metres per second).

The initial range of the A-9 was to be over 800 kilometres, and it was hoped, by the time development work was completed, to have achieved a range of 2,500 kilometres. That would have been an enormous achievement for a single-stage rocket of the period, and would have placed the A-9 on a level with the medium-range rockets we have today.

During its flight, the A-9 was to be precisely monitored and controlled. While in the stage of initial ascent, control was carried out by means of an accelerometer; after this the subsequent control was carried out by means of a new type of rocket long-range radar system (see section 'Flight Monitoring and Calibration' in Volume 3). As the flight proceeded further, it was then the intention to monitor the flight of the A-9 by means of two radar stations, and after re-entry into the thicker layers of air it was intended to control the gliding flight to the target by means of radio. Over the target, a signal would then have placed the A-9 in its final vertical dive.

It was hoped that this vertical dive would make it more difficult for enemy observation and aerial defence, because, in the case of the winged rockets, as a result of their lower speed during the gliding flight phase, they were (at least in theory) susceptible to being successfully intercepted by air defence.

Although during 1944 discussions also took place in Peenemünde with Professor Dr Eugen Sänger to achieve more rapid progress in development of the winged rockets, because of its new technology, the rocket proved to be very difficult to manufacture. On 30 September 1944, Wernher von Braun therefore ordered that shortcuts should be taken in the A-4 programme to achieve the first launch more quickly.

Two versions of the A-9 were known. The noticeable differences between the A-9A (14,030 mm) and the A-9B (15,030 mm) could be easily distinguished because of the different length of the fuselage, since the A-9B had an additional fuselage section to hold more fuel. This design variant was adopted in 1947 for the development of the Russian R-2 rocket.

There were plans to increase the 30 tons of thrust achieved by the propulsion system of the A-9 to 60 tons of thrust in the A-9B. The propulsion system of the Russian EKR also later 'happened' to have the same performance characteristics.

While the wing surfaces of the A 9A ran along the entire fuselage, those of the later developed version began further down the fuselage.

According to one account, the long wings of the earlier version tended to catch fire in the re-entry phase, so that the shorter wings proved to be more effective. This is another indication that flight tests of the A-9 (two-stage rocket?) had already taken place.

The A-9 programme was not under the direction of Arthur Rudolph, and to date it is unknown who had overall control.

The rocket was principally to be manufactured in smaller 'development plants'. Whether it was possible to produce an improved version of the A-9B is, however, doubtful, because its fuselage and its more powerful propulsion system in comparison to the A-9 presented further risks in developing the weapon, which would have required time to solve.

It is unknown how many A-9 rockets were actually able to be built. Successful flight trials are said to have taken place in January and March 1945, and a reliable report, based on the statements of one of the most senior former Peenemünde officers, even makes reference to a U-boat version of the A-9 which is said to have been successfully tested in December 1944 in conjunction with the U-boat A-4.[115] But it is not clear whether this test was only to demonstrate that the A-9s were suitable for use with the U-boats, or whether it involved an actual U-boat launch. Based on the same source, it is unclear whether a few A-9s were actually used in combat, because most of the relevant information fell into Russian hands or was destroyed by the Germans to prevent the data falling into Allied hands.

In addition to being used as a rocket in its own right, the A-9 was principally to be used as the second stage in the A-9/A-10 America rocket.

Alternative plans also envisaged the A-9 being launched from a gigantic catapult, in the same way as the V-1, into a flat orbit, in order to give this single stage rocket a range of thousands of kilometres. But to achieve this it was calculated that the catapult would have had have achieved a launch velocity of 1,290 kilometres per hour. This too must have caused immense technical problems!

In the post-war period, the Americans made urgent efforts to obtain data and material concerning the A-9. Thus, from August 1945, the former Peenemünde engineer Rudolph Daniel was working for the Americans. He was instructed by them to obtain details of the development work in EMW Karlshagen, and to obtain components not only for the A-4 but also for the A-9, and to send these to the headquarters of the 7th US Army in Frankfurt.

Unfortunately we do not know what came of this hunt for technology. Some elements of the A-9, however, later turned up in the American Redstone rocket, and an American design from 1948 has been published which shows an A-9 with duck wing configuration.

The Russians, too, evidently adopted A-9 characteristics in their own rocket design programme.[116] The Scud missile, which became famous from being used in several wars during recent decades, was developed in the 1950s under the Russian designation R-11. Thus, the R-11 originally had the same 'Visol'/ 'Salbei' propulsion system as the A-9 and the same payload. Its fuselage structure also looks suspiciously similar to the A 9! The only thing that was missing was the wing surfaces.

Seen from a certain perspective, the Scud missile is therefore the last remnant of the Peenemünde wartime rockets. In the case of the Scud missile it is today completely beyond dispute that, in addition to conventional warheads, it can also be fitted with chemical, bacteriological and nuclear warheads. But what was the case with its predecessor, the A-9?

II) Special armaments for V-1s and V-2s

1) Fieseler Fi-103 'V-1': Special warheads and special payloads

The design of the Fi-103 allowed it to carry warheads with a payload of up to 1000 kilograms. As an alternative to conventional explosive, consideration could be given to loading a flying bomb with sensitive payloads such as, for example, the super explosive Trialin, the effect of which was the equivalent to an aerial mine weighing 2,000 kilograms. It was also possible to fit underneath the fuselage a small number of individual bombs, such as the one-kilogram B-2 incendiary bomb.

As the war progressed, the payload of the Fi-103 varied according to availability and the armaments situation. Thus, some SC-800 aircraft bombs were also fitted instead of the standard warheads, and towards the end of the war the deterioration of the general situation in the armaments industry compelled the use of less and less effective explosives, such as, for example, Donarite, which was used in mining.

In addition to these conventional explosives, however, the Fi-103 could also transport special payloads.

Were there Biological Warheads for V-Weapons?

When in June 1944 the V-1 offensive was launched and the first flying bomb detonated with a loud explosion, revealing that it only contained normal explosive, the members of the General Staff all let out a great sigh of relief.

Brock Chisholm, Canadian General

In 1944 the Allies feared that the Germans were planning to release biological weapons in the centre of London using V-weapons. There were secret service reports of which suggested that the V-1 would be loaded with anthrax bacteria or botulinus toxin. Thus, in a V-1 attack with the weapons on London, there would be no normal large explosion, but a gentle puff could be expected which would scatter a liquid or a fine powder.

Professor Dr Kurt Blome, who was the co-ordinator for Herman Goring of the German activities connected with defence against biological weapons, was questioned after the war, together with Wernher von Braun, about the existence of biological payloads for the V-1 and V-2. Both experts categorically denied such plans existed.

According to the view of experts today, the Allied secret service reports concerning bacterial weapons charges in V-weapons may well rest upon a linguistic misunderstanding.

In 1944, the Anglo-Americans had apparently understood that the German plans were proposing *N-Stoff* for the weapons. *N-Stoff* was a high performance incendiary substance. In the Anglo-American reports, however, the letter 'N' was used as the code designation for anthrax bacteria.

Because, on the basis of incorrect reports from emigré circles immediately after the National Socialists came to power, the Allies assumed that Hitler planned to use anthrax bacteria and botulinus toxin as bacterial weapons, their suspicions may well have been aroused that it was also planned to use Germany's most modern carrier weapons to carry the bacterial material.

Did von Braun and Blome tell the Allies the whole truth? The assumption was that Hitler's refusal to use biological retribution weapons would have meant that any scientists would be risking his head in developing 'biological retribution weapons' in contravention of an express order from the Führer.

But the Allies had received, from trustworthy German sources in Switzerland, reliable information that the *Reichsführer-SS* Heinrich Himmler was preparing sinister projects on his own initiative. This information came from representatives of Admiral Canaris' *Abwehr*. Thus, the Allies found out that (indeed!) German scientists, working on the orders of the SS, had begun to develop spray distribution containers for the agents causing *Papageienkrankheit*, psittacosis, typhus, plague, and other pathological germs. It was planned that these containers for bacteriological weapons would be mounted on the V-1 and V-2 *Vergeltungswaffen*.

Because, from mid-1944 the SS increasingly had control of everything which had to do with *Vergeltungswaffen*, it is conceivable that there were developments of deadly super weapons carried out by the SS on their own initiative against the 'official' line. But whether this research could have been done without the expert knowledge of the Peenemünde scientists and engineers is doubtful, even if the latter were able to state in the post-war period that they had not received any official orders or commissions to develop such weapons.

Precise documents concerning the final status of SS research into bacteriological V-weapons at the end of the war have not yet come to light.

Gas and nuclear isotopies:
V-1 with combat agent warhead

Even if in expert circles the experts are unwilling to discuss it, there is nevertheless proof that, at least on the drawing board, a version of the V-1 existed which was intended for gas warfare.[117] [118] [119] Possibly even worse things were planned! In this version, which was designated Fi-103D-1, there was a great similarity to the B-1 design. But the D-1 could easily be recognised by the new truncated wooden nose. Its warhead had been developed in Münster, probably in collaboration between the Army and the Luftwaffe, and contained a series of distribution containers of *K-Stoff* (combat agent) capsules which would be ignited by detonators over the target. The impact detonator which was normally accommodated in the nose of the V-1 was not present in this version. Instead of this, the explosive capsule detonator was fitted over and in the middle of the *K-Stoff* warhead charge in order to achieve optimum distribution of the gas. To achieve this, detonation could be fixed to take place at a predetermined height over the ground.

One experiment which was carried out indicated that this arrangement would achieve the effect of a 1,000-kilogram phosgene bomb. Of course, instead of phosgene, the new, significantly more effective nerve gases such as tabun and sarin could be carried in the distribution containers.

Apart from the warhead, the Fi-103D bore a basic resemblance to the B-1 design and was largely constructed of wood. Another special characteristic was a new assembly to enable it to be dropped from aircraft. The available drawing dating from 19 September 1944 shows that in the fuselage there was only a relatively small space for fuel. This indicates that the Fi-103D-1 was probably intended to be used mainly to sterilise territory in areas close to the front and for retribution purposes, being dropped by aircraft.

Whether the Fi-103D was actually manufactured is not known. There is a remarkable silence on this subject in the published literature – or is it better to say a remarkable cover-up? – but the assumption can be made that appropriate chemical warheads for the V-1 were produced and stored in order to be immediately available for the 'doomsday scenario'.

Although the radius of devastation of such automatic long-range weapons with nerve gas could be exceeded by the effect of the atomic bomb, it is known that Hitler specifically refused to use such weapons as first strike weapons. Moreover, the D-1 version could have been used without much alteration for use with radioactive isotopes, so that it is possible to make assumptions in this regard.

It is known that efforts were undertaken by the Germans to produce so-called 'radioactive gases'. This dreadful weapon was a mixture of phosgene with radioactive isotopes (see Volume 3). Was it planned to use the Fi-103 to carry such payloads?

The Fi-103 could also have been a possible candidate for carrying radiological isotopes pre-absorbed in carbon dust, sand or similar substances. The particle size of the carrier materials used in this radiological weapon would have had to be between one and ten micrometres (one to ten micrometers are 'absorbable by the lungs' – particles larger than one micrometre will be breathed out again, and those larger than 20 micrometres fall to the ground too quickly and do not hover in the air for long enough). In addition to strontium and caesium, suitable isotopes for this purpose would also have been plutonium, uranium and especially thorium. Possibly this is a reason for the remarkable stockpiling of thorium by the Auergesellschaft in 1944 (see Volume 1).

Because, unlike conventional and nuclear bombs, isotope weapons are fully active almost without limit, after they have been manufactured, these charges would have represented a constant deadly danger for everyone and everything around them (manufacture, storage, service personnel, pilots and aircraft). Launching them by using unmanned rockets and missiles would have at least made it possible to reduce some of the risks inherent in these substances, if it is assumed that this payload was unloaded shortly before launch from a secure container. To achieve this it would simply have been necessary to exchange the space within the Fi-103D-1 reserved for conventional gas weapons for the famous, and much talked-about, 'spherical containers' which were produced in a factory in the southern Harz mountains, the location of which remains unknown. Fitting the planned 1,000 kilogram radiological bomb for use with aircraft would also have been feasible.

Because the isotope bomb is a weapon whose existence continues to be contested in modern historiography, it is useless to look in official documents and archives for drawings or photographs of these Fi-103 versions. Possibly, in some private albums or collections there are still unknown and 'forgotten' proofs that they actually did exist.

The military purpose of the radiological V-1 would have been to sterilise territory (for days, weeks or months) with only moderate fatalities, in contrast to the use of chemical weapons which would have had a fatal effect, depending on their concentration, within minutes or hours. Because of their long period of effectiveness, however, the radiological V-1s would have been suitable for a long lasting blockade of enemy-occupied hinterland, and as terror weapons for making enemy metropolitan areas uninhabitable.

It can therefore be assumed that if Churchill had carried out his intention in 1944 and attacked Germany with poison gas bombs in response to the conventional deployment of V-weapons, the German retribution against Britain, in addition to conventional bomber and fighter-bomber attacks, would have consisted principally of Fi-103D-1 missiles, some of which would have been armed with the new deadly nerve gases and radiological substances. At that time the British had no idea that there was any such thing as these deadly nerve gases, against which there was no defence at the time. By contrast, however, they were fully aware of the threat from potential German nuclear weapons, as will be outlined in more detail below.

At Monterolier (Somme-Seine) there existed, hewn into the rock in a wooded area near the Grotte de Clairefueille, two storage and service installations for V-1 gas warfare warheads. Kilometres of the 'Beaumont I' tunnel complex had already been developed, while 'Beaumont II' was in the early stages of being extended when the Germans evacuated the district. In 1994, 'Beaumont II' was mentioned in the press as the scene of an accident in which 3 children playing inside and 6 members of the rescue services were tragically killed by a 'mysterious' gas.

Fortunately, a German retribution offensive using weapons of mass destruction did not take place against Britain in summer/autumn 1944, because Churchill had thought better of his plans. The reason for this was fear of British public opinion if unconventional retribution measures were taken by Germany in response to British gas attacks.

In January 1945, the subject of V-1s armed with gas was once again under discussion. At that time, the SS were finally achieving what they had long desired: complete control over the entire V-1 weapons programme. For the V-1 this meant that various command structures were interrupted and that the V-1 launch teams, which had until then only consisted of Luftwaffe personnel, were reinforced not only by Army but also by *Waffen-SS* units.

Further details regarding these 1945 plans for using isotopes and gas have yet to be researched. Another interesting point is whether these were plans for using the weapons against cities or whether they were desperate efforts to stabilise the fronts. But it seems that the Fi-103D-1 armed with gas and or isotope warheads was to be deployed not only on the Western Front but also on the Eastern and Southern fronts.

On this basis, it can be assumed that, if Hitler's 'all-round defence' had actually been carried out 'at the last moment', the Fi-103D-1, or a version derived from it, would have played an important part in the operation.

V-1 with Uranium Warhead: "… it was called the German V-3"

13 June 1944: Immediately after the first V-1 struck London, leading members of the ALSOS mission rushed with Geiger counters to the impact crater created by the robot bomb! With relief, they confirmed that the weapon had contained only normal explosive.

Where did the British get their knowledge that the Germans were planning to mount uranium warheads on the V-1 flying bomb?

Like the A-4, the Fi-103 was able to carry up to one ton of explosive to the target. With the state of technology at the time, this payload would have been sufficient to carry a uranium warhead of the Hiroshima type, working on the shell principle.

In contrast to the rocket, the flying bomb had the advantage that the uranium warheads needed no special protective measures to be taken against the heat caused by friction and also required less ambitious detonator designs such as were necessary for the rocket because of its ballistic flight behaviour and impact speed.

Even *Reichsmarschall* Hermann Goering had plans to launch Germany's atom bomb at Britain in 1944, using the V-1.[120] And it was precisely this which ALSOS feared!

But as 1944 progressed, conditions had developed quickly in favour of the planned deployment of nuclear Fi-103s.

The great disadvantage in transporting atomic warheads with the standard V-1 to Britain was that the flying bomb was at great risk from Allied aircraft and anti-aircraft defence. Only two out of every ten Fi-103s reached their target! For the few available V-1s fitted with uranium warheads, this would have been far too unfavourable a probability. Added to this was the fact that after the loss of the French launch bases in August 1944, the main intended targets were already outside the range of the flying bombs.

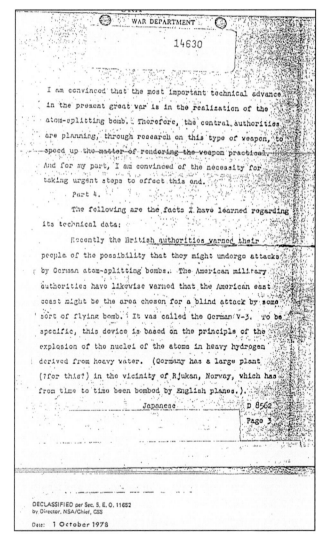

Extract from the document of 9 December 1944 (released by the American National Security Agency in 1978) which refers to the existence of V-1s with 'bombs based on the splitting of the atom' which were intended to be launched from U-boats at New York.

Apart from dropping the bombs from He-111 aircaft, the only remaining option was the use of increased range V-1s. But this would have made it necessary to considerably reduce the size of the payload, with the result that normal nuclear warheads could not have been accommodated in the long-range version. The only option that remained was to fit a 'small uranium bomb'. Whether there were actually plans to do this is a question for which, to date, there is no evidence.

But there is evidence that efforts were underway to improve the performance of the Fi-103 so that it would once again be superior to that of enemy defences. The super V-1 which resulted, which was also called the *Hochgeschwindigkeitszelle* ('high-speed cell'), was only produced in small numbers. It could have carried all the warheads (including the uranium bomb) which were intended to be carried by the standard V-1.

It was planned that the standard Fi-103 with nuclear warheads would also have been able to be launched from U-boats and thus successfully used against only lightly-defended targets (see Volume 1).

Although there is documentation indicating that the top leadership of the Third Reich intended to use the V-1 to carry nuclear weapons, it would be futile to look for official construction plans, photographs and the like. It is also quite likely that during the postwar period no designer wanted to associate himself publicly with such plans. The only exception to date is the statement made by the V-1 specialist engineer Kirfes while he was a prisoner of the Soviet secret services in 1946.

Unfortunately, it is not possible to reach any definitive conclusion as to what degree of success was actually achieved in producing nuclear-armed Fi-103 missiles. There are initial indications that in April 1945 in Berlin-Lichterfelde Süd there did exist warheads for this purpose without detonators (see section 'V-1s and V-2s on the Eastern Front').

Whilst to date only a little is known about the nuclear land version of the Fi-103, there is more material relating to its naval version (see Volume 1).

On 26 October, 1944, the American OSS Secret Service reported from Stockholm that there were reliable reports concerning a U-boat which was to set sail for the port of New York in order to launch a single V-1 for propaganda purposes.

As early as 30 October 1944, the Allied Special Force Headquarters reported to General Eisenhower that not just one, but four U-boats armed with V-1s had been transferred from Germany to Bergen (Norway) in order to set sail to attack New York on an unknown date. This report was confirmed once again on 7 November and gave rise to a flood of telegrams from SHAEF which warned everybody to be on the alert for for a V-1 (V-3) attack on New York.

When, on 28 June 1944, *SS-Gruppenführer* Jakob Sporrenberg went to Norway as General Plenipotentiary, the organisation of the V-1 attack on New York was one of

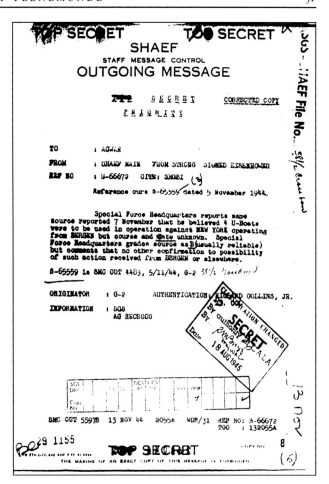

SHAEF report of 5 November 1944 relating to four German U-boats which were planned to set sail at an unspecified date to attack New York.

his special tasks during the last months of the war – together with plans to carry out 'special evacuations' of secret weapons and high technology. Probably, the Allies wanted to smoke out the hornets' nest in Bergen before the four U-boats were able to set sail for New York. On 2 November 1944, General Eisenhower asked General Spaatz whether a new type of Allied rocket bomb could not be tried out against 'some important' U-boat bunkers in Bergen or Trondheim ... But this attack did not take place – evidently the Allied 'rocket bomb' was not ready for operational service.[121]

An ULTRA/MAGIC secret document of 9 December 1944 addressed to the deputy chief of the US General Staff indicates that the American military authorities (and also the British - *author's note*) had also warned "that the eastern coast of America could be the planned target for a blind attack by a type of missile. It is said to be called the German V-3. To be more precise, this weapon is based on the principle of the explosion of nuclear particles in the atom ..."

The actual proofs concerning the threat of V-3 attacks must have been very convincing to the responsible authorities. The senior American military authorities decided to take a comprehensive series of measures which included military action, but also plans for psychological preparation of the American population.

According to an American document mentioned by Air Force General Arnold after the war, and which reported on the conference of 8 December 1944, these measures were taken to prevent a German victory.

In the light of this knowledge of the possibility of German nuclear attacks against New York, the material which was actually officially announced by senior members of the US military concerning the imminent threat of a V-1 attack against New York was scarcely likely to prepare the population psychologically for the danger of an imminent catastrophe.

Thus the Supreme Commander of the American Atlantic Fleet, Admiral Jonas II Ingram, warned the American population on 8 January 1945 that within the next 30 to 60 days the Germans would launch some flying bomb attacks against New York and Washington. Ingram went on to state that the flying bombs could be carried to America by aircraft, U-boats, or conventional ships, but evidently did not want to give too much away. He stated that the attacking forces would take up positions within 200 miles of New York and use as their target the Empire State Building (100 storeys high). He stated that all possible preventative measures had been taken and that there was no need to panic. The bombs, he said, would be smaller than those which had been launched against London, and 10 or 12 of them might strike at the same time, but the casualties would be nothing in comparison to those which London had suffered. He stated that six or eight U-boats would be necessary to attack New York.[122]

Whilst these and a series of other psychological preparatory moves might have succeeded in mitigating the element of surprise in a V-1 attack, the expected nuclear-armed V-3 attack against New York was – given the evidence, unwisely - played down in order to avoid general panic.

In actual fact, the Americans had discovered from reliable sources how treason and espionage tend to play things down. There is no other explanation for the fact that the senior American officers had been informed of the planned German V-1 attacks almost at the same time as the senior authorities in the SS had planned V-1 attacks against the New York from U-boats (see Volume 1). The (German?) source of information about the U-boat missile attack was classified by Special Force Headquarters as Category B (which usually meant reliable). The accompanying commentaries in the Allied SHAEF reports indicate that these reports did not come from Bergen, so the informants must have been based in Germany itself.

The betrayal of the secret plans also contained what, for example, Otto Skorzeny let slip in his memoirs, namely that to bring about Himmler's 'opportunity for turning the course of the war', Fi-103 flying bombs with nuclear explosive charges were to be used!

Although Armaments Minister Speer announced on Berlin Radio that on 1 February 1945 V-1 and V-2 rockets would strike New York, nothing in fact happened. Today the process of Allied warnings and fears would be likely to be dismissed as grotesque horror stories which involved unnecessary waste of personnel and material. But was not every effort justified in trying to prevent a nuclear attack on the USA?

The reports outlined in Volume 1, which indicate that in 1945 German U-boats armed with V-1 missiles were already on course for America could indicate that perhaps the implementation of these German plans was further advanced than has been admitted to date.

2) EMW A-4 'V-2': Special warheads and special payloads

A) Non-nuclear and radiological special warheads for the A-4

The nose cones carrying the payloads for the A-4 were not only limited to this rocket, but also served at the same time as armament for other EMW rocket developments such as the A-4B, A- 9 and A-9/A-10.

The V-2 rockets, which would strike their target at 3.5 times the speed of sound, were fundamentally different from the other bombs and missiles which had been deployed until that time. Their strength was simultaneously also their weakness. The strike momentum of the body of the missiles alone, without any additional explosive charge, caused a crater 10 metres deep and 25 metres wide. The impact locations of the sharper rockets were correspondingly considerably bigger.[123]

It was confirmed that the crucial factors in the destructive effect of the V-2 were not the effects of the explosive or of blast, but the tremendous shaking of the ground. The impact had the force of 50 locomotives each weighing 100 tons all colliding simultaneously at a speed of 100 kilometres per hour. In London, in heavily built up areas, one single V-2 missile could destroy or damage 600 houses.

Apparently, the scientists and engineers at Peenemünde had for a long time overlooked the problem of what warhead to fit to the A-4. According to Dr Dornberger, it was due to Adolf Hitler that any operationally viable warhead at all was able to be developed for the A-4. When, on 7 June 1943, he and von Braun gave their famous lecture on the planned rocket programme, Hitler's questions persistently homed in on the effect and the force of impact of the rocket, so that the scientists at Peenemünde were forced to consider something in their design which until then they had not considered. This led to the development of a new detonation system for the V-2 without which it could not have been deployed.

Later, by using a further developed electrical impact detonator, it was possible to achieve a significantly shallower crater similar to those created by the aerial mines used by both the Germans and the Allies, so that the warhead carried by the rocket could create a considerably greater lateral blast effect.

At the end of the war in Peenemünde a separation detonator had been developed for the V-2 which worked on the basis of the FuG 101. Separation detonators of this kind were principally intended for ABC special warheads which had to be detonated in the air to create their full effect, because they would lose some of their force in impact and the creation of an impact crater.

The nose cone of the rocket normally consisted of 6 mm thick steel plate and contained an explosive charge with an impact detonator. Initially, the quantity of explosive which was carried was 738 kilograms of Amatol, but later it was possible to increase this to 990 kilograms. While Amatol was a very effective explosive, it was not possible to load the A-4 with Trialin high explosive, which was twice as effective, because during flight the outer skin of the rocket reached a temperature of 650 degrees centigrade as a result of friction. This would have caused the warhead to explode prematurely.

It was therefore necessary to take account of the characteristics of the rocket by using payloads which were less sensitive, or isolated.

In later operational versions, the explosive effect was significantly increased by an additional 240-kilogram hexogen mixture ring charge. This charge extended back into this section of the rocket which contained the guidance equipment.[124]

V-2 with 'Röchling' projectile

After the war, Wernher von Braun admitted[125] that in Summer 1944 he had received a commision from the *Heereswaffenamt* (Wa Pruef 1) to investigate the possibility of using 'Röchling' projectiles instead of the normal explosive charge in the V-2. The question was whether the V-2 could transport 'Röchling' projectiles over large distances and discharge them within an effective distance of the target. After some trials and tests, according to von Braun, a favourable result had been achieved and it would have been possible to provide the *Heereswaffenamt* with plans, drawings and test results. But then, he said, the Wehrmacht had decided against using the Rochling projectile without telling him the reasons for this sudden change of mind.

Von Braun told his British interrogators that 'Röchling' projectiles were able to penetrate the thick concrete walls of air-raid shelters and fortified bunkers and also very thick armour plating. In doing so, they would explode at the moment the projectile had penetrated the walls and had reached the interior of the space in question. At the same time, he referred them in this connection back to Armaments Minister Speer.

What was all this about?

The 'Röchling' projectiles were not new developments of the last years of the war. These shells, made of chrome

vanadium, were extra-long missiles which were fired using a sabot and which were stabilised in flight by four thin steel aerofoil surfaces. Their penetrative capability was considerable. In France, German experiments carried out on the fortifications of the Maginot Line had indicated that a 21-centimetre 'Röchling' projectile was not only capable of penetrating four-metre-thick steel-reinforced concrete but also penetrated an additional five metres into the floor of the casemate.[126]

On 1 April 1943, 1,383, 580 'Röchling' shells of various calibres had been produced, from 3.7 centimetre anti-aircraft shells to the shells for the 34 -centimetre K 647 cannon. But for fear that the enemy might be able to capture an unexploded 'Röchling shell', copy it and use it against Germany, Hitler had reserved to himself responsibility for authorising deployment of 'Röchling' shells and had only given such orders in individual cases. Thus, in 1944, there must have been large quantities of the special shells in German arsenals. It is therefore not known whether a completely new 'Röchling' projectile was to be designed for use with the A-4, or whether, instead of this, converted projectiles of unspecified calibre were to be built in to the nose cone of the rockets.

In September 1945, Albert Speer was also questioned on plans to arm A-4 rockets with 'Röchling' projectiles. In replying, he contradicted both Wernher von Braun's statements and also his own information. The former Reich Armaments Minister had stated that in the case of the V-2 what was being planned was a 'Röchling' cartridge which would be filled not with explosive but with gas. But in the subsequent discussion it was not clear whether this referred to the same 'Röchling' cartridge which Speer had discussed as early as 29 March 1943 with Hitler. This discussion concerned a new highly concentrated substance called *Nebelsäure*, the acidic cloud from which was to cause blindness in enemy troops and render them unfit for further combat. According to Speer, Hitler decided at that time that this highly concentrated acid cloud could be construed as a poison gas and therefore forbade the use of the 'Röchling' cartridge.

But at the end of the interrogation, the British were not able to decide whether the contents of the 'Röchling' cartridge which was planned for the A-4 were really to be *Nebelsäure* or whether this was simply a term used to conceal a far more dangerous substance! From a military point of view there would have been little sense in using in *Vergeltungswaffen* a gas which was not deadly and which was only intended to be used in anti-tank defence.

There are still many details which remain unclear about the project planned during the war. The first of these concerns the type of 'Röchling' projectile. Was it planned to use 'Röchling' projectiles with (unconventional?) explosive or 'Röchling' cartridges with (unknown) gas? Neither Wernher von Braun nor Speer were very clear on this point and the relevant plans have 'disappeared without trace'. It is also not clear whether one single 'Röchling' projectile weighing about 1 ton was to be used, or a multiple payload consisting of several smaller projectiles.

The purpose for which the special warheads were to be used also remains unclear. 'Röchling' ammunition was intended to destroy precise targets, whether these were bunkers or tanks. But the V-2, because of its inaccuracy which could run into kilometres, would have been unsuitable for use against precise targets, at least until more precise guidance and control systems had been developed.

Even if it is assumed that the 'Röchling' V-2 rockets were to be loaded with non-conventional explosives or gases, the question arises why it was important to achieve such penetrative depth on impact. Was it perhaps the intention to attack the centre of government in London, with its deep bunkers? The hypothetical question could also be raised as to whether there was in existence a weapon, to date unknown, which could achieve its full effect only

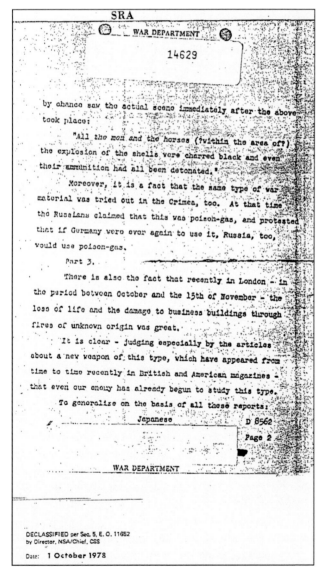

V-2 armed with N-Stoff? Extract from the document of 9 December 1944 (released by the American National Security Agency in 1978) reporting on unusually heavy fires in London said to have been caused by German bombardment.

after an impact in which it penetrated deep into the earth. If this were the case, the 'Röchling' A-4 would have provided the Third Reich with a special 'crater weapon' of the highest penetrative capability.

According to von Braun, orders were given in 1944 to discontinue the 'crater weapon' project, without any further reasons being given. Unfortunately, to date, no further documentation has emerged either to confirm or to explain this statement.

V-2 with N-Stoff

N-Stoff was an inextinguishable accelerant which consisted of chlorofluoro-carbons and other materials. It is one of the minor riddles of the Second World War why this substance never came to be used properly in weapons (see subsequent volume). If the possibility considered by Hitler of adding N-Stoff to the V-2 warhead as an incendiary material had been properly realised, experts think that the V-weapons bombardment would have caused far higher casualties.

But is it in fact the case that rocket prototypes with nose cones for carrying N-Stoff payloads had already been converted and tested in action? A document released by the American NSA (National Security Agency) in 1978 concerning the fear of German nuclear V-weapons attacks on New York and London reports in another place that in London, in the period between October and mid-November 1944, there had been great loss of human life and infrastructure, caused by extremely fierce fires, the origin of which could not be explained …

V-2 with combat agent warhead

In hearings after the war, Wernher von Braun admitted that there were no plans for warheads for the V-2 filled with combat agent.

But it seems like the German High Command, with or without knowledge of the process of splitting the atom, which at the time was new, were completely aware of the suitability of the long-range rockets as carriers of weapons of mass destruction. Initially, poison gas was considered. Even if these considerations are apparently missing from the documents, nevertheless there are clear indications that such considerations were given. Thus, the former General Chief of Staff of the Wehrmacht, Generaloberst Franz Halder, in his war diary, gives an account of a trip which he took together with the then rocket General Karl Emil Becker. On this journey, on 29 September 1939, the two generals visited a factory producing gas weapons (Tabun?). Halder mentions in his diary at this point both poison gas and the deployment of the long-range rockets against London.[127]

Then, later, there is evidence that a recommendation was made to arm a V-2 with a payload of 2,500 kilograms of phosgene. To go from this to arming the rocket with the deadly nerve gases Tabun, Sarin and Soman would have been no great leap. The effect of a V-2 with a nerve gas payload can be compared to a V-2 armed with nuclear explosives.

The same special warheads were also suitable for fitting to the A-4 B and the A- 9/A-10 America rocket.

How much progress was made in developing combat agents for the V-2 rocket is, unfortunately, unclear.

Had the preparations for the production off combat agent warheads for the Peenemünde rockets already progressed further, as has been suspected to date? In any event, on 19 April 1945, the British newspaper the *Daily Mail* gives a report of a remarkable event: soldiers of the 1st Commando Brigade shortly before the end of the war captured a secret German poison gas factory which in the middle of the forest of Rehburg, about a mile north of Leese on the eastern bank of the river Weser. The poison gas factory was so well camouflaged that it could not be seen at a distance of 50 yards either from the air or from the road. Its large concrete bunkers were provided with massive steel doors and perfectly camouflaged.

The British commando units saw that on a railway connection which ran right into the heart of the factory there were many a destroyed V-2s on their transport wagons. Other rockets were intact, but none of them had warheads. In a subsequent search, other destroyed V-2s were found in the woods nearby.

The reader of this book must now decide for him or herself whether to accept the concluding lines of the *Daily Mail* account, which soothingly state that the rockets were only in Leese by chance and had nothing to do with the factory …

In capturing the great combat agent arsenal near Espelkamp, the British also found a train loaded with rockets. Was it only an oversight that it had been left there?

What sense would it have made to leave V-2 rockets, which had to be launched as quickly as possible after their manufacture, in such out-of-the-way poison gas factories?

In the photograph collection of the Imperial War Museum in London, the British researcher Phil Henshall

discovered other photographs which showed the V-2s in Leese. According to the caption with the pictures, they had been bombed there by the Allies. Was this bombing to prevent the combat agent V-2 from being manufactured in time? And from whom did the Allies know that there were V-2s there? If the unlikely coincidence theory is not accepted, then we are forced to the conclusion that these rockets at Leese were intended to carry combat agent warheads.

Only if the British secret archives are opened again can we clarify the questions as to how much more progress could be made with the tests, the production and the filling of the C-warheads. Even if these weapons had a massive potential for destruction, it remains doubtful whether Hitler, with his well-known dislike of gas weapons, would have agreed to using them.

This German project was the grandfather of the later gas-carrying 'Scud' rockets used by Iraq's president Saddam Hussein in the Gulf War. It is a matter for discussion even up to the present whether such gas rockets were not jointly responsible for the 'Gulf War Syndrome' suffered by many returning US soldiers. How narrowly did those who took part in the Second World War escape this fate?

V-2 with 'P.K' gas?

In microfilm only recently released from American archives there was also a report dated 14 August 1944.[128] This report contains a summary which states that the Montecatini factory in Italy was to produce an explosive and incendiary gas known as 'P.K', which was intended to be carried in V-2s.

Unfortunately, no other clues relating to 'P.K gas' are known. But it appears remarkable that this short report has been kept classified for so many years. Was this report merely a 'duck', or was there something more behind it?

'Liquid Air' as a V-2 payload

According to an American OSS report dated 9 October

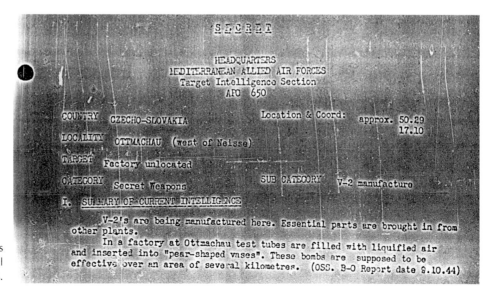

V–2 with liquid oxygen bombs and an effective radius of several kilometres.

1944, there was a factory in Ottmachau (west of Neisse) which was involved in producing a special armament for V-2s. According to the report, at the factory test tubes were filled with liquid air and used in pear-shaped containers. These bombs were intended to be used as a payload in the V-2 and to have an effective radius of several kilometres.

The same report also states that the Americans at the time did not succeed in precisely locating the factory, which was somewhere in the territory of the former Czechoslovakia. Unfortunately there is still no additional information about how far developments had progressed by the end of the war. The method of operation of the German oxygen bomb will be described in Volume 3.

V-2 with radiological warhead

Although it continues to be disputed whether there were any German atomic bomb developments at all during the Second World War, in modern literature more and more consideration is being given to the possibility that there was at least a radiological weapons project in the Third Reich.

Thus it is no surprise that the thought that Germany's revolutionary rocket weapon was to be loaded with isotope warheads is finding more and more credence among even more critical authors.[129]

In contrast to the procedure which involved filling the fuselage, in the case of this V-2, instead of the normal explosive charge, separate radiological warheads would be fitted. According to various reports, these were in the form of spherical containers. These containers were then to be filled with radiological pollutant isotopes.

Strongly radioactive isotopes such as, for example, strontium or caesium, would be used, which after they had been produced in nuclear reactors, cyclotrons or linear accelerators would be mixed with silicon, carbon, sawdust or suitable fluids. Their production, mixing and storage would have required extremely stringent safety measures to be taken because of the strong radiation which would be present. The same precautions would have had to be taken for transporting the materials in special protective containers to the deployment areas and for fitting them in the rockets.

Despite all these difficulties, the production of these malicious weapons is said to have begun as early as 1944, and it is very significant that completed containers were stored in an underground factory run by the SS in the Harz mountains, the precise location of which is still unknown. It is not hard to imagine under what sort of dreadful conditions this production took place.

However, during the last months of the war, a research team under Professor Albert Dreuzel had been transferred to a location close to Salzburg, and worked there right up until the end of the war not only on miniature atomic weapons but also on isotope payloads for ground-to-ground rockets.

In operational use, radiological isotope charges had to be distributed by the explosion of conventional explosives. The ideal distribution of this substance was achieved by the detonation of the bomb about 30 metres above ground level. A great disadvantage of using this type of weapon on the A-4 or similar rockets was therefore that a normal impact using a conventional impact detonator would only create a radioactive crater. But by the end of the war, in Peenemünde, separation detonators had already been developed which would have also allowed the A-4 to be exploded at a predetermined height above the ground. This detonator, codenamed Schnabel, which has been mentioned elsewhere, was based on the FuG 101 radio altimeter and in addition had the useful characteristic of preventing premature explosion of the rocket payload in the case of failed launches. To what extent this separation detonator (which would very probably also have been suitable for use with normal uranium bombs) was already under mass production is not known.

We do not yet know how great a risk these V-2s armed with radiological warheads posed by the end of the war. Possibly the V-2 with a radiological charge within the fuselage represented a simpler alternative to the V-2 with separate radiological warheads, because it did not require a separation detonator and did not involve the dangerous procedure of fitting the radioactive warheads directly at the launch site.

But the truth about these malicious victory weapons may still be hidden in Allied archives. One of the reasons why they have been kept classified for so long may be that, for example, during the post-war period the Russians brought into service a direct descendant of the A-4 called the R-2 (Nato: SS-2 'Sibling').[130][131] The R-2 came into operational service from 1953 and had a radiological isotope warhead called 'Geran'. Wouldn't it have been more honourable, in fact, to call it 'German'?

Dangerous fuselage loading procedures: 'Tornado' V-2 and 'Corset' V-2

From as early as summer 1942, under conditions of the greatest secrecy, the engineer Dr Mario Zippermayr had been developing artificial tornadoes (see Volume 3). This weapon involved creating tornado-like atmospheric effects by the use of special techniques involving the explosions of mixtures of gases and pulverised carbon. Zippermayr and the SS considered this project to be a genuine alternative to the atomic bomb.[132]

Apart from various other offensive and defensive applications of the Zippermayr system, it seems that consideration was also given to the production of V-2s with Zippermayr explosive. These were based on the so-called liquid oxygen bombs version of the Zippermayr project, the bombs consisting of 60 percent fine lignite dust and 40 per cent liquid oxygen. The V-2 was particularly suited for use with these weapons, because even after the longest flight there was always a certain amount of oxygen

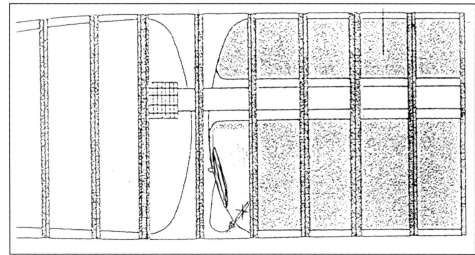

Diagram showing the attachment of a breakable membrane to the A-Stoff (oxygen) container of the A–4 in order to make use of the oxygen remaining at the end of the flight by allowing it to saturate the *Oxyliquit*.

remaining in the tubing, in the fuel compartment and in the heat exchanger.

In December 1943, the then *Oberleutnant* Frenk at Peenemünde had the idea to use the remnants of this liquid oxygen at the end of the flight of the V-2. He planned to fix a membrane at the top of the lower fuel tank, which shortly after the conclusion of the burn would break and allow the remaining liquid oxygen to penetrate into the space between both tanks. This space had been previously purposely filled with a mixture of cork dust and carbon powder, the so-called *Oxyliquit*. After the membrane had broken, there then remained about four minutes before the rocket impacted, during which the *Oxyliquit* could become soaked in the liquid oxygen. This then formed an explosive which, depending on the distance of the target and the remaining oxygen in the tanks, would have multiplied the explosive effect of the normal rocket nose cone. When the impact of the V-2 occurred, the *Oxyliquit* mixture was ignited by the explosion of the normal rocket payload. Dr Zippermayr indicated that the effect of his system would be considerably increased if the impact took place from a great height. This condition would have also been ideally fulfilled with the A-4.

Then, in reports of American hearings dated 23 July 1945, the statement is made that Dr Zippermayr had been working in Lofer (Tyrol) on special explosives for the rockets, which were possibly atomic explosives.

Does this mean that the carbon dust mixture in the V-2 fuselage was also going to be replaced by a radiological isotopes? And what became of the 'Tornado V-2'? According to Frank, it never reached the production stage, but only underwent a few test explosions which had shattered a few window panes in Peenemünde.

But there are clues that the Tornado V2 could have already been developed to a far greater extent:

One of the last known photographs from Peenemünde show in a series of photographs the preparations for launch of a V-2 which indicates a massive iron structure like a corset in the middle of the rocket between both fuel tanks.

This corset happens to be located exactly over the place which normally would have contained the oxygen liquid mixture. This structure was constructed on a considerably greater scale than the *Halskrause* or *Bauchbinde* which Kammler ordered to be fitted to V-2 rockets to prevent them being destroyed by 'aerial destructive elements'. Their dimensions, too, were completely different.

This special corset-like structure, the material composition of which is to date unknown, is likely to have served to generate high pressure before the explosion of the liquid oxygen-carbon dust mixture.

Unfortunately, it is unknown how many corset V-2s were actually produced.

Were they really plans to develop rockets with such dangerous supplementary explosives? Dr Zippermayr states that the order to produce his substance was only issued on 3 March 1945. This date turned out to be too late to be able to bring V-2s armed in this way into operational service. But nevertheless, experiments were made in filling the V-2 with this substance or with similar substances. There are indications that this was also the case with trials using radiological isotope mixture supplements.

Thus, in 1945, scientific search teams of the Red Army succeeded in capturing intact the underground German factory 'Weser' in the former Czechoslovakia. In the 'Weser factory', several fuselages of V-2s and a large quantity of design documents and reports were found. But why were there V-2 fuselages there? The thought suggests itself that this connection between cyclotrons and V-2s was no coincidence, and that the cyclotrons were to serve to provide isotope material to fill V-2 fuselages. Because the V-2 payload-carrying nose cones were manufactured separately and were only fitted to the rocket shortly before launch, the mere mention of rocket fuselages without nose cones suggests that there were plans to fill the the intervening spaces within the fuselage. The alternative possibility that these spaces were for fuel is counted out, because fuel could only be pumped into the tanks immediately before launch.

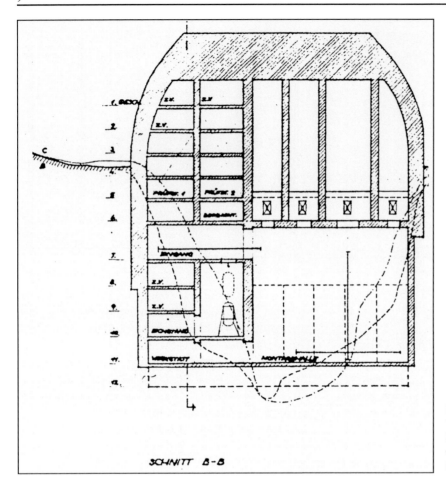

SCHNITT B-B

Preliminary sketch dated 19 December 1944 for the giant bunker 'Salamander Z' in Ebensee for A–4s, A–4Bs and A–10s with water-cooling system and probably nuclear isotope generators. (DM Peenbild B65/45)

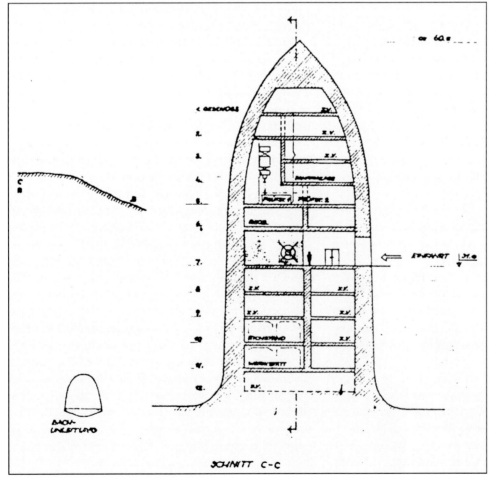

SCHNITT C-C

Corset V–2 before launch! (Official text: A–4 with single-colour paint scheme on the launching pad by the lowered launching tower, 1945). (Raumfahrtsarchiv, Peenbild, B49/45, Photo Deutsches Museum, Munich)

After the American atomic bomb attack on Hiroshima, the 'Weser factory' is said to have resumed work under Soviet control with all the former engineers, supervisors and workers. To date, nobody has finally succeeded in identifying the exact location of the Weser factory. According to the information which is available, it was located in the district in which the River Elbe breaks through the barrier of the Sudeten and flows through the Podmokly plain. But Podmokly is not on the Elbe but on a small tributary called the Berounka. This description would better apply to the district round Hradek Kralova or Usti (codenamed Richard)!? Will this riddle ever be able to be solved?

The British author Philip Henshall gives an account of a British sergeant who, when Germany was occupied, inadvertently entered a hall in which there were several V-2 fuselages filled with a 'coloured dust'. The British soldier told his family that this must have been 'a kind of chemical'. In entering the hall, the man came into contact with this substance and died painfully in 1952 of a mysterious illness.[133] From the unusual symptoms, his relatives concluded that he had been suffering from a kind of 'radiation sickness', and so demanded from the British Government precise information and sight of the relevant documents. But such information has been withheld from them even to the present day. The research carried out by the soldier's son produced surprising results: his father had been assigned as a soldier in the Espelkamp/ Lübbecke arsenal.

Approaching from the West, units of the VIII Army Corps of the British Second Army were advancing at that time into the remaining area of the Reich. Their targets were assigned codenames such as 'Mississippi' (Lübbecke) or 'Milwaukee' (Minden). The most important target was called 'Adelph'i and was situated at co-ordinates 60/21. This target was reached on 4 April 1945 at 1730 hours by the Royal Tank Regiment. On 5 April, the British entered in their diary: "The munitions store which was discovered yesterday at co-ordinates 60/21 proves to be an underground factory filled with high explosive substances".

Possibly, in these subterranean plants, work was being carried out on the nuclear/radiological weapons programmes of the SS. There was talk of secret Third Reich armaments projects and of loading rockets with combat agents.

In a British VIII Army Corps document from October 1946, there is mention that in that area there was a factory which was involved in the production of a German atomic bomb. The fact that ALSOS was there later on is also documented, as is the fact that on 3 January 1946, the senior German atomic scientists were also staying in the village of Alswede. These scientists included, in addition to Otto Hahn, Werner Heisenberg and Karl-Friedrich von Weiszäcker, also Walter Gerlach, Max von Laue, Erich Bagge, Kurt Diebner, Paul Harteck, Horst Kosching and Karl Wirtz. In short, the *crème de la crème* of the most illustrious

German atomic scientists up to that time. Why the British brought them to precisely this place remains a secret even today.

It is conceivable that there were connections with the underground factory in Espelkamp and its likely nuclear/radiological weapons programmes. This is particularly the case since there is evidence that as early as March 1946, the British met in Alswede with the head of research of the Kiel firm Anschütz & Company. Under the Third Reich, the Anschütz company provided ultracentrifuges for the enrichment of uranium. In a document relating to the meeting between the British commander Roland Frazer and the head of research of the Anschütz company, mention is made, among other things, that Frazer had considered the question as to whether this subsidiary plant had not taken an active part in development after Beyerle had produced the Ultracentrifuge 3B. What did he mean by 'this subsidiary plant'?

Does this mean that in Espelkampt/Lübbecke, work was being carried out underground on the nuclear/radiological weapons programme of the Third Reich using ultracentrifuge plants?

The prototype UZIII model which was planned for production in January 1944 was to produce more than 20 grams of U-235 per day. This was a quantity which, in a year, would alone have produced by the end of 1944 the material required for several (small, sub-critical) atomic bomb charges!

The enriched uranium could then either be used to build nuclear weapons or, mixed with sand, carbon or another substance, be placed into V-2 fuselages as a radiological weapons material. Were there plans to mix chemical combat agents together with radiological isotopes and use them as 'annihilation charges'? There may well be definitive evidence for the existence of such a project (see Volume 3).

The British sergeant who died after the war in unusual circumstances may have possibly had the misfortune to have remained inadvertently too close or too long in the proximity of such a filling plant. The British then evidently panicked when they realised what they had found here. There is an indication that at the time, because of their inexperience (*vide* the example of the sergeant) and the danger of the materials, the British drove a train loaded with V-weapons and nerve gas shells into available tunnels. From their point of view at the time, this would have been the easiest way to get rid of the problem and to save risking their own lives. The remains of the train may be still there today and represent a danger which cannot be underestimated.

What is surprising and puzzling is that, according to the present-day official German Federal authorities, there are said to have been neither tunnels nor deep bunkers in the arsenal, although these tunnels are marked on British maps and the deep bunkers are expressly mentioned in a letter dated 24 May 1950 (Staatsarchiv Düsseldorf)! What is going

on here? Taken all in all, there is every indication that in the case of the Espelkamp arsenal we are dealing with a 'rocket fuselage filling plant' similar to the plant in the 'Weser factory'.

It is possible that the third plant of this type was to be built in a bunker above ground in a tributary valley in the Alps. When it was built, the rocket bunker which, as a result of its construction, would have been proof against the heavy British 'Tallboy' bombs, would have been able to house A-4B, A-9 and A-10 rockets which would have been delivered by rail. The large rockets would have been lowered into the tubes by means of a crane. At launch, the exhaust gases would have been discharged down a slope into the valley, but the bunker had its own water cooling system, to provide which a mountain stream had been channelled and diverted into the bunker.

Was this cooling system only necessary for the launch? The large bunker could have had another function besides preparing rockets for launch! Its remarkable underground spaces do not resemble those of a fuel storage plant. In the case of 'Salamander Z', these tanks were to be stored separately outside the launch bunker. But the tanks in the underground spaces shown on the plans display a great similarity to the heavy water containers in the atomic storage cellar in Haigerloch. But this is only one of the remarkable things about this plant. Thus, the plants accommodated in the underground sections of the bunker look suspiciously like they have been designed to house untrue ultracentrifuges.

This suggests the conclusion that both the British and the Russians captured German secret factories in which enriched uranium material produced by ultracentrifuges was to be placed in V-2 fuselages. The 'radiological' rockets could be recognised immediately by their corset, and had already been subject to flight tests at Peenemünde. It is possible that the remains of such special rockets are still underground at Espelkamp/ Lübbecke even today.

Definitive proofs that this weapons development programme existed might therefore still turn up, thus providing a information which would be urgently necessary, even if only because it presented a possible environmental hazard.

Additional containers for radiological payloads

Certainly, the system the Germans tried out of filling the A-4 with additional payload charges in the space between the fuel tanks was the simplest solution. But there seems to have been a second method which was considerably more flexible.

When, on 26 May 1949, the first Russian R-1 rocket was launched, in this successor to the A-4, two containers were attached to the side of the rocket's fuselage in addition to the normal complement of instruments. These payload canisters, called FIAR-1, were about 1 metre long and 40 centimetres wide.

After the conclusion of the burn by the main propulsion

system, they were released from the fuselage by a mortar-like explosive charge and then descended on their own parachute.

But the civilian payload containers used on the Russian R-1 and R-2 rockets had a serious background. Thus, a military version existed which contained 600 kilograms of radiological isotope fluid.[134] Here too the containers were to descend on their own parachute and distribute their deadly cargo over a wide area. These radiological detachable missiles were used on the Russian R-2 and R-5 military rockets as additional payloads.

Nobody has yet shed light on the question as to whether these detachable missiles fixed to the side of the rockets were primarily Russian invention, or whether in this case, too, the Russians had once more adopted German ideas. The fact that in 1949 the first Russian rocket (a copy of the V-2) was fitted with these additional missiles gives pause for thought, because at this time the Russians were not yet able to produce there R-1 copy of the V-2 on an industrial scale. The German preference for radiological isotope weapons and for mounting these on the V-2 also gives pause for thought. The reports which continually emerge concerning V-2s with additional charges fixed to the fuselage could thus also be attributed to this kind of weapons project having been carried out by the Germans. In addition, side-mounted payload containers had the advantage that, as a result of the braking action effected by the parachute, they were not exposed to the same physical conditions on descent as the warhead of the standard A-4.

It would not be surprising if one day drawings from Peenemünde or even photographs of rocket flight tests were to turn up in which these kinds of side-mounted payload containers can be seen on the A-4 rocket.

B) Nuclear 'V-2': Special Warheads and Special Payloads

Nuclear warheads for the A-4

The intended use of the A-4 to carry nuclear warheads created at the time it was developed a series of new problems which had to be solved before the weapon was used. The high external temperatures of up to 650 degrees centigrade which affected the nose cone during the flight of the rocket presented the designers with great challenges, because premature destruction or self-detonation of the explosive charge had to be avoided at all costs. This series of problems had made it impossible to use the highly effective explosive Trialin, which had originally been the intention in the case of the V-2. We do not know how in 1944/45 the expected problem of the high external temperature during the descent of the rocket was to be solved. But one published photograph proves that Germany was already experimenting with alternative forms of payload-bearing nose cones. Possibly this work was intended to solve the temperature problem.

After the war, Wernher von Braun found a surprisingly simple solution. He circumvented the difficulties by using flattened wooden nose cones for the sensitive nuclear warheads in the rockets.

Does not the mention of this remarkable replacement material necessarily raise the suspicion that this solution had been discovered during the war?

But there was a second problem with which the designers had to deal. The nuclear warhead had to be definitely detonated as the rocket impacted. But it was not only the scientists of the Third Reich who had problems finding a solution to this difficulty. The Americans and the Russians also thought for years after the war about the conditions under which the effectiveness and certainty of the nuclear rocket warheads could be, so to speak, to a certain extent guaranteed. In the 1950s, specifically to solve this problem, the Americans created their own type of research rocket designated as the Lockheed X 7. The X 7 was also well-known because in 1957 it was used in Project 'Argus'. But even by using such research techniques, it was not possible to solve all the problems. Thus it was only during the 1970s that it was realised that most of the atomic warheads in the early American 'Polaris' submarine missiles were so insensitive that when it came to being used they would not have exploded on impact!

The question therefore remains whether the relevant German Second World War designs for nuclear warheads for A-4 rockets would have been operationally viable at all. Fortunately, it was never necessary to discover the answer to this question under real operational conditions.

'All untrue?' - Wernher von Braun and the atom

The British, who to some extent were in stubborn competition with the Americans in researching and making use of the German secret projects, evidently also had doubts after the war what the ultimate purpose of the German rocket programme actually was.

This is evident from a report published on 8 July 1947 concerning questions addressed to Wernher von Braun. In addition to being asked technical questions, Wernher von Braun was asked about such sensitive issues as his membership of the SS. To the surprise of his British interrogators, Wernher von Braun initially denied that in 1942 he had any rank in the SS, although it must have been clear to him from the attitude of the British that this was something which they had already known for a long time. It was only later, in the course of further hearings, that he admitted that he had become a member of the SS in 1940.

The primary purpose of the British was to obtain information as to whether any experiments or projects relating to special warheads for biological, chemical or nuclear weapons had been planned or had been already carried out in Peenemünde-Ost or later in Bad Sachsa, or whether any such plans had existed or been implemented for other remotely controlled rockets. Wernher von Braun categorically denied that he had not even heard any rumours about the existence of such charges for remote-controlled rockets. He pointed out that this subject had not been discussed with anybody in the United States because up to that point nobody had asked him any questions about it. But the British would not let it drop! When von Braun was again persistently questioned on the subject he said that, apart from the already well-known high explosive warheads in 1944, the only work that had been carried out was on a project to mount 'Röchling' projectiles on the V-2 (see the relevant section).

This statement by Wernher von Braun, however, is demonstrably false! Thus, according to the Peenemünde scientist Dr Frenk, during the visit of a delegation of senior officers to the Peenemünde Army research establishment, Wernher von Braun was asked in Frenk's presence by one of the officers why, instead of the normal one-ton warhead, an atomic bomb could not be mounted on the A-4. In response, according to Frenk, von Braun pressed his elbows in his sides and and said: "Because we don't have any yet". So the subject of nuclear warheads was in fact officially raised by the Germans!

When his British interrogators later again asked von Braun the question as to whether there had not in fact been a possibility that atomic charges were to be used as warheads for V-2s, once again this option was energetically rejected by him: "I had *nothing* to do with atomic energy". But at the end of the hearings, he stated that in 1943 he had given some consideration to 'atomic energy'. But, he said, this had only been for the purposes of providing propulsion, and nothing had come of it. He said that he had merely wanted to establish whether atomic energy could be used as a propulsion system in the V-2 as it could in U-boats.

As will be outlined in the section concerning atomic propulsion systems, there was an official commision given to Peenemünde to carry out research into atomic energy and atomic decay with a view to their use in rockets! and this had been the case not only from 1943, but from as early as 1942! The statements made Wernher von Braun after the war, which are so eagerly viewed as 'proof ' that a German nuclear weapons programme did not exist, are thus anything but credible, because on this subject they bear no evidence of truth.

Unfortunately we do not know whether the British interrogators believed Wernher von Braun's assurances. But their stubborn questioning could indicate that they had already received very different information from other sources.

Rockets fitted with small uranium bombs - were flight tests carried out as early as 1944?

On 2 February 1956, a Russian R-5M rocket successfully transported and exploded a nuclear warhead (0.4 kilotons). But was this really the first successful USSR test of an atomic rocket, or had such a test perhaps already taken place much earlier in another country?

Hitler himself mentioned small uranium bombs as

armament for rockets. Thus, Picker mentions that in his table talk Hitler had spoken about plans to provide the New York rocket with several small uranium bombs and to launch it against the American metropolitan city.[135] Because the A-9/A-10 and the A-4 had the same rocket nose cone, Hitler's own words thus referred to the relevant conversion of the V-2.

But, as has been mentioned earlier, the designer of the V-2, Wernher von Braun, said that he had not even heard any rumours about plans to fit nuclear payloads to the V-2. (A more detailed history of the development of the Third Reich is small uranium bombs is given in the first volume). Probably there were plans, as a variant of this development, to equip the rocket nose cones of the A-4 four and A-9 with one or several of the small nuclear warheads, which respectively weighed 250 kilograms or 400 kilograms. This weight was comparable to that of the small uranium bombs developed by the Luftwaffe.

Although many sources indicate that they did exist, the technical feasibility of this kind of small atomic weapon with at least 100 grams of atomic explosive is always disputed by conservative experts. But in fact, on the basis of official American publications, the researchers Thomas Mehner and Antonio Chover have demonstrated that the smallest quantity of plutonium which is required to achieve critical mass in detonation is about 100 grams …

But successful tests using different sizes of small uranium bombs took place between October 1944 and March 1945 not only in several ground trials (see Volume 1) but also in all probability using a V-2. In his capacity as head of the Northern Italian RSI (Republica Soziale Italiana), Benito Mussolini received on his desk an interesting report on the subject. On 28 September 1944, under reference number 1078/1, the secret SID (Servizio Informazioni Difesa) information service provided information concerning a new German weapons experiment that had been carried out shortly before. A man by the name of 'Ambrosi' reported after his return from Germany - where he had been previously working in a factory near Kattowitz which was located in a massive area of forest - that he had been present at the test of a new kind of explosive.

In this test, he said, a large rocket had been set up in a wooded area which had been sealed off by the SS. After the preparations for the launch of the specially converted V-2 rocket had been completed and the crew together with some observers, including 'Ambrosi', had gone into a bunker, the V-2 was launched. When the rocket reached a predetermined height, it was exploded. According to Ambrosi, the observers who were present were disappointed by the fact that at first nothing happened apart from the fact that the warhead fell to earth. After its impact in a wooded area there was a remarkable pause of half a minute, apparently with no reaction. But then it happened! A dreadful explosion could be heard which even shook the floor under the feet of the observers in the bunker like an earthquake. There was a deafening noise, followed by a great cloud of dust, but no fire. After about an hour, the test area was examined. Ambrosi saw a huge crater, and round about it in a radius of about one kilometre, all the trees had been knocked over like matchsticks.

Unfortunately, Ambrosi could not say whether the test in Poland had been completely satisfactory in the eyes of the people who had carried it out. Was it intended to test the effects of the airborne explosion of a small uranium bomb, and had the test resulted in the fact that the explosive only detonated after it had hit the ground?

According to Ambrosi, a super bomb called the 'V-4' had been installed in the nose cone of the test rocket at Kattowitz.

In the British publication *Flight* of 26 July 1945, the Australian Wing Commander A G Pither also confirmed the existence of a German 'Uranium Disintegration Bomb' for the V-2 which had a far more destructive effect than the normal V-2, with a 24-pound uranium bomb having the same destructive power as the entire conventional one-ton explosive payload of the V-2. It is true that at the end of the war this weapon would still have needed another six months to be completely ready for operational service.

What is interesting is the question as to where Wing Commander Pither obtained the information relating to the effects of the new weapon which he describes. The data relating to the first 'official' atomic test explosion at the American Alamagordo testing ground, which had taken place only a few days before on 15 July 1945, could certainly have not yet been known to the Australian, because they must have been one of the most closely guarded American war secrets at the time.

Unfortunately there is no indication as to whether it would have been possible to mount the small uranium bombs on the V-2 by the end of the war.

The possibility can therefore not be excluded that the manned German rocket which, according to astronaut Gordon Cooper would, at the end of the war, only have needed another week to be ready to launch at New York, was intended to carry such a payload. (see Volume 2B).

Uranium-sphere warheads for rockets

From the period of the Third Reich there are various statements made by important people which expressly emphasise the suitability of the new rocket for transporting atomic bombs. In actual fact, at that time there was also an uranium project which appears to have been specifically tailored for the V-2's special characteristics.[136]

The first volume of *Hitler's Miracle Weapons* told the story of the two spherical 1000 kilogram uranium containers which were burnt by French troops after they had been captured, in order to prevent them falling into their hands of the ALSOS Mission. But were these only bombs for aircraft, or was there more to it than this?

The containers had a diameter of 0.65 metres and consisted of two hemispheres which were screwed together in the middle. They contained 10 layers of U-235/238

plates with a total weight of 551 kilograms. These lightly enriched uranium layers were composed of round plates of various thickness and were fitted in the lower half of the sphere. Between each of the layers was a layer of paraffin. Paraffin was to serve as a neutron absorber, so that the uranium plates did not react with each other. According to other accounts, instead of paraffin liquid, kerosene was used. On impact, the kerosene would have either been immediately ignited by the diesel effect or the liquid would have run away so that the plates could enter into direct contact with each other.

The designer of such a uranium container, which is shown in David Myhra's book,[137] also has shows a tube which penetrates through the middle of the sphere, in the centre of which there is a small round object called 'Präparat'. This object, called P, was strongly radioactive. It may have been a small ball-shaped object composed of beryllium and polonium. This fragile object would then probably act as the detonator for the fission process by releasing neutrons.

The upper half of the container contained a solid hemispherical mass of ballast. Taking into account the total weight of 1000 kilograms, the remaining weight for the mass of ballast seems to be too light for uranium and too heavy for so-called heavy water. It may well have been composed of iron or steel. It will be explained below that this mass of ballast was intended to have a quite specific function in setting off the weapon.

Was it planned to use these containers as the payload in the nose cone of a V-2, A-4B or A-9/A-10 rocket? As far as size is concerned, it would have been relatively easy to install the uranium sphere in the standard nose cone. In terms of weight, too, the container 'happened' to correspond to the weight of a normal V-2 warhead payload.

How were the uranium containers to function? It may have been the intention to generate the critical mass required to release a nuclear explosion by the impact momentum of the rocket. The momentum of a rocket impact would involve velocities and forces which were many times greater than the impact speed of the Little Boy atomic bomb used at Hiroshima. The uranium plates in the sphere would have collided with the mass of ballast with such force that they would have been instantaneously melted. Under these conditions it is very lightly that a fully-fledged nuclear explosion would have resulted.

Moreover, the impact velocity of the V-2 corresponded relatively exactly with the velocity of 3000 ft per second which the American atomic bomb team in Los Alamos saw as being required to create fission in plutonium.

But even if critical mass was not achieved on impact, the discharge of the payload in the crater would have created radioactive contamination of the impact site and its surrounding area. This nuclear contamination, however, would not have been as extensive as it would have been in the case of an airborne explosion approximately 30 metres

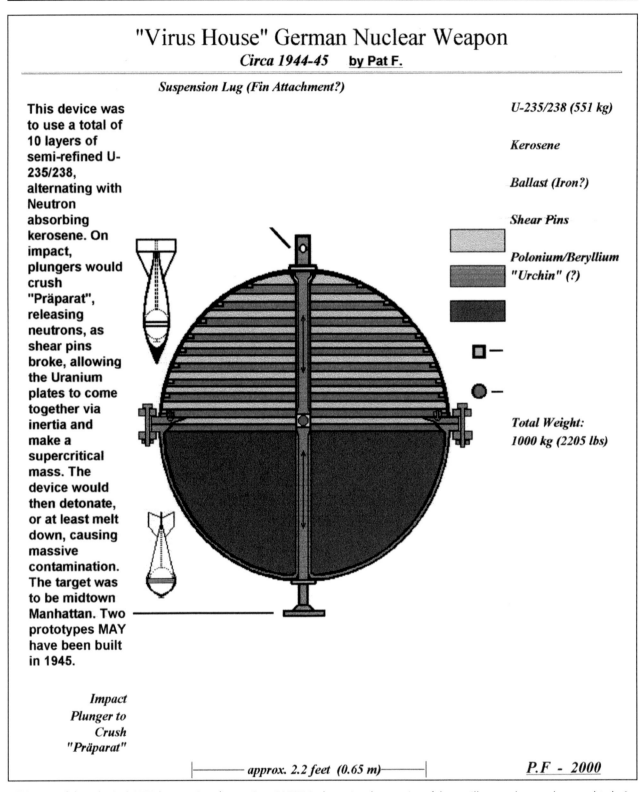

"Virus House" German Nuclear Weapon
Circa 1944-45   **by Pat F.**

Suspension Lug (Fin Attachment?)

This device was to use a total of 10 layers of semi-refined U-235/238, alternating with Neutron absorbing kerosene. On impact, plungers would crush "Präparat", releasing neutrons, as shear pins broke, allowing the Uranium plates to come together via inertia and make a supercritical mass. The device would then detonate, or at least melt down, causing massive contamination. The target was to be midtown Manhattan. Two prototypes MAY have been built in 1945.

Impact Plunger to Crush "Präparat"

U-235/238 (551 kg)

Kerosene

Ballast (Iron?)

Shear Pins

Polonium/Beryllium "Urchin" (?)

Total Weight: 1000 kg (2205 lbs)

|———— *approx. 2.2 feet (0.65 m)*————|

P.F - 2000

Diagram of the spherical 1000 kg container for uranium–235/238 plates. Are the remains of these still somewhere underground today? (Pat Flannery, www.Luft46.com)

above the ground. The result, in any event, would be to render the area uninhabitable.

Scientists such as Dr Edse, a leading member of the staff of the atomic bomb researcher Dr Harteck, confirmed during the course of Allied hearings that consideration was given to developing bombs consisting of uranium plates with paraffin layers and beryllium detonators. In doing so, Dr Edse stressed that the V-2 would be particularly suitable for transporting this kind of weapon ...[138]

It is surprising that post-war censorship let these hints about the spherical container weapons, later mentioned by Myhra and Flannery, slip through the net so easily!

Fi–103 'High-speed cell' with atomic warhead, distance detonator and remote control. Colour scheme: Upper surfaces: RLM 82/83, Lower surfaces: RLM 'weissgrau 1945'. (Igor R. Shestakov)

Arado Ar–234-C–5 twin system with Fi–103 D–1. Armed with 1000kg spray container for Tabun nerve gas. Colour scheme: Ar–234-C–5: Upper surfaces: RLM 82/76 cloud pattern, Lower surfaces: RLM 76. Fi–103 D–1: Gas warhead: RLM 78, rest of missile RLM 65 overall. (Igor R. Shestakov)

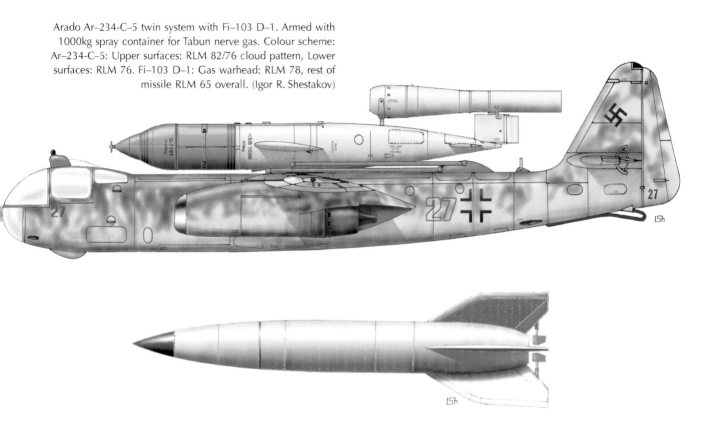

A–5 test rocket for aircraft launch trials (Peenemünde 1943). Colour scheme: fuselage RLM 74, tail wings: RAL 3000/RAL 9001, instrument nose cone: black (RAL 9005). (Igor R. Shestakov)

A–4 standard version – late model (Art.Rgt.z.V.901), Westerwald 1945. Colour scheme: splinter camouflage RAL 6003/RLM 83. (Igor R. Shestakov)

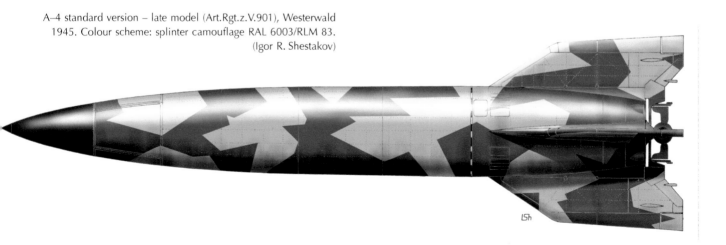

V–2 two-stage ramjet rocket (project, 1945). Colour scheme: V–2: irregular camouflage RAL 9003, signal white (RAL 6003), olive green with cloud pattern camouflage RLM 99/RLM 82; Ramjet stage: RLM 'weissgrau 1945', nose: black (RAL 9005). (Igor R. Shestakov)

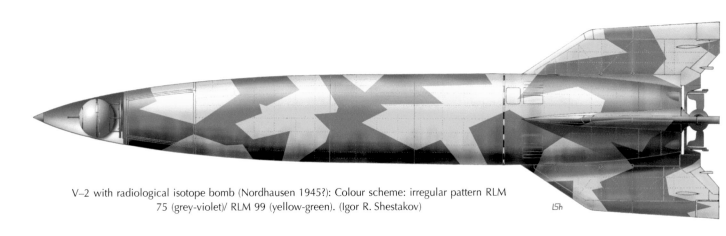

V–2 with radiological isotope bomb (Nordhausen 1945?): Colour scheme: irregular pattern RLM 75 (grey-violet)/ RLM 99 (yellow-green). (Igor R. Shestakov)

Corset V–2 for radiological fuselage charge (Peenemünde 1945). Colour scheme: Rocket: RAL 6003, protective corset: metallic grey, nose: black (RAL 9005). (Igor R. Shestakov)

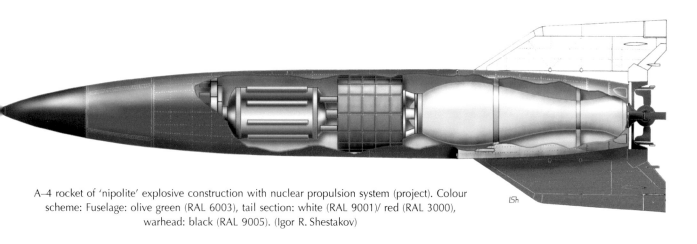

A–4 rocket of 'nipolite' explosive construction with nuclear propulsion system (project). Colour scheme: Fuselage: olive green (RAL 6003), tail section: white (RAL 9001)/ red (RAL 3000), warhead: black (RAL 9005). (Igor R. Shestakov)

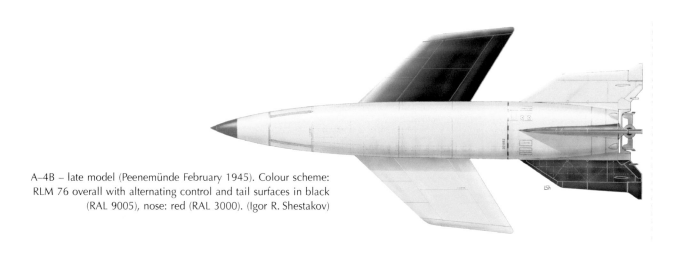

A–4B – late model (Peenemünde February 1945). Colour scheme: RLM 76 overall with alternating control and tail surfaces in black (RAL 9005), nose: red (RAL 3000). (Igor R. Shestakov)

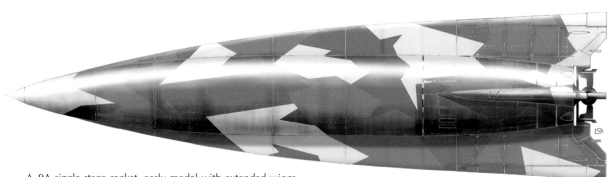

A–9A single-stage rocket, early model with extended wings (Peenemünde March 1945). Colour scheme: splinter camouflage consisting of RLM 81/82 and RLM 'weissgrau 1945'. (Igor R. Shestakov)

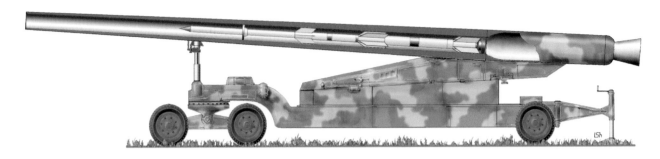

'Rheinbote RH.Z5' with isotope charge on rocket gun. Colour scheme: 'Rheinbote': ivory (RAL 1001), gun: cloud pattern (RAL 6003/ RAL 8017/ RAL 7028). (Igor R. Shestakov)

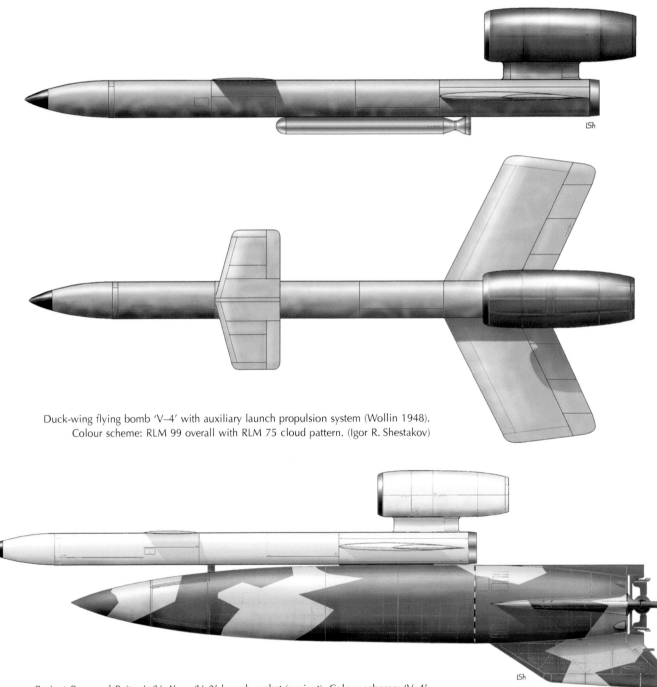

Duck-wing flying bomb 'V–4' with auxiliary launch propulsion system (Wollin 1948). Colour scheme: RLM 99 overall with RLM 75 cloud pattern. (Igor R. Shestakov)

Project *Ross und Reiter* I: 'V–4' on 'V–2' launch rocket (project). Colour scheme: 'V–4': RLM 'weissgrau 1945', 'V–2': jagged camouflage pattern consisting of RAL 9003/ RAL 7028/ RAL 6003). (Igor R. Shestakov)

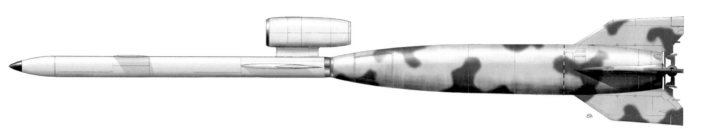

'V–2/ V–4' two-stage rocket (project). Colour scheme: 'V–4': RLM 'blaugrau 1945' overall, V–2: irregular camouflage consisting of Luftwaffe and armour colours RAL 6003/ RAL 7028/ RLM 76. (Igor R. Shestakov)

Junkers Ju–488 long-range bomber with Zippermayr/ Messerschmitt 'Enzian' air-to-ground missile attacking Middle East oilfeields.
(R. Mendes)

above Giant battleship H–44 launching an 'Enzian' victory
weapon. The final guidance of the missile was to be carried out
by a large Dornier Do–216 flying boat. (R. Mendes)

right Postwar further development of the German 'Flying Man'
project. (Renaud Mangallon)

Fokker V.21 remote-controlled glider bomb. (Author's model)

Savoia Marchetti SM.79 ARP, remote-controlled flying bomb (1942). (Author's model)

Tupolev TB. 3, remote-controlled flying bomb (1942). (Author's model)

Battle of the 'weapons of the future' over England! The Allies deployed the most modern weapons they had at the time against the V-weapons. The illustration on the box of this vintage AMT construction kit recalls the meeting of the first Allied jet fighter aircraft, the Gloster 'Meteor' Mk. 1 (616 Sqdn. RAF), and the V–1 robot bomb as the harbingers of 'push-button-warfare'.

Fi–103 'High-speed cell' with TV camera guidance system and Stealth colour scheme. (Author's model)

Fieseler Fi–103 with Porsche 109–005 jet propulsion system on transport carriage, towed by an HKL 6P half-track vehicle. (Author's model)

Mobile launch ramp for Fi–103, loaded on a 'Panther' ('Langholz Principle') mobile trailer. (Author's model)

above Mobile launch ramp for Fi–103 in launch position with Fi–103 (nerve gas warhead) and launch rockets. (Author's model)

left There were plans for this, too: 'Tornado' high-performance remote-controlled explosive boat – the V–1 of the sea. (Author's model)

above left A–4A 'long-range fuselage' with 'Visol'
propulsion system (model: Herminio Pimentel Espinoza,
photo: Aescala models ®, ww.geocities.com/aescalamodels)

above right EMW A–4A standard fuselage.
(model: Herminio Pimentel Espinoza, photo: Aescala
models ®, www.geocities.com/aescalamodels)

EMW A–8 high-pressure rocket (Author's model)

Medium (8-ton) towing vehicle (Sd. Kfz. 7) with prototype of an EMW hydrogen propulsion system on trailer. (Author's model).

left A–4B early version (model: Herminio Pimentel Espinoza, photo: Aescala models ®, www.geocities.com/ aescalamodels)

right A–4B late version (model: Herminio Pimentel Espinoza, photo: Aescala models ®, www.geocities.com/ aescalamodels)

EMW A–9A on trailer with Breda Tipo–61 towing vehicle. (Author's model)

left EMW A–9B, late version with extended fuselage (model: Herminio Pimentel Espinoza, photo: Aescala models ®, www.geocities.com/aescalamodels)

right Vehicles from a rocket launching battery with EMW A–4 (filled with 'Tabun' nerve gas). (Author's model).

Himmler's never-realised 'silent apocalypse': EMW A–4 with biological weapons warhead and service crew in protective clothing. (Author's model)

above left EMW A–4 with fuselage section opened to show the spherical isotope container. (Author's model)

above EMW A–4 with flattened nose cone – test version for a nuclear re-entry missile? (Author's model)

above right EMW A–4 with separable multiple warhead for small uranium bombs. (Author's model)

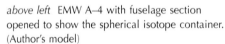

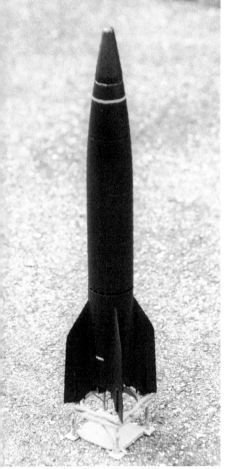

left 'Atomic' A–4: the definitive version. (model: Herminio Pimentel Espinoza, photo: Aescala models ®, www.geocities.com/aescalamodels)

right A–4A standard payload, adapted for beam guidance system (tail fin antennae). (model: Herminio Pimentel Espinoza, photo: Aescala models ®, www.geocities.com/aescalamodels)

A–4B U-boat rocket in transport tube, loaded on trailer with 'Famo' heavy 18-ton towing vehicle (Sd. Kfz. 9). (Author's model)

Proposal for a ballistic rocket U-boat project based on the Type XXI U-boat with rocket launch tubes in the conning tower. (Author's model)

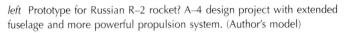

left Prototype for Russian R–2 rocket? A–4 design project with extended fuselage and more powerful propulsion system. (Author's model)

right Sd-Kfz –251 self-propelled carriage for EMW *Wasserfall* artillery guided missile (small). (Author's model)

Pz IVJ self-propelled carriage for EMW *Wasserfall* artillery guided missile (large). (Author's model)

Blohm & Voss BV–246-F glider bomb loaded with 'Sarin' nerve gas under Focke-Wulf 190-A–8 carrier aircraft. (Author's model)

Henschel HS–293-B guided missile loaded with 'Sarin' nerve gas compared to an HS 293A with normal explosive (above).
(Author's model)

Gotha Go–299 B
with four
R–300Bs onboard
rockets. (Author's
model)

above Junkers Ju–388-J–2 Tagzerstörer
with Henschel HS–117-H 'V–3' rocket.
(Author's model)

left EMW A–4 'flak rocket' with Visol
propulsion system (1944). (Author's
model)

If the uranium containers were to be used in the 1000-kg bomb to be carried by the HOXVIII 'New York Bomber' and the Sänger bomber, a cylindrical container measuring 0.75 metres in diameter and 3.63 metres in length would have been developed. It would have been shaped like a smaller V-2. On release, it would have reached a velocity greater than the speed of sound, but not the same strike velocity as that of the A-4.

American Colonel Don L. Putt, who was responsible for investigating German military secrets for the postwar Allied military government, also mentioned, when his mission came to an end in 1946, that the Germans had two atomic bombs which were to be mounted on the V-2.

It is not clear or whether by this he meant that the Third Reich had two different types of bombs for mounting on rockets or that there were two bombs of the same type. Were the spherical containers filled with U 235/238 one of these weapons?

Work was also being carried out on various miniaturised versions of the uranium containers, which would have allowed them to be fitted to other weapons, such as the atomic rocket developed by engineer Matzka. After Stadtilm had been captured, staff from the atomic laboratory revealed to the ALSOS mission details of this 'Diebner bomb'. But the weapons themselves could not be found, because they were to be developed in a laboratory in the south.

Nothing is known about whether the Allies made any use of this idea after the war. It is likely that the perfection of the uranium bombs of the Hiroshima type and the plutonium bombs would have made this 'temporary solution' unnecessary.

Unfortunately, up to the present day, nobody has succeeded in identifying the location of the secret laboratory with the two experimental containers. In the opinion of the American researcher Flannery, the fact that they were stored in a water tank would indicate that they were perhaps already ready to be tested.

As has already been outlined in the first volume, the destruction of the two containers could possibly have caused radiological contamination of the surrounding area with the resulting negative consequences for the population. For this reason alone, it would be still important today to determine the former location of this atomic bomb laboratory.

In any event, rumours about the buried atomic bomb components surface every few years in the area around Haigerloch. But taking into accounts the reports about these Swabian atom bombs, it must have been clear that Haigerloch could never be the location in question.

The representative of the Atomic Bomb Museum at Haigerloch said to the American researcher Flannery that although no atomic containers had been found in Haigerloch, this did not mean that they did not exist. So the search goes on!

Atomic A-4A: Uranium warheads for the V-2

Contrary to everything which is written today about the V-weapons, leading German atomic scientists, officers and politicians of the Third Reich and also informed Allied experts saw that the purpose of the German rocket and missile programme was quite clearly to transport nuclear warheads.

As early as 15 October 1942, that is, only a little less than two weeks after the first successful launch of an A-4 rocket, a secret development commission was issued direct to *Postrat* Kubicki at the German *Reichspost* research establishment.[139] This commission must have been extremely important, because, bearing as it did the second highest level of urgency - *Sonderstufe* - it had the same degree of urgency as the entire A-4 programme. The commission came from *Abteilung 11* of the *Amtsgruppe fur Entwicklung und Prufwesen* (Development and Testing Group) of the *Heereswaffenamt (WA Pruf 11)* in Peenemünde.

The commission required the development of new rocket fuel mixtures with the highest energy content in order to increase performance and achieve a greater range than the range of 200 kilometres which had hitherto been the maximum range of the A 4. It also required that 'investigation should be given to the possibility of using atomic decay and the chain reaction to provide *R-Antrieb* (propulsion for rockets)'.

In addition to research into nuclear propulsion systems for rockets, the order issued to Peenemünde also clearly contains a concealed requirement for research to be carried out into nuclear explosives for rockets. In this connection it should not be forgotten that 'the designation new sources of energy for *R-Antrieb*' was, as early as 1939, demonstrably used as a codeword for nuclear weapons research by the Diebner/Harteck group working on behalf of the Wehrmacht. Was this also the case here?

The commission of 15 October 1942 was evidently considered to be so important that - as is clear from the document - it was to be carried out despite the Führer's order, in force at the time, that only permitted research which would lead to the relevant developments being ready for front-line service within one year.

But were the researchers ready anyway to produce a nuclear explosive charge which would have been suitable for a German rocket? The A-4, the A-9/A-10 and also the flying bombs of the type Fi-103 were only designed to carry a maximum explosive payload of 795-1000 kg. Was not this value in itself too small a weight for an A-bomb?

Let us consider the state of technical developments at the time. From a technical point of view, at the end of the war, there were two types of atomic bomb. The first was the uranium bomb of the Hiroshima type which worked on the projectile principle, and the second was the plutonium bomb of the Nagasaki type which worked on the implosion principle. For reasons of space, only a uranium bomb would have been suitable for mounting on the V-weapons.

Photograph of the construction of a nuclear-payload rocket nose cone from 1944? The official caption of the German Museum reads: 'Workshop with payload-bearing nose cones (special design) for the A–4 rocket, 1944'. (Raumfahrtarchiv, Peenbild B2046/44, Photo Deutsches Museum München).

Although during the post-war period the Americans never announced what the critical mass of the Hiroshima bomb actually was (it is estimated that it was 50 to 60 kilograms of uranium 235), nevertheless we do know that the main weight component of the bomb design was composed of-as it turned out-unnecessary armoured materials. The actual functioning explosive mechanism including the explosive charge may have been no heavier than 530-850 kilograms.[140] [141]

Thus in 1944/45 it would have been possible, after appropriate refinement and removal of all necessary armour plating, to transport a fully functioning Second World War nuclear bomb of the Hiroshima type with Germany's rockets and missiles. On the basis of the measurements, too, it would have been feasible to build it in with a suitable detonator to the nose cones of the V-1 and V-2.

To serve as detonators, impact detonators (for crater formation) and a separation detonators (for effect over a greater area) would have been considered. Is it coincidence that both types of detonator had been developed for the A-4 by the end of the war?

The main problem may have been to build the sensitive warhead into the rocket in such a way that it would not have been damaged or destroyed by the heat created by friction during the flight, and on the other hand would not be too insensitive to be detonated as planned at the target.

In order to clarify the question as to whether work was actually carried out on nuclear warhead nose cones for the A 4, we must look for German rocket specialists who had significant knowledge of atomic physics and who apparently for no reason remained in places which can be connected with German atomic weapons research.

Has this question already been answered?

When on 12 April 1945, together with the first Allied troops, the American ALSOS mission arrived in the small Thuringian town of Stadtilm, the American nuclear experts already knew that they expected to find an atomic research laboratory there.[142] [143] Surprisingly, however, ALSOS also found Dr Ernst Stuhlinger, who had occupied a prominent position at Peenemünde since 1943 and who was a specialist in ballistics, speed measurement and guidance for the rockets. Stuhlinger was one of the closest associates of Wernher von Braun, and the question must expressly be asked what the Peenemünde rocket technician together with his working group was doing at the atomic laboratory. His presence in Stadtilm becomes even more difficult to understand when it is considered that no activities connected with rockets ever took place in the town. What, then, was Stuhlinger doing there during the

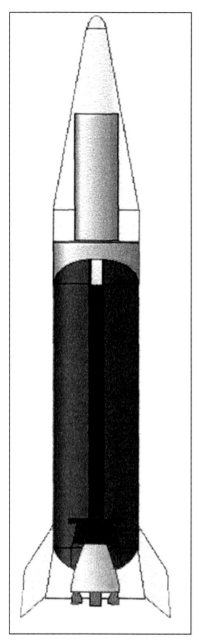

South African 'Type 1' rocket which carries a 1000 kg uranium warhead (1971) – a copy of designs developed by Germany during the war? (according to Mark Wade).

their work without the equipment which they had built and tested ever being taken away. Are we to believe this?

To date it has not been clarified where exactly Dr Stuhlinger's working group stayed in Ilmenau. But he himself admits that one day he 'happened' to meet there his old colleagues from the Berlin Technical University, including Dr Otto Haxel, Dr Helmut Folz, Dr Luise Schützmeister and Dr Erika Leimert, and had been invited by them, together with his group, to stay in the school building in Stadtilm. This, he said, had been in March or April 1945. It is known that the school building in question was the so-called *Mittelschule* which was situated behind the town hall and in which the atomic laboratory was located.

This post-war legend prompts the conclusion that the rocket and atomic specialist Stuhlinger had worked with his working group on the site of a German nuclear laboratory together with his old colleagues from the Berlin Diebner group. And this is surely not without basis. In the cellars of the *Mittelschule* there were, according to eyewitness accounts, some of which were given on oath, scale models of the later German atomic bombs and also possibly even original warheads.

Of course, having regard to the fact that both German atomic and rocket specialists were actually present in Thuringia, it is not possible to continue to believe that all this was just an amazing coincidence of coincidences. But it is more credible to assume that Stuhlinger's team were working in Ilmenau together with the Diebner group and an SS group of atomic researchers on the adaptation of atomic warheads for mounting on rockets.

Is it not remarkable that after the war Stuhlinger worked on similar projects in the USA? For example, he carried out research on nuclear propulsion systems for rockets for NASA and the US Atomic Energy Commission (AEC) ...

That there was a connection between German rocket development and atomic research can no longer be disputed. This is demonstrated, for example, by the fact that Pascal Jordan, a leading nuclear scientist and an old colleague of Professor Dr Heisenberg, worked within the rocket testing ground of Peenemünde. In addition to this, there are other clues which indicate that Peenemünde was directly connected with nuclear research (see Volume 1).

Fortunately, in the meantime, it has even become known what Hitler's 'rocket surprise' actually looked like. According to reliable information from a former leading member of staff at Peenemünde, the nuclear version differed externally from the normal rocket. *The A-4A with nuclear armament* had the same fuselage length as the A-9b (15,030 mm). It could be recognised externally because of the greater diameter of its fuselage-warhead assembly (1690 instead of 1651mm) and a more sharply defined nose. Besides being a medium-range rocket, it was also intended to serve as the second stage of an A-4/A-10 combination fuelled by Visol and Salbei.

By the end of the war, work on this project appeared to have been at a very advanced stage. This is confirmed by

period from January to April 1945?

Again, is it only coincidence that Dr Stuhlinger was one of the specialists who were involved with atomic research as well as with rocket technology? Before he worked at Peenemünde, he had worked from 1939 in Berlin with notable nuclear physicists under Professor Heisenberg on Germany's atomic programme. Even before that, Dr Stuhlinger was involved from 1935, first in Tübingen and later in Berlin, in the successful production of the first devices for measuring radioactivity.

After the war, Dr Stuhlinger said that it was pure coincidence that his working group was moved to Ilmenau and Stadtilm. It is remarkable that this only happened in January 1945, that is, before the official evacuation of Peenemünde! Stuhlinger wrote in his 'Recollections of Stadtilm' that he had 'no contact whatever' with his 'superiors' and that the working group were simply continuing reliable American experts.[144] [145] [146] Thus, after the war ended, the US Army Air Force (USAAF) created Operation 'Lusty' (Luftwaffe **S**ecret **T**echnology) which was under the command of Colonel Don L Putt, and which began the hunt for German aircraft designers, engineers and aircraft captains. Colonel Putt's investigation only really got under way in mid-1945, but then rapidly increased in intensity. 'Lusty' looked for material and specialists even in the British and Soviet occupation zones, and was later continued by the Allied Military Government. Don L Putt, who later became one of the leading representatives of Operation 'Paperclip', rose to the rank of Lieutenant-General in the 1960s, not least because of his success in the hunt for German technology and the relevant specialists.

After his mission in Germany had come to an end, in July 1946 Putt made a statement which must silence all doubters. He said: 'Only a few more weeks and the Germans would have deployed a decisive weapon. Atomic bombs, of which they had two, would have been built into the V-2'.

During the period after the war, the German plans for uranium warheads to arm the V-2 and A-9 rockets turned up, to all intents and purposes seemingly unchanged, in another part of the world even decades later.[147] Between 1971-1989, the then white Government of South Africa developed atomic warheads for its Types 1 to 4 nuclear rockets.

Seven of these A-weapons, which could also be used as flying bombs, were built by South Africa. They each weighed 1000 kg, had a diameter of 65 cm and a length of 1.8 m. Their explosive power was between 10 and 15 kilotons.

Is it not remarkable that this cylindrical warhead had also had a place in an EMW V-2?

V-2 with neutron warhead - only rumours, or is there more to it?

According to the information provided by several American researchers, by the end of the war the Germans had even succeeded in producing V-2 rockets with neutron warheads. It is said that these special V-2s were equipped with new types of astro-navigation equipment and that they were to be launched from U-boats. For this purpose, the rockets were to be housed in the underwater towing containers of the 'Laffarenz Project', towed to a position off the US coast and launched from there.

The same information suggests that the Germans succeeded in launching several of these U-boat rocket towing units across the Atlantic towards America. On the orders of Grand Admiral Doenitz, however, these vessels scuppered themselves shortly before the German surrender and sank with all hands.

Before we consign this story immediately into the realm of fantasy, we should note the reports and rumours which repeatedly turn up suggesting that apart from the uranium and plutonium bomb in Germany, there were also other developments of the same kind.

The research and salvage ship 'Glomar Explorer', built by Howard Hughes for the Americans, became famous when it salvaged a Russian nuclear submarine which had sunk near Hawaii. But originally it was said to have been specially designed to salvage the former German rocket U-boats which had sunk at the end of the Second World War, in order to get access to the technology of their warheads. According to the same reports, the 'Glomar Explorer' actually succeeded in raising the German secret rockets.[148]

Whatever the case may be, will we ever get to know the truth about these alleged events?

3) How were the V-2 Victory Weapons to be deployed?

The 'Special Installations' - the secret of the large underground rocket bunkers in France

As early as 1941/42 there were fierce discussions about how the A-4 was actually to be deployed.[149] The questions involved whether the rockets were to be launched with the aid of mobile camouflaged batteries or whether they were to be launched from fixed bunkers and underground bases. Although after the war Dornberger wrote that the designers at Peenemünde had vehemently preferred the mobile launch procedure, there are indications that in actual fact the development team for the A-4 rocket came down strongly in favour of launching the rocket from large bunkers. How can we explain this?

The main advantage of fixed positions in bunkers as against mobile batteries was that in the bunker positions complicated preparations for launch and tests could be carried out in peace. Even with other special operations procedures, the point at issue is seen repeatedly to be the need for an undisturbed period of preparation before launch (see relevant chapter). The disadvantages of such bunkers was

that they would automatically attract enemy counter-measures as soon as their position became known. This was a dangerous issue in the light of Allied air superiority which was continually increasing!

Even before the first successful launch of the A-4, Wernher von Braun and his colleague Stegmaier prepared a document which ordered for 1943 the construction of both mobile batteries and the installation of launch bunkers. As early as 18 December 1942, the first models of bunkers for 'fixed operational batteries' were presented to Adolf Hitler.[150]

The original plan for the deployment of the V-2s from fixed positions and their further enlargement envisaged two large launch bunkers in the Pas de Calais and two further bunkers on the Cherbourg peninsula. All four were to be able to accommodate between 30 and 100 V-2s and were to have been equipped with oxygen production plants and storage facilities for alcohol, HTP and catalytic fluids. Above all, they were to be completely bomb-proof and to be able to guarantee complete checking, fuelling and arming of the rockets, irrespective of the kind of planned warheads (whether conventional or ABC). The following launch bunkers were planned: Watten (codename: Kraftwerk Nord-West), Wizernes (codename: Schotterwerk Nord-West im Pas de Calais), Sottevast (codename: Reservelager West – Bauvorhaben 51) and Brécourt (codename: Ölkeller Cherbourg), both on the Cherbourg Peninsula.

Later there was added a combination of four lightly protected open launch positions and 50 unprotected launch positions.

In 1944 a further network of simple launch positions with light protection was created, which could be used as needed for the launch of the V-1, V2 and the *Rheinbote* rocket.

In his research into the German large rocket bunkers projects in Watten, Wizernes and Brecourt, the British rocket specialist Philip Henshall demonstrated that these were far too big and expensive for the mere storage and launch of individual V-1s or V-2s. The real purpose of the bunkers, he said, was to store additional special nuclear or chemical materials, to prepare them and to house the A-9/A-10 America rocket and other future rocket projects.

Is this the secret behind the large bunkers and at the same time also the reason why the people from Peenemünde did not want to have had anything to do with them after the war?

The Allies discovered that the gigantic concrete bunkers begun in 1943 were precisely aligned on London or – as, for example, in the case of the Martinvast bunker – on Bristol.

In this connection, the bunker of Wizernes had a special position. In scrutinising the reconnaissance photographs, the terrified photo reconnaissance evaluators noted that the front end of this construction project was oriented to within half a degree of the Great Circle leading directly to New York. When the former German Reich armaments Minister was asked for the reason for this when he was a prisoner, he bitterly contested the allegation that he had ever had the intention of launching rockets at New York from Wizernes. Just as the other bunkers 'happened' to be oriented towards London and Bristol, this bunker just 'simply happened' to point towards New York.[151]

The Anglo-Americans did not want to expose themselves to any risk at all and submitted all the bunker projects which had been spotted to a determined bombardment which increased to such an extent that eventually the majority of the Allied air strike capacity was being deployed against the German large bunker projects in France. But the building project at Brecourt was never identified and was not attacked even once.

The Allied air forces deployed everything in their arsenal against the German rocket and missile bunkers – fighter-bombers, medium and heavy bombers, 'Tallboy' bombs –

the largest bombs that had been dropped up to that time during the Second World War -, remote-controlled aircraft from the 'Aphrodite' project filled with explosives.

These measures met with considerable success. But they did not succeed in destroying the large bunkers such as Watten and Wizernes from the air. Nevertheless, a large part of the other building projects had to be abandoned while they were being constructed. Watten and Wizernes were then systematically 'stifled'. In doing this, the Allies were acting on the correct assumption that if direct annihilation of the plants was not possible, it would be sufficient to transform the surroundings of the large bunkers into a moonscape, so that, short of necessary supplies, the bunkers would never be able to resume their normal operations.

The Allied air raids resulted in the largest and most complex plant at Watten becoming no longer suitable for its purpose in Winter 1943, and instead of this, taking over responsibility for special tasks such as the important production of oxygen.

But after the beginning of the Allied invasion in France, in an order dated 18 July 1944, Hitler gave orders that, since it was the only fully protected launch position for the V-2 (and A-10?), *Bauwerk 21* at Wizernes must be completed as quickly as possible. Despite the many air raids which were now principally directed at Wizernes, the urgency classification of the B21 bunker was retained. This can be seen from the increases in the number of workers on the building project from 1106 men in April 1944 through 1280 in May and up to 1381 in the middle of June 1944, 60 percent of whom were German.

But here, too, it was not possible to complete the construction before the Allies captured the bunker in September 1944. When the British occupied Wizernes, they found a bunker construction site which had been completely evacuated and cleared.[152]

The conclusion is that it was not possible for the Third Reich, despite a very large input of material and personnel, to bring the planned large rocket bunkers in France to a state of combat readiness. The bunkers were either destroyed by the Allied air forces during their construction phase, or air raids by allied aircraft slowed down their construction to such an extent that they were not able to achieve a state of combat readiness before the Allies occupied France.

But what danger did these rocket and missile bunkers in France really represent? This has remained a mystery even up to the present day.

To serve the large bunker complexes in Watten and Wizernes, *Artillerieabteilung 953* had already been formed. It was set up on 15 August, 1943 in Greifswald and Karlshagen (see section entitled 'The 3rd V-weapons Regiment').

All the items of the equipment and installations necessary for the bunkers were already standing by – once again there had not been enough time! The Allies were clear that the rocket and missile bunkers in France were to play a special part in the German programme.

As early as 10 September 1944, that is just four days after the launch site at Watten had been captured by Canadian troops, a small group of Allied scientists and experts arrived there to inspect the interior of the complex.[153] [154] This group included Duncan Sandys, who led the British rocket specialists, and Frederic Joliot-Curie, the most illustrious French atomic researcher of the period. During the war, Joliot-Curie played a role which is still unclear, in which he probably also carried out tasks for the German nuclear weapons programme.

Details of what the Allied inspectors found at that time in Watten remains unpublished even today. But only a few weeks later attempts were made to destroy the building with 'Tallboy' and the even bigger 'Grand Slam' bombs. A German document dated 4 November 1943 mentions that Watten was intended for 'special operations'. This raises the question what was meant by that term. Was it, as the British researcher Henshall suspects, even planned to install nuclear reactors in Watten? When the Germans evacuated Watten in September 1944 they had previously switched off all the drainage pumps to the deep levels within the building, and these shortly afterwards filled with water. Early French tourist guides to the present-day memorial site of Watten said at the time that in these deep levels nuclear and laser laser experiments had been undertaken. The present day museum guides at Watten 'happen' not to mention this piece of information. Is it no longer politically correct to mention this possibility?

It is also worth noting that Dr Dornberger, who worked on the planning of the bunker at Watten, makes as little mention of that site in his post-war books as he does Nordhausen.

On 2 October 1944, Professor Joliot-Curie and other French scientists once again inspected Watten. In December 1944, it was Wizernes' turn and in January 1945 Mimoyeques (see Volume 3). At that time the French also 'happened' to meet the British Colonel Sanders. As a result of this meeting, the hypothesis that these bunkers were factories for producing Type V-3 atom bombs was rejected. But does this conclusion also apply to plans to launch nuclear rockets and missiles?

It is quite clear that what has been said to date about large bunkers in France is not the whole truth. While most of the British secret documents concerning the German secret weapons in the Second World War have been published in recent years, there are also in existence many other secret documents, for example a file under the codename 'Operation Crossbow'. This file, which very likely contains the truth about the German rocket projects, cannot be opened until 2019! This seems remarkable and raises suspicions! The fact that documents concerning bunker construction projects are to be kept classified for so long shows that a great and probably dark secret is behind it all!

The riddle of the 'Regenwurm' installations

When in summer 1944, despite the ever increasing risk of an invasion of Normandy and under the hail of Allied bombs, the Germans tried to bring at least one of the large bunkers to combat readiness for rocket launches, suddenly a completely new project emerged. It was codenamed *Regenwurm* (earthworm).[155]

This project was apparently so important that in the assignment of priority classifications to building projects on 1 July 1944 it was given priority over the new bunkers for factories producing oxygen at Euville and *Bauvorhaben 21* at Wizernes.

As far as is known today, the *Regenwurm* project involved creating tunnel-like galleries or special construction projects underground, in which motorised rocket batteries, with all their supply and service vehicles, were to be transported by rail. The dimensions of these galleries were relatively small. Normally, a *Regenwurm* tunnel would therefore need to be no more than 3.8 metres wide, while its main gallery was to measure 5 metres wide and 5 metres high. The distance between the entrance and the exit of such a tunnel would have been no more than 43 metres. The maximum length was not to exceed 75 metres. The vehicles belonging to the battery would circulate in a network of galleries which were connected with the outside world by means of many tunnel openings. The *Regenwurm* installations were to have ventilation, energy supply, lighting and fire prevention provisions. The rockets, once ready to launch, would be pushed out of the tunnel system, set up vertically outside only a few metres away from the tunnel opening. The *Regenwurm* system also planned for three rockets to be launched successively in a very short time from the same tunnel opening, before the mobile rocket battery moved to another launch position in order to reduce the risk of being spotted.

On 1 June 1944, the *Organisation Todt* (OT) was ordered to construct three *Regenwurm* installations as a matter of urgency. According to the conference of 1 July 1944, these installations would enable operations to be carried out with certainty, even if Projekt B-12 (Wizernes) could not be completed in time.

What could this phrase 'be carried out with certainty mean? Certainly not the conventional deployment of the mobile rocket batteries which presented few problems. The fact that the *Regenwurm* installation must have involved a project of more than usual scale is probably evident from the fact that to date not a single plan or precise project specification concerning *Regenwurm* has ever come to light. A perspective view of *Bauvorhaben 21* (Wizernes) dated 1 August 1945 shows on the right a network of underground galleries with extended curves which is marked with the codename *Regenwurm*.

Where the two other *Regenwurm* installations commissioned in July 1944 were to be built (or were built?) has not to date been clarified. It has been suggested that a similar

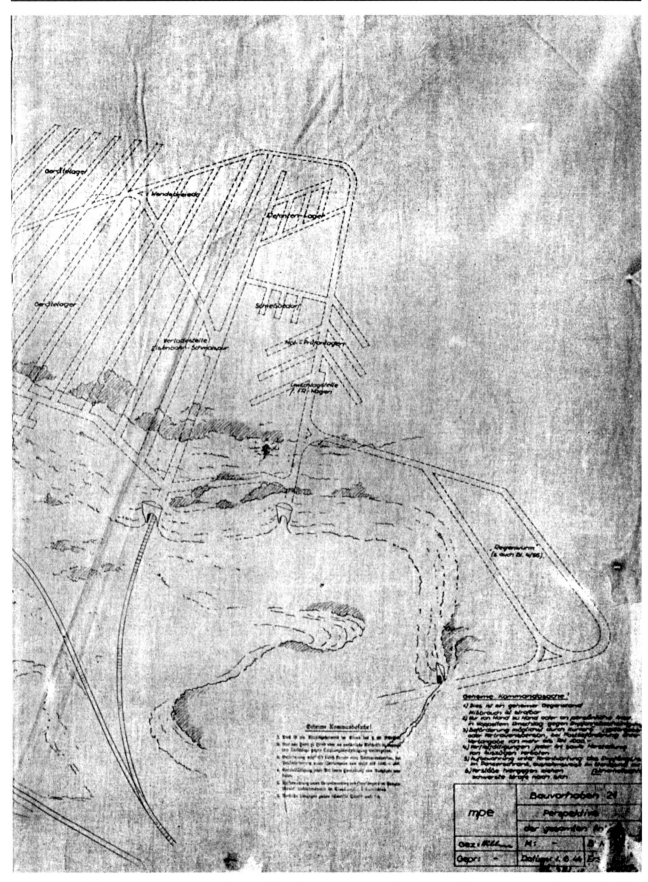

Part of the plan for Building Project B 21 ('Schotterwerk Nordwest'), Wizernes, with a recognizable Regenwurm installation on the left. (Bundesmilitärarchiv)

installation was to be provided in Rapallo (see section 'V-Weapons in Italy').

The remarkable shortage of data, plans and drawings relating to this project which was so important in 1944 almost automatically raises the suspicion that the *Regenwurm* project was a project which could have involved the planned deployment of weapons which are said not to have existed.

It is very probable that the *Regenwurm* project was the ancestor of the later American idea from 1978, when the new MX atomic rocket was to be transported around an enormous underground network of galleries. The galleries which were planned for this project were to have a diameter of about 3.96 metres and, in contrast to the German project, to extend underground for some 4,828 kilometres. As was the case with the German project, the MX rockets would have been launched from predetermined windows outside. Because of the exorbitant cost (by today's standards 10.2 billion US dollars for the construction of the underground tunnels alone), the modernised version of the former German *Regenwurm* project of 1944 was not pursued by the Americans.

Mobile A-4 batteries for Special Operations

As far as is known to date, mobile deployment was the only method by which V-2 rockets came to be used operationally during the Second World War. The basic principles of this idea had been developed as early as 1941/42. These involved mobile launch units which were completely independent. *General* Dr Dornberger wanted to create 45 mobile launch units comprising hundreds of different types of vehicle.

The actual rocket launch would be carried out by the so-called *Schiess-Zug* (launch detachment).

The vehicles in the rocket batteries were characterised by their capability of operating on any kind of terrain. For the most part, they were not new developments, but conversions of types of vehicles which were already in existence.

The entire preparation procedure for the launch of the V-2 lasted about 90 minutes. As a foundation for the launch pad for the rocket, simple woodland tracks or even firms sandy ground were suitable. The launching positions were constantly changed and were mostly in woodland or parkland.

The launches themselves were mostly carried out from small clearings in the woods in the hours of twilight, which guaranteed the greatest level of protection against discovery by the enemy. Later, some launches were even carried out from urban districts around Den Haag.

The V-2 batteries moved almost exclusively at night, sometimes they and their supply units moved with the help of infra-red night sight equipment. The batteries were extremely mobile. Thus, after the launch, the entire detachment would be able to leave its launch position within 30 minutes.

To date, the hunt for mobile rocket launch batteries has been comparable to the search for the notorious needle in a haystack. No single instance is known in the Second World War of a V-2 launch being prevented by Allied air raids. After the war, Wernher von Braun stated that no instance had been known in which even a single V-2 had been damaged in an air-raid. In the 1990s Gulf War, too, it proved to be almost impossible to destroy in time the Iraqi Scud rocket launchers which operated on the same principle.

Fortunately for the wartime Allies and the Gulf War alliance of Americans, Israelis and Saudis, the rockets launched against them by Hitler and Saddam Hussein did not contain nuclear warheads. But were the German mobile rocket launch batteries really so harmless or were there other batteries among them which had worse things up their sleeve?

On 4 November 1943, the *Beauftragter ZBV (Heer)* issued an extremely important document which described the planned rocket operations in France. The document indicates that certain V-2 units were also designated for special operations (which are not described in any more detail than this!). These were to have their supplies and logistics base in 'Ölkeller Cherbourg' which was to provide bombproof underground accommodation for personnel, vehicles, fuel and 30 V-2s. This rocket base called 'Ölkeller Cherbourg' is also known as the combined rocket base of Brécourt, and was also to provide launch ramps in bunkers to launch (special?) V-1 flying bombs.

Research carried out by the British rocket and atomic specialist Philip Henshall has indicated that in Brecourt there was room for at least 300 V-2s. This raises the question why in the German document only 30 V-2s are designated for 'special operations' for Brécourt and why much too large an area in the valuable bunker was reserved for just these few rockets.

'Ölkeller Cherbourg' fell into British hands as early as July 1944 without ever having been able to begin its intended function. Its true significance had never been recognised until the Allies captured it, and it is probably for this reason that it was never bombed. What would have happened if the invasion had only taken place a few months later?

Unfortunately there are no later documents which could provide an answer to the question as to what became of the mobile V-2 'Special Operations' batteries after France fell. It is not likely that the German plans to form such 'special operations' units were simply abandoned after the loss of one uncompleted bunker. Therefore, today, we would have to search for example, in Holland, for any traces as to whether the one or indeed another V-2 battery was located there for 'Special Operations'. (see section entitled 'Were there already nuclear test units?').

Rockets for secret 'Special Operations': the Railway V-2

From summer 1944 in Peenemünde, work was being carried out on two unusual transport procedures for the V-2. The first procedure involved railway trains being used as a mobile launch system, while the second planned to tow V-2 containers by U-boats across the Atlantic underwater to bombard New York (see Volume 1).

While the U-boat V-2 of the Laffrenz Project was in competition with other long-range weapons such as the America bomber, the A 9/A 10 and the Sanger bomber, the purpose of railway rocket batteries is not clear at first sight.

But the plans to launch V-2s from railway wagons were not an idea originating during the last stages of the war. When the development of the V-2 began in 1939, consideration was given to the various railway operations. In doing so, in addition to examining the possibility of launching from fixed bunkers and with the help of mobile all-terrain vehicles, the possibility of launching the rockets from special wagons which moved by rail was examined.[156] [157]

At the end of 1942 the first railway launch wagons were ready as experimental prototypes for testing in Peenemünde. As part of this process, the A4 rockets were carried on newly-designed Meiller wagons on the train. These wagons were very similar to the mobile launch arrangements which are already known, and in addition had demountable launch pads. The particular characteristic of these launch pads was a long base plate shaped like a saddle which would divert the blast of the exhaust to right and left alongside the tracks during launch, so that the rail infrastructure was not destroyed by the massive pressure of the glowing exhaust gases.

The main preparations to launch the A-4s were to take place in twin-rail railway tunnels. Afterwards, the transport and launch wagons would be driven with the rocket launch pad immediately outside the tunnel exit. There the rocket, which had been prepared for launch, would be raised by means of the lifting arm and launched. Thus, outside the tunnel, only a very short period of time of a few minutes was required for the launch.

Because of the increasing deterioration of the air war situation in the West and the advantages of mobile launch bases which had emerged in the meantime, work on the rail -based launch procedure was discontinued.

In 1944, however, Hans Kammler had ordered that this development work be resumed. According to Dr Dornberger, his reasons for doing this remained unknown. So, during the last months of 1944 in Peenemünde thorough experiments were carried out using the railway V-2s. But the eight wagons of an autonomous railway battery which

V-2 railway battery in trials on the Peenemünde testing ground 1944. (Raumfahrtarchiv, Peenbild, B1965/44, Photo Deutsches Museum München)

had been planned at the beginning of the war had now increased to trains of 70 to 80 wagons carrying all the vehicles and equipment for the launch battery and also the necessary rocket fuels of alcohol and liquid oxygen. These trains could be several kilometres long. They were comprised of two parts: the first was for personnel, accommodation wagons, laboratories and workshops, and the second transported the fuels, rockets and launch vehicles. Whilst the fuels were carried in special tanker wagons, the launch vehicles were the same as for mobile A-4 batteries apart from the fact that they were mounted on *Reichsbahn* wagons. The crew of the railway batteries consisted of about 100 men. Depending on their design, the trains could carry two, three or six rockets. For taking measurements in the initial phase of the rocket flight, the 'Messina' system was also carried on board the railway trains. The rocket trains were pulled by modern diesel locomotives of the type WR 360 C14, each providing 360hp.

Dornberger wrote that shortly after the development work for these rail-based rocket bases could be completed at the beginning of 1945, all further work was stopped and the preparations abandoned. But this assertion is demonstrably incorrect! Is it the case that this to all intents and purposes incredible legend of a pointless project which was stopped, begun again, and stopped yet again, conceals something entirely different?

On the contrary, it appears certain that one of the V-2 railway batteries, allegedly stopped on Dr Kammler's direct orders, was in central Hesse in January 1945 and that in February 1945 tunnels were being converted specifically for V-2 railway batteries. Published photographs indicate that there were least three different Meiller railway wagons, so that they must also have been at least three railway batteries which together composed a long-range artillery unit. Probably this was the training and reserve unit for *Eisenbahn-Artillerie (mot)* 100. From 1 October 1944, this unit was under the command of Dr Kammler's *Division z.V.*

As early as Autumn 1944, the then *Oberleutnant* Heinrich Schaus, a member of V-2 *Artillerie-Regiment (mot) z.V.901*, had received orders to look for railway tunnels suitable for the railway V-2. Thus, even at that time there were specific plans for rail-based rocket operations in central Hesse, even though the front was still a long way away.

In actual fact, then in January 1945, a (combat-ready?) rocket train unit was to have been moved westwards to a tunnel specially converted for the purpose. But then something must have gone wrong! Because from about 15 January 1945, this train had been placed on the eastbound sidings parallel to the main line to Giessen. The hermetically-sealed train, kilometres long, was redirected several times on the orders of the Frankfurt railway directorate, but always kept returning to the same sidings in Gardenheim. It seems that every time something was

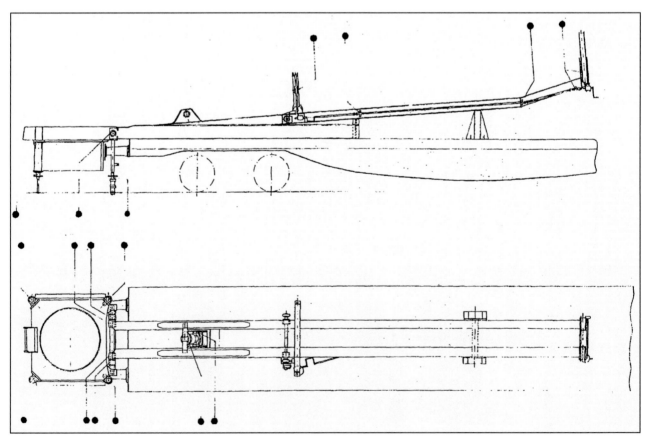

Design sketch for a railway rocket launch wagon with lifting arm and lowering launch platform. (Deutsches Museum München)

preventing this train from carrying on its journey into its tunnel base!

The rocket railway battery finally met its end on Sunday 21 January 1945 on the goods station at Gardenheim, when suddenly a flight of twin-engined American 'Marauder' bombers deliberately (!) attacked the train and blew it sky-high. Even as the first bomb struck, a jet of flame several hundred metres high shot into the sky. Eyewitnesses reported that for days afterwards explosions could be seen and heard!

This raises the question what (or who) had once again prevented the A-4 railway battery from continuing its journey. It must have been clear to all those responsible that, given Allied total air superiority, such a valuable train waiting for so long in the same place was as good as lost. Did treason and sabotage perhaps play a part here? Normally, until shortly before the end of the war, the Allies hardly ever succeeded in hitting V-2 railway transports directly from the air, and in this instance it was one of the rare battery trains which was hit! Even from a conservative point of view this appears remarkable.

Evidently, even after the destruction of the railway rocket battery at Gardenheim, plans for further operations had not been abandoned. Even in February 1945, there were plans to convert the former railway tunnel at Hasselborn in central Hesse to house rocket trains. From June 1944, an armaments company had taken over the tunnel. At this time, the rails were removed from the entire tunnel and the floor of the tunnel was concreted. In February 1945, instructions came suddenly from Berlin that the tunnel being used by the armaments firm VDM was to be evacuated within 14 days, because, after removing the concrete floor of the tunnel, the Wehrmacht wanted to build new rail tracks for military purposes. When the military then realised that it was not possible to carry out such conversion work in a short time, everything remained as it was.

Unfortunately, it is unknown whether other railway tunnels were also to be converted to take V-2 rocket batteries and how far these plans had progressed. Even before the failed movement of the V-2 railway train at Gardenheim, at least one or other tunnel base must have already been prepared. Where was this tunnel and why it did the rocket train never reach it? It would be entirely in keeping with the situation if the tunnel or the approaches to it had perhaps 'happened' to have been rendered unusable shortly before this time.

Any search for secret rocket tunnels must also take into account the fact that there were posibly plans for such operations in other districts than central Hesse, even on the Southern and Eastern Front.

The fact is that two V2 rail-based rocket batteries were driven in Spring 1945 westwards into the Bleicherode area when Peenemünde was evacuated. There the Russians discovered them in a damaged state after the war had come to an end. On the orders of the Soviets, former Peenemünde scientists of the RABE Organisation brought the trains back to working order again. Under the codename FMS (mobile meteorological station) the first train left Bleicherode in December 1946, followed by the second in January 1947. According to technical reports, the trains are said to have been first moved to the Peenemünde area for launch trials, but then evidently travelled directly to the Soviet Union. What eventually became of them remained unknown for many years.[158] [159]

It so happens that the first Soviet ballistic rocket units were also formed in the same year. Their launch units, such as the '23rd Guard Special Operations Brigade', were originally entirely equipped with captured German technology and used V-2 rockets which were launched from FMS railway launch units. This may shed some light on the question as to what became of the German rocket trains.

Another German special train for the evaluation of rocket launches was captured in a damaged state in Prague by the Russians. This train, too, later provided an important foundation for the commencement of the Soviet postwar rocket programme.

In this connection, the question is raised as to why the SS had transferred the evaluation train to Prague. Unfortunately, no pictures exist of this 'Crown Jewel' belonging to Kammler.

Even up to the present day there have been repeated attempts to deploy rail-based strategic rockets for terror purposes. So, here too the former German V-2 railway batteries are the direct forerunners of these rail-based weapons of mass destruction. Were Dr Kammler's railway-V-2s to be used to launch victory weapons? He must certainly have had important reasons for investing so much effort, time and labour in developing the risky railway-launch version.

One advantage of the V-2 railway batteries was that the rockets could be checked and loaded ready for launch in the relative security and peace of the railway tunnels. This must have involved a longer preparation period than for the normal method of launch. Unlike the procedure in a mobile battery, the rail-based rockets could have only been launched individually. This, too, represents a remarkable expenditure of resources for one single one-ton warhead. Could it have, however, have been precisely this warhead which was important enough to justify all the expenditure of resources?!

It is very probable that a rail-based launch procedure from railway tunnels was regarded as a supplement or replacement for launching from large bunkers. That this assumption I am making is not mere speculation is evident, for example, from a document which was issued by OKW on 4 November 1943. This related to the planned distribution of the V-2 units in France and contained precise details concerning storage, launch and oxygen production. There appear for the first time in this document references to various 'special tasks' and 'special operations' for the V-2s.

These concepts of 'special tasks' and 'special operations' often appear in this type of German secret documents from the Second World War as a coded reference to ultra-secret special weapons and operations (such as, for example, nerve gas), so that in the case of the railway rocket launch units, something special must also have been planned.

Transport of V-2s by aircraft

The already great mobility of V-2 launch batteries would in turn have been considerably increased if it were technically feasible to fly the weapons to their launch positions by means of aircraft.

Calculations made in 1944 indicated that there was already a suitable type of aircraft available for this purpose. This was the six-engined Messerschmitt Me 323 large transport aircraft. This aircraft had a wingspan of 55 metres and, with a weight when empty of 27.3 tons, could be loaded to a total weight of 43 tons. Even a V-2 rocket would have fitted into the fuselage of this transport aircraft called the 'Gigant'. It was calculated that to transport one single V-2 battery and its accompanying vehicles, an entire squadron of Me 323s would be needed. The Third Reich did happen to have one squadron of this type of aircraft, TG 5. So all the aircaft of this type in Germany would have been needed to transport five or six V-2 rockets to their launch positions,

quite apart from the organisational difficulties and time-co-ordination problems associated with this type of large-scale transport operation. It is thus clear that this kind of transport operation would never have been considered for normal V-2 batteries. Such a 'gigantic' expense (in the most literal sense of the word) simply to transport 5 or 6 tons of conventional explosive would have been completely inefficient, even under wartime conditions. By contrast, the position is very different if in actual fact it was planned to transport nuclear, radiological or chemical combat agents by air to suitable corners of the Third Reich.

Originally it was planned to continue the production of the Me 323, together with its new, strengthened variants the ZMe-423 and the Zme-323H, far into 1945. In hindsight, the ZMe-323H version, which could carry a considerably larger payload at the expense of range and speed, seems to have been particularly suitable for transporting rockets. Was this in fact the operational purpose for which it was designed?

In actual fact, however, production of the Me-323 had already ceased as early as April 1944, and it would have been impossible, in view of the shortage of fuel and Allied air superiority, to try to transport a V-2 battery by air without ending in a complete fiasco.

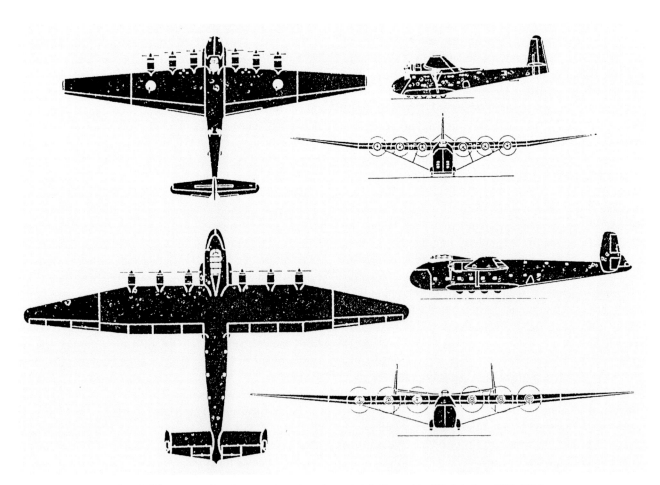

Special V-weapons aircraft transport versions for rockets? Above: Me 323 F, below: ZSO 523A.

Launching the A-4 from aircraft?

It is well known that a comprehensive programme of tests was carried out on launching A-5 rockets from Heinkel He-111E aircraft.

The A-5, designed as a test weapon, normally served as a test vehicle for the more ambitious A-4 project. It was designed on a smaller scale with a simplified guidance system and a propulsion system which proved to be excellent.

But the interesting aspect of these tests carried out with the aerial launch A-5 is that simulated drop launches from aircraft were also carried out using the 'miniature A-4'. It is very likely that these tests were used to develop direct launch procedures for the A-4 after dropping from the carrier aircraft. Doubtless the aerial launch would have been a completely novel way of increasing the range of the A-4 and of giving it even greater operational mobility and flexibility. The aircraft would have had to fly within 300 kilometres of the target, to then release the rocket by parachute and turn for home. Finally, the rocket would have been detonated by signal at a pedetermined height.

But the great disadvantage of the drop launch procedure would have been that it would have been necessary first to devise suitable rocket navigation and guidance systems. Also, the A-4, with its launch weight of 12.8 tonnes, could not have been carried by any of the bomber aircraft types used by the Luftwaffe.

The only alternative possibility here would have been to use the six-engined Messerschmitt Me-323 'Gigant' transport aircraft. From its F1 version, the 'Gigant' would have been able to carry the A-4 without any problem. But Messerschmitt's large transport had the problem that it was extremely vulnerable to enemy aerial defences and thus from the beginning of 1943 in the West could not operate near to the front by day. The best that could be done would be to carry out Me-323/A-4 night operations, but these would have been extremely risky because of the capable Allied night fighters operating at the height which would be required to to launch the rocket. So it would have been necessary first to create new more suitable rocket transport aircraft such as the Junkers Ju-290E (maximum bomb load 20 tonnes) and the Daimler Benz Project (maximum bomb load 30 tonnes).

If ever there had been the intention to use the revolutionary drop launch procedure for the A-4, the procedure would have failed if only because of the question of the carrier aircraft. Even the production of the stronger Me-323 version and its further development by the Zeppelin factory was not, as originally planned, continued to 1945, but halted as early as spring 1944.

After the war, the Americans and Soviets attempted to launch intercontinental rockets from Lockheed C 5 A 'Galaxy' aircraft and Antonov large transport aircraft. But as far as we know, here, too, as had been the case at Peenemünde, no progress was made beyond simulated drop launches.

A-4 Laffarenz Project

(See Volume 1)

U-boat A-4B/A-9

Notes of interrogations of former members of the crew of U-boat U-234 published in the USA in the year 2000 raise the question whether, apart from the V-2 rockets of the 'Laffarenz' Project (see Volume 1, Part 2 D), there was another U-boat ballistic rocket project. Thus, at the hearing of the captured German *General* Kessler, one of the main areas of interest to the Americans was the question whether Germany had yet succeeded in developing ballistic submarine rocket technology. Kessler was questioned in great detail on a report which stated that from 1945 U-boats were stationed in Norway which could launch a V-2 rocket under water! But Kessler had no knowledge of such a naval development. But the naval officer Kay Nieschling, who was on board the same U-boat,, is said to have given an account of relevant German rocket U-boat plans. Was there in fact a ballistic submarine rocket project? And what were the real facts about the development of special U-boat rockets?

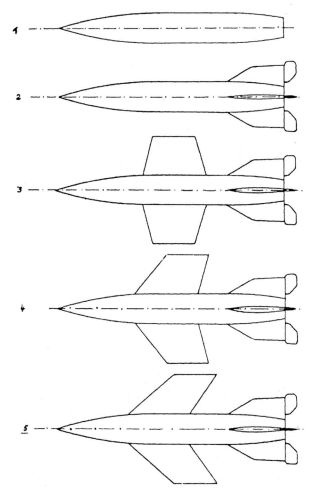

Wind tunnel sketches of the A–4B family. Was Sketch 1 the model for the planned U-boat version?

The existence of separate ballistic U-boat rockets of the A-4 series is not even mentioned by any of the people who wrote memoirs about Peenemünde. On a German drawing of wind tunnel test models of the new A 4 B rocket dating from the end of 1944, five different rocket fuselages with different gliding wings and tail control surfaces are shown. But the first rocket to be shown is an A 4 B model which has no tail fin guidance surfaces, exhaust rudder or anything of that kind. Was a thrust vector steering system planned as the guidance system in this case? Although it is known that work was actually carried out in Peenemünde on techniques of this kind, unfortunately the state developments had reached by the end the war remains a mystery.

In the first versions of the American 'Polaris' A-1 submarine rocket, at the end of the 1950s a simple elevator ring was fixed to the end of the gas exhaust of the propulsion system. The rocket was then steered by moving the ring in all directions with the aid of four piston cylinders. Available drawings showing this simple type of thrust vector guidance system clearly show a liquid fuel propulsion system. But the 'Polaris' - in contrast to the A-4 - had a solid-fuel propulsion system. The A-9 - which externally resembled the A-4 - is also connected with U-boat plans. Here, we can be only be talking about variants from which components had been removed to make them suitable for launching from rocket silos. In this way, the diameter of the launch tubes could be kept to a minimum.

Given the war situation in spring 1945, and the fact that the Reich was now only about 300 kilometres wide, land-based rocket silos for the A 4 no longer had any purpose. Things would have looked different if these silos had actually been installed on U-boats. But until now no naval plans have turned up which show U-boats with silo launch installations. Nevertheless, in order to examine the possibility of the existence of such a German project, we must check whether in the first years after the war among the former allies remarkable projects emerged whose existence can actually only be traced back to previous German developments.

Such developments, supposedly by individual countries other than Germany, existed at that time in many military fields, and until today the predecessors of these developments have been kept secret. With the ballistic submarine rockets there are also such indications that they had foreign ancestry.

After the war, the Soviets succeeded remarkably quickly in being the first major power, even before the USA, in bringing into service rocket submarines. How was this sudden technical quantum leap possible? From 1950, Russia brought the 'Whiskey' class submarines into service. This was nothing other than a Soviet version of the former German Type XXI Electro U-boat from 1944/45.[160] On some submarines of the 'Whiskey' class and the subsequent 'Zulu' class, which were based on the same XXI technology,

in the 1950s individual rocket tubes were accommodated under an enlarged deck superstructure.

The first Soviet trials took place using adapted land rockets of the 'Scud' type, which happened to have a payload of 800 kilograms.

Before the launch, the 'Whiskey' or 'Zulu' submarine had to surface, open the silo, lift the rocket platforms and with the help of three stabilisers lift the rocket into position for launching. Using this process, the rockets could only be launched at a windspeed less than Force 5. At the same time that the naval 'Scud' missile was brought in to service and work was being carried out on its successor system, the SS-N-4, which, like the A-4 and the 'Scud', was also powered by liquid fuels. It is remarkable how precisely the dimensions of this Russian submarine rocket which was brought into service in 1958 resembled those of the A-4B. Thus, its length was 14 metres and its diameter 1.8 metres. And so in the rocket silos of the Soviet Type XXI derivatives 'Whiskey' and 'Zulu', German-produced A-4s or A-9s would have fitted comfortably. A coincidence? In actual fact, during the years 1949/50, the Soviets were actually planning to use a U-boat version of the R-1. Because it would be eight years after the war ended before the Soviet Union had been able to absorb German rocket technology to such an extent that the first Russian derivatives of the V-2 could be brought into the service under the name R-1, it will be clear that the new naval version of the R-1 in 1949 was based on German Second World War naval technology.

If we follow the development of American submarine rocket projects, it is noticeable that the 'Polaris' A-1 rocket was developed by the German scientists Wolfgang Noggerath (rocket), Dr Karl Klager (propellant) and Willy Fiedler (underwater launch system). While in the case of Dr Karl Klager it was only announcedn that he had 'worked during the war in various research establishments and laboratories in Germany', nothing at all has been published concerning what Wolfgang Noggerath did under the Third Reich. This strange silence concerning the father of the 'Polaris' rocket has prompted further research which, it is true, to date has not reached any conclusions. This research should answer the question whether Noggerath had also played a leading role in the project for German ballistic U-boat rocket. As with all important German secret weapons projects, here, too, there must have been a senior high-ranking officer in the Navy who, like *General* Dornberger (Army) or *Obergruppenführer* Dr Kammler (SS), was responsible for solving the problems related to the rocket atomic bombs and atomic U-boats. This officer was *Generaladmiral* Carl Witzell.

In fact, in 1947, the French scientist Dr Albert Ducrocq, who is very well-respected today, reported that at the end of 1944, after lengthy experiments on the Toplitzsee, the first German V-2 rocket submarine was designed. The work, he said, must have been nearly completed when the German surrender on 8 May 1945 intervened.

The Navy rockets and the
Generaladmiral's secret

At any early stage, the Navy was interested in the development of the German rockets. Thus, the artillery specialist, *Generaladmiral* Carl Witzell was present together with other important people on 13 June 1942 at the famous A-4 test in Peenemünde. Although this particular test was a failure, this date is regarded as the day on which the Peenemünde programme received the full support of the Armaments Ministry, the Army and the Luftwaffe. But nothing is said about the reaction of the Navy. This seems all the more remarkable given that *Generaladmiral* Witzell was Chief of the *Marinewaffenhauptamt*, and thus responsible for naval armaments policy. Probably, however, 13 June 1942 also marked the beginning of plans for suitable naval versions of the Peenemünde rockets (see Volume 1).

Shortly before this, on the evening of 4 June 1942, Witzell had been at the famous night meeting of the *Uranverein* in Berlin. *Generaladmiral* Witzell retired from active service in August 1942 and in autumn 1942 became a member of the *Reichsforschungsrat* (Reich Research Committee). Almost nothing is known of his further activities during the war, apart from the fact that on 5 October 1942 he was awarded the Knight's Cross with Swords and in 1945 was taken prisoner by the Soviets.

But Witzell must have carried out an important task in the *Reichsforschungsrat*, because in 1946, while he was in detention at Nuremberg, *Grossadmiral* Raeder wrote in a letter the significant lines: Witzell - Russia (atomic bomb). Thus the *Generaladmiral* was acquainted with the rocket armaments policy and also with the atomic bomb research carried out within the Third Reich. In addition to questions of armaments, the main thrust of his work for the RFR could have been in the field of developing nuclear-powered U-boats.

For the Russians he must have been an important catch, because he was to remain a prisoner of war for 10 years. Witzell eventually died in 1976 in Berlin without having uttered a single syllable to clarify the riddle surrounding the Navy's rocket plans, nuclear-powered U-boats and German atomic research.

'By their fruits shall ye know them' - or were there after the war 'Nuclear Children' of the German V-Weapons among the Allies?

Insofar as it is a valid hypothesis that Hitler ultimately planned to arm his V-weapons with nuclear warheads, in the postwar period there must have also existed among the former Allies similar projects for arming their weapons with atomic warheads in the form of copies and further developments. This becomes even more credible if the East and West at the same time also again 'happened' to develop identical ideas.

While none of the victorious powers used copies of the 'Rheinbote' rocket during the post-war period, the case was very different with the V-1 and V-2. Thus, from 1948, the US Navy used derivatives of the V-1 as LTV N-2 'Loon'. Although it was claimed to be only a research project, a so-called 'war reserve' of foreign 'Loon' missiles was assembled, for which an atomic uranium warhead of the Type TX 10 was being developed from May 1948. Whether the idea for this really can only be traced back to US Minister of the Navy Forrestal (see Volume 1) has to be more than questionable!

The Soviets brought their V-1 copies into service under the designation 10 X and 16 X for launching from aircraft types Pe-8, IL-4 and TU-2. Ground-based variants were launched from tanks, lorries and fixed ramps. Nothing is known of the explosive power of the X-series flying bombs. The nuclear warhead for them, weighing 1000kg, was then developed by the NIL-6 Institute. But because at that time the X- series missiles were no longer in service, the TK-1 was mounted on the KS-1 (NATO: AS-1 'Kennel') missile, which went into mass production from November 1952.

Long before the Americans, as early as 1947, the first ballistic rocket units in the Soviet Union were set up using V-2s captured in Bleicherode, and further developed by the RABE organisation acting on behalf of the Russians. These were initially equipped with F M S railway launch ramps of German manufacture and were deployed by the 23rd Guard Special Operations Brigade. Later this brigade was provided with mobile units, which used Soviet derivatives of the German Meiller wagon.

The Russian rockets which were brought into service were a direct V-2 copy under the name R-1 and the lengthened V-2 version R-2.

Whilst to date the R-5 has always been regarded as the first Russian rocket developed to carry a nuclear warhead, in the meantime it has become known that as early as the early 1950s the Soviet GAU (main artillery administration) was working on the development of nuclear, radiological and chemical warheads for the SS-1A and SS-2.[161] [162]

According to his own statement, the German atomic scientist Professor Manfred von Ardenne had had discussions with Russian Colonel-General Sawenjagin about equipping ballistic rockets with atomic warheads. In his memoirs, Professor von Ardenne of course never mentioned what previous experience in rocketry he had recourse to in this case. But von Ardenne seems to have been somewhat disappointed, because in actual fact as early as 19 May 1945 in the visitors' book of Professor von Ardenne's research institutes in Berlin-Lichterfelde, the name of one Abraham P. Sawenjagin is entered, so that this subject must have been discussed by the two gentlemen very shortly after the end of the war.

The fact that this was so shortly after the end of the war makes clear that the discussion can at that time only have been about taking over former German plans for equipping rockets with atomic bombs.

In fact, production of this uranium warhead commenced in 1954, and it was carried on an R-2 for the first time in November 1954. One year later, uranium warheads for the R-1 and R-2 were first brought into front-line service.

A radiological isotope warhead was also produced for the R-2.

How far development plans for nuclear warheads for the R 1 and R-2 rockets progressed is unknown. In any event, a radiological isotope warhead was ready for them!

It may be fairly probable that this attempt to fix atomic warheads to the Russian V-2 developments was also based on German plans, as were the American plans of 1949 to mount the 850 kilogram nuclear uranium warhead TX 8 on the United States V-2 development Hermes.

The American T X 8 warhead with an explosive power of 15 to 20 kilotons was to be exploded by an impact detonator when the rocket hit the ground. It happened to have the same weight as the T X 10 warhead in the V-1 Loon, which could release an explosive power of 12 to 15

kilotons at a predetermined height above the ground by means of a separation detonator.

Even if the successors of the German V-1s and V-2s only had a brief transitional existence among the former Allies, nevertheless this proves that as early as the immediate post-war period nuclear versions of the German *Vergeltungs-waffen* were in service in both East and West. And so, here too, there was a seamless transition of former German projects into the hands of the victors. Or should we continue to believe that the former allies had the same idea at almost exactly the same time, immediately after the war, of mounting nuclear warheads on their pirated German rockets and missiles? And this despite the fact that it would be years before East and West had been able to properly understand the normal technology for these rockets and missiles!?

Table: US postwar developments of German uranium bomb projects from the Second World War?

US designation	Year	Weight of warhead	Explosive power in KT	Detonator mechanism	Planned US carrier system	Original German system
TX8	1949	850kg	15–20	Impact	'Hermes' rocket, air bomb	Nuclear V–2 (Hiroshima bomb?)
TX9	1950	250kg	15	Separation	28cm atomic projectile on the T–131 self-propelled carriage	28cm atomic projectile on the DüKa self-propelled carriage, small 'uranium bomb' on the A–9 rocket
TX10	1950	850kg	12–15	Separation	'Loon' submarine missile, air bomb	Nuclear V–1 (U-boats, land version)

Table: Russian postwar developments of German nuclear weapons projects

Russian designation	Year	Type of weapon	Planned Russian weapons system	Original German system
Geran	?	Radiological 1-ton isotope warhead	R–2 rocket	Radiological isotope warhead for V–1 and V–2
?	?	Radiological 600kg additional side-mounted charge	R–2, R–5 rocket	Radiological side-mounted charge for V–2
FK–1	?	10,000 kg nuclear charge (uranium bomb?)	Missile KS–1 (and 10/16?)	Nuclear uranium warhead for V–1

III) Were there yet more weapons?

1) Rockets (ground-to-ground and ship-to-shore)

On 27 January 1945, *Oberst* Wachtel, the commandant of *Flakregiment 155 (W)*, which was responsible for launching the Fi-103, was given command of the 5th Flak Division (W).

Then, when *Oberst* Wachtel wanted to disband the

divisional Staff of the 5th Flak Division, because he felt that the division was no longer needed, Dr Kammler replied to him that the Divisional Staff was in fact needed, because soon other weapons with new kinds of propulsion system were to be placed under its command!

But these other *Vergeltungswaffen* have never come to light. What could Kammler have meant by saying this?

There now follows a series of other rocket and missile developments from the last phase of the war which appear to be connected with the victory weapons.

A) Special versions of Rockets in service

The atomic 'flaming arrow' ('Rheinbote')
The long-range 'Rheinbote' rocket was the first multi-stage solid-fuel rocket in the world to be deployed in front line service. The development of this rocket, the design of which had been developed from the beginning of 1941 by *Arbeitsgruppe* Z under the direction of director Professor Hans Klein was extensively described in several publications. But it is little known that it was one of the last projects of *SS-Obergruppenfuhrer* Dr Kammler to equip the 'Rheinbote' rocket with an atomic warhead. The existence of this plan was mentioned in a book by Joachim Engelmann, who unfortunately died too early to be able to give further details.

However, in considering the various sources which refer to the 'Rheinbote', there are a series of facts which indicate that this weapon system was by no means the harmless dust-squandering 'toy rocket' which the literature often asserts that it was.

What is clear is that the development of this large solid-fuel rocket suffered front the petty jealousies of the advocates of the V-2 programme. Although the rocket was entered into the official V-weapons programme in 1942 as a ballistic rocket, in April 1944 it still had been assigned no official category of urgency, so that it is said that even the tireless Professor Klein as director of Development Group Z was almost about to give up his work …

In clear contradiction to this is the fact that the British author and atomic specialist Philip Henshall in his researches for traces of German rocket positions in Normandy discovered that, in addition to the positions for V-1s and V-2s which were already known, there were many other concrete launch positions for a third type of rocket.[163] From 1943, these completed launch platforms were specially designed for solid-fuel rockets and therefore showed great differences to the launch platforms for V-2s which were often nearby. Both types of launch installation, for V-2s and for solid-fuel rockets, pointed north-westwards in the direction of Britain. It was also the case that the launch platforms planned for solid-fuel rockets, in comparison to the V-2 installations, had additional security bunkers.

The 'Rheinbote' was also to be launched in France from bunker positions. New research indicates that the great launch bunker in Brecourt was to accommodate the Rheinmetall-Borsig rocket as well as V-1s and V-2s.

The only solid-fuel rocket which Germany possessed which had the range to reach Britain was the 'Rheinbote'.

But the existence of a considerable number of solid-fuel

rocket positions in the Cherbourg peninsula demonstrates that the 'Rheinbote' programme was assigned considerably greater military value than is generally assumed. Thus, as early as 1943, there must have been well developed operational plans for the use of solid-fuel rockets against Britain. The *Organisation Todt* must also have been provided with precise data on this rocket before they constructed these launch positions.

In this connection it is remarkable that in the publications after the war nothing was said about solid-fuel rockets in Normandy. Even Professor Dr Klein, the leading light in 'Rheinbote' development, conceals this circumstance, although such plans could never have been developed without his collaboration. This suggests parallels with the behaviour of Wernher von Braun in the period after the war!

It seems remarkable that Professor Klein does give an account of his stubborn battle against the overwhelming Peenemünde lobby and as a result, so he says, was almost about to discontinue his programme in Spring of 1944, although along the Atlantic coast positions had long since been built for his rocket to attack Britain. In this case, there must have been good reasons for his silence, because the Allied reports are strangely silent about the solid-fuel rocket launch positions in Normandy.

This denigration of the 'Rheinbote' project was also practised by Dr Dornberger, the head of WA Prüf 11, that is, the establishment which was responsible for all questions relating to rockets. Thus, in 1952, in his book 'Der Schuss ins Weltall', he writes about the 'Rheinbote' rocket: 'We agreed that this weapon, with its launch performance and minimal effect would be useless - yes, completely useless. But despite this, on Hitler's orders (he didn't know the weapon) and Dr Kammler's it was to be brought into service'.

What reasons did Hitler and Dr Kammler have for advocating the deployment of the 'Rheinbote'? From the point of view of armaments economics, to use the 'Rheinbote' with its ratio of 40 kilograms of explosive to almost 15 times that amount of solid-fuel being used in its propulsion system, would be a waste of money. Even if the effect of a conventional 28 centimeter artillery shell could be expected from this warhead, overall it would not have justified a such waste of solid-fuel.

But there were also serious points which favoured the solid-fuel rocket. These were that it was easy to produce, it could be stored for a long time and it needed few personnel and little material to launch it. If then the 40 kilogram conventional warhead is exchanged for a warhead filled with radioactive isotope material, then the 'Rheinbote' would have been an interesting weapon. All the more so if it was possible to fire four rockets an hour from every 'Rheinbote' launch position. This would have soon caused extensive radioactive contamination in the target country. Nothing comparable could have been achieved with the V-1 or V-2!

220 conventional 'Rheinbote' rockets were launched

from September 1944 against Antwerp. Nothing is known of any other operational use.

Public opinion insists that the entire process of development of the 'Rheinbote' was discontinued in February 1945 on the orders of *SS-Obergruppenfuhrer* Dr Kammler. In clear contradiction to this is the fact that in Spring 1945, Armaments Minister Albert Speer received instructions from Führer Headquarters to give Professor Klein full powers which recognised the V-4 rocket as the most urgent weapons development of the German Wehrmacht. Professor Klein, from whom this report comes, then in the post-war period always called the 'Rheinbote' the 'V-4'.

On 1 March 1945, Professor Klein finally received appropriate powers from Berlin. during this period, the designer had been practically uninterruptedly travelling from Berlin via the Unterlüss firing range to Duneberg, Walsrode, Gottingen, Sommerda and Wittenberge to the various manufacturing firms, to carefully supervise the individual production processes and to achieve the closest possible co-ordination. Unfortunately it is not known what the rocket which was to be the result of all these efforts was actually to look like. But we do know that in addition to the 'Rheinbote' I there was to be the so-called 'Rheinbote III', a large rocket which was created at the same time as the V2. This rocket had a 785 kilogram warhead, weighed eight tons and was 15 metres long. For the launch carriage 30 tonnes were necessary which were to be moved by motorised vehicles in two sections.

From what is said in the last paragraph it will be noticed that the 'Rheinbote II' is not mentioned, although it must at least have existed as a plan. Is it perhaps Kammler's atomic rocket?

Possible candidates for the mysterious designation 'Rheinbote II' would most likely be the Rh. Z5 three-stage rocket or the 56 centimeter long-range rocket produced by Rheinmetall-Borsig. The Rh Z 5 was a three-stage non-guided rocket which was able to transport a 220 kilogram warhead over a distance of 160 kilometres and a 570 kilogram warhead over a distance of 100 kilometres. The planned weight of the rocket was 2405 kilograms and its length was 10.53 metres. The launch installation was planned as a 880 mm thick tube as a result of which it was necessary to use unfolding telescopic stabilisers in the first stage. The launch of the Rh. Z5 could either take place from a stationary concreted 80 ton launch installation or via a mobile artillery piece. The mobile version was a massive rocket gun with a triple axle carriage weighing 40 tons. It was planned to launch the 'Rheinbote' rocket from this gun at a velocity of 250 metres per second. It was hoped that in this way it would be possible to save solid-fuel and to achieve improved accuracy and a considerably greater payload than that which was achieved with the 'Rheinbote I'. It is said that the Rh. Z5 system never got beyond the project planning stage.

But there are indications that at the end of the war, Rheinmetall were engaged in producing a further version of the 'Rheinbote' rocket. Thus, an official document from 1945, which gives details of various rockets, makes reference to a 56 centimeter long-range rocket produced by Rheinmetall-Borsig. It was 9.7 metres long, had five rocket stages and was planned to have a range of 350 kilometres. Nothing more was known about this rocket.

Which of these rockets was Dr Kammler's atomic rocket? Or would the expression isotope rocket be more appropriate? As has already been outlined, there is said to be a train with radiological V-2 or V-4 rockets even today under the former Espelkamp/Lübbecke arsenal – a train which, after the war, the British simply allowed to disappear for fear of radiation …

B) Special versions of rockets which were not used operationally

The 'Paris Rocket'

Even before the Second World War began, in March 1939, the Army Research Establishment at Peenemünde received a commission to build a rocket which could be used to bombard Paris. This 'Paris Rocket' was to be a modern version of the *Wilhelmsgeschütze* of 1918 (see Volume 3).

After the end of the campaign in the West in 1940, work on the rocket was slowed down and eventually given up altogether.

Unfortunately, apart from the planned weight of 1000kg, only a few details are known of the 'Paris rocket'. At the moment, therefore, it is not possible to reconstruct it as a drawing or a model.

The FR-35 long-range rocket

This was a design produced by the Rheinmetall-Borsig company in 1944. The FR-35 was a solid fuel multi-stage rocket which, in comparison to the 'Rheinbote' rocket produced by the same company, incorporated considerable simplifications and improvements, but worked on the same principle. With this rocket it was hoped to create a smaller weapon which was easier to store than the V-2, and which in addition would have a better propulsion/explosive ratio than the more cost intensive V-2. The 5.45 metre-long rocket with a diameter of 0.5 metres consisted of a 1.23 metre-long warhead shaped like a projectile which could carry a 200 kilogram charge, and five identical propulsion stages which fitted into each other on the building block principle. Depending on the desired range, the number of propulsion stages could be varied, with the maximum range using all five solid-fuel propulsion stages being 350 kilometres.

The FR-35 only weighed two tonnes and carried five diglycol-powder charges each weighing 208 kilograms. Each stage of the rocket burned for about 2.5 seconds. The long-range rocket could thus be accelerated to a maximum of 7560 kilometres per hour. For the sake of simplicity, stabilisers were dispensed with, and these were to be replaced by jets set at an angle. Nothing is known about the launch procedure for the rocket. It is rumoured that it was planned to use a mobile self-propelled carriage.

As far as is known, after the war there were no successors to the idea of the FR-35.

V-6 atomic rocket

Even up to the present day there exist serious rocket projects from the final phase of the Third Reich, the fate of which is largely unclear. One of these is the so-called V-6 *Vergeltungswaffe*. In November 1944, a Bohemian SS engineer by the name of Matzka sent a secret technical report to his chief Heinrich Himmler. In this report, following a series of discussions with some scientists from the Vienna L F W Aviation Centre and the Institute of Physics of the University of Vienna, suggested immediately commencing the mass production of an atomic rocket in some factories of the then *Ostmark* (Austria), based on a design the which technicians from the Strasbourg atomic laboratory had developed. They had only just managed to flee in time before the Americans marched into Strasbourg.

Even today almost nothing is known about the mysterious Strasbourg rocket team! Despite this, the team must have played an important role in the Third Reich, because, when in Autumn 1944 the data of Professor Sänger's 'Space Bomber Project' was sent to a few selected people, firms, and research institutes, on the distribution list of the 70 official recipients under number 36 is listed 'Inst. f. Treib- u. Schmierst. – Strassburg' (see also Volume 3). To all appearances this Institute could have been the creator of the 'Matzka rocket'! Is it a coincidence that this Strasbourg Institute is listed between the 'KWI Berlin, Prof. Heisenberg' (No. 35) and the 'TH Wien, Prof. Richter' (No. 38)? All these institutions had something to do with Hitler's atomic project.

Reich Propaganda Minister Dr Josef Goebbels was informed about Matzka's proposal and immediately gave him unreserved support. He even gave this weapon design the provisional name of *Vergeltungswaffe* 'V-6'. According to two articles by the military reporter William Connor, which appeared at the end of 1945 in the American magazine *Crusader* and the Italian periodical *Rivista Aeronautica*, the 'V-6' rocket project was specially planned for nuclear warfare and is actually said to have been developed near Strasbourg.

With a weight of six tonnes, the rocket was less than half the weight of Wernher von Braun's V2 and was not to be mass-produced but was to be produced in individual sections. In contrast to the V2 it was not possible to influence it by external radio signals and it was thus completely immune to possible enemy attempts to scramble signals. Despite its reduced size, the V-6 was able to annihilate an entire metropolitan area with one single direct hit.

Unfortunately, nothing much has ever been known about the V-6. William Connor, whose articles were prin-

cipally about the possibility of scrambling the radio signals of future post-war long-range projectiles, said that the Germans had decided of their own accord not to use this weapon. Connor placed a question mark behind this statement given to him by the German side in connection with the Matzka rocket, because he felt that too much 'humanity' in using atomic weapons seemed to be a contradiction in terms.

If we examine more closely this information which has subsequently never been contested, we are forced to the conclusion that the atomic rocket proposal of SS engineer Matzka, who may well have belonged to the Kammler staff, was not simply a paper project. Unfortunately, precise details about the weapon are likely to remain hidden for ever.[164]

The V-101 long-range rocket

On 23 March 1942, Heinrich Himmler issued a letter which, in accordance with an instruction from Adolf Hitler, gave approval to the establishment of a research and development centre for the Waffen-SS at the Skoda factory and the Brunn weapons factories. This was a beginning of the so-called SS think factory, also called the Kammler group.[165]

Many activities went on there which resulted in secret projects, for many of which we know few details even today. But it is known that among the tasks of the Kammler group was a rocket testing programme in an SS-controlled research centre in Pilsen. Some of these activities were connected with Hitler's instruction to Kammler to construct a subterranean launch base to test a smaller long-range rocket, which was planned as the prototype of an intercontinental ballistic weapon. This rocket may have been the V 101.

This three-stage rocket was to have a length of 30 metres and a diameter of 2.8 metres, and was to weigh 140 tonnes. It is known that the solid-fuel propulsion system for the first stage was designed to produce a thrust of 100 tonnes and its calculated range was 1800 kilometres at a maximum height of 200 kilometres

This would have brought all European targets within the range of the V 101. Because of its solid-fuel propulsion system it was also, in contrast to the V2, more suitable for use in launch silos. The design of the V 101 is said to have been only a broad-brush sketch of the main principles. There are also today no documents or plans of any kind relating to the V 101, except perhaps in American archives. We also do not know where General Kammler's underground launch base for the V 101 was to be created.

But it is conceivable that progress on the V 101 was considerably more advanced than is assumed today. Evidence of this is an American secret report dated 19 January 1945 which consists of an evaluation of the German weapons developments which were to be expected during that year. The report, among other things, states that it is known that larger rockets than the V2 did exist and that these might turn up in smaller quantities during the current year. These rockets, it said, would have a considerably larger warhead than the V2. The size of the rocket was said to be 68 ft (compared to 45 feet for the V2).

From these are dimensions it is clear that the report was not referring to the A 9/A 10! The America rocket could only carry the same one-ton payload to as the V2. We must therefore consider the question as to whether, in addition to the A 9/A 10 'America rocket' produced by E M W Peenemünde, there was also a 'Europe rocket' being designed in the SS Skoda works in Pilsen!

Wasserfall artillery rocket
The EMW *Wasserfall* was Germany's most advanced anti-aircraft rocket.

It appears that in addition to the large rockets and missiles, a series of guided anti-aircraft rockets was also planned for operation from the ground. But these rockets were rejected by the HWA because of their range, which was too short. As a result, versions were created with the stern of the A-4 and also glider rockets with wedge-shaped aerofoils as on the A-4B. This series of various proposals was to carry 200-300 kg of explosive under remote control to hit a target at a range of 100-175 km. The final version with wings was to carry 200kg of explosive over 175 km, and still to hit its target at 1.5 times the speed of sound. This high impact velocity was - as we shall see below - not without reason considered very important.

Another proposal was the '1000 rocket gun'. This weapon would use launch rails for normal *Wasserfall* rockets on the so-called *Behelfslafettenkreuz 3742* (an auxiliary gun carriage).

As in the case of the *Wasserfall*, at first glance it seems to make no sense to use rockets which are urgently needed for aerial defence for ground-based attacks. And this is particularly the case because it was likely that there would never be enough rockets for decisive mass deployment in the final battle. But, here too, there is an explanation. This may well have been that it was planned to carry special payloads by means of these fast rockets which had a high impact velocity. Such a system of warheads was available on the Zippermayr principle (see following Volume). For his artificial tornado weapons, which were to have an effect similar to that of the atomic bomb, Dr Zippermayr needed special rockets with high impact velocity. Within the context of the 'all-round defence', the use of these weapons, even in

small numbers, would perhaps have been extremely effective.

The Americans took the *Wasserfall* rocket launcher extremely seriously. Thus Colonel Keck reported at the famous press conference in Paris on 28 June 1945, that in addition to other monster weapons such as the A-10, the atomic bomb and the orbital station project, there was also a new type of German rocket launcher with a number of rockets which were to have a launch weight of 5000 pounds and a range of 100 miles.

But it was nevertheless not possible to bring any of the artillery versions of the EMW *Wasserfall* into front line service by the end of the war.

EMW A-7 shipborne rocket
The A-7 was a design for the Navy, using the glider model of the tried and trusted A-5, which was taken up again in great haste in 1944. Whilst the basic fuselage of the A-5 was used, new aerofoil fins with a span of 1.61 metres were added. The A-7 was to produce 1.8 tons of thrust. The total length of the shipborne missile was 5.9 m.

The A-7 would have been suitable for using as a *Vergeltungswaffe* on large surface ships such as light and heavy cruisers. Well aware of the experience that the large ships could no longer be deployed in the West because of the total Allied air superiority, the OKM asked the EMW company to produce a smaller version of the A-7. This could then have been installed on board destroyers, speed-boats and U-boats. But in this case too there was no longer enough time between October 1944 and the end of the war to be able to achieve any definitive progress with this weapon.

Thus it was left to the US Navy to launch the first Peenemünde rocket from a surface ship. This operation took place on 6 September 1947 under the name 'Operation Sandy' and comprised the successful launch of a V-2 from the deck of the aircraft carrier *USS Midway*. The purpose of the tests may have been to see whether it was technically possible to bring A-4 type rockets in large surface ships, such as, for example, aircraft carriers, close to enemy coasts and launch them. At that time the US Navy was in a bitter struggle with the Air Force over who in future would carry out nuclear attacks on enemy targets. Apparently, transporting V-2 rockets rght up to enemy coasts was attractive enough for the Navy planners! Here, too, it may be otiose to ask where this idea originated.

2) Air-to-ground rockets and missiles

A) Special versions of operational missiles

Blohm & Voss BV-246 close-range glider bomb with combat agent warhead 'the poisonous hailstone'
The bridge at Remagen on 9 March 1945. Two days previously, the 9th US tank division had succeeded in capturing the strategically important Ludendorff Bridge at Remagen

and crossing the Rhine. An American bridgehead was immediately formed on the eastern bank of the Rhine, which was constantly being extended. Military police with loaded weapons guided the chaotic traffic over the bridge, but the roads leading to the entrance to the bridge were blocked for kilometres by fully-loaded lorries. Because of the pitifully narrow roads and the deep mud, this left some of the American vehicles up to their axles in mud. The previous day, the Germans had mounted four air raids against the bridge, which were all repulsed. So, on the morning of 9 March 1945, hardly anybody paid any attention to the single Focke-Wulf F W 190 which went into a dive from a distance of several kilometres. It released a remote controlled gliding bomb, on the nose cone of which three small green bands were visible. The bomb was released at a distance from the target of 8000 metres and exploded with a harmless pop near to the bridge. This released a colourless liquid which smelled sweet and fruity. Within 5-10 minutes after the impact the first cases of fatal poisoning turned up. Within a very short time, nothing was alive within a radius of 2500 to 3000 metres around the bridge, and up to 10,000 metres away from the point of the explosion, all troops were completely unable to continue fighting. The few survivors fled in panic across the Rhine, and the bridgehead over the Rhine, contaminated by the new German nerve gas Tabun, had to be evacuated. Afterwards German broadcasting stations announced that this was a test operation and that in the future all Allied attempts to cross the Rhine would meet with similar action to repel them.

The weapon here, fortunately, described only in a hypothetical operational scenario was the Blohm & Voss BV-246 close-range 'Hailstone' glider bomb, which was originally developed as a cheap alternative to the V-1 flying bomb. It was intended that the BV-246 would be transported by aircraft such as the Ju-88 and the He-111. In action, the bomb was to be dropped from a height of 7000 metres at a speed of 550 kilometres per hour, as a result of which it was expected to reach a range of 210 kilometres. Because in the first tests its inaccuracy was unsatisfactory and many serious development difficulties emerged, a research and production was halted several times and again resumed. The results were chaos and wasted time!

But on 14 August 1944 approval was given to resume testing on all versions of the BV-246 and a new testing location in Fassberg near Celle was also planned.

Because of the Allied air superiority, from December 1944 efforts were made to use the high-performance aircraft Tank Ta-15 and Arado Ar-234 to transport the BV-246.

By the end of the war, a total of around 1100 BV-246s had been produced, of which 599 were available on 1 January 1945.

The last version was the BV-246 F, which was tested with various target search devices, radio and TV guidance systems. Of the F types, on 1 January 1945, there were about 200 in production, of which, according to report number 211/06 produced by the Karlshagen testing centre, some were designated as carriers for combat agent. It appears that this measure took place more or less at the same time as the SS took over all secret weapons research and production. It was planned that the Focke-Wulf F W 190 would carry this victory weapon. A F W 190 A4 had already been tested for this purpose and a targeted drop of the combat agent

BV-246 had been planned by Stuvi 5 of the CZ company. It was intended that a gliding angle of 1:11 should be achieved, and at a target distance of 8000 metres, with the BV-246 F, it would have been possible to strike 50 per cent of all targets within an ellipse of 440 metres and 560 metres width. This was completely sufficient for gas warfare.

On 1 January 1945 another new commission for the production of long-range glider bombs of the E series was issued, of which 2300 were to be produced. A large number of these, in the version E2, were also planned to carry combat agent. It was principally the Arado Ar-234 which would have been considered a suitable aircraft to transport the long-range version. At the beginning of 1945, there were 218 BV-246s available. How many more produced by the end of the war is not known.

In the case of the BV-246, as in the case of the combat agent V-1, what is notable is the close connection in time with the takeover of secret weapons development by the Waffen-SS. But Hitler would never have allowed the possible deployment of this gas weapon missile.

On 9 March 1945, towards 8 o'clock in the morning, an attack was actually carried out by a single Focke-Wulf F W 190 against the bridge at Remagen using the remote controlled Type BV-246 glider bomb. The detailed circumstances are not known …

Henschel HS-293 Vergeltungswaffe?
There are many clues which suggest that there was also a *Vergeltungswaffe* version of the Henschel HS-293.

The Henschel HS-293 had been developed by Professor Wagner and after its first operation on 25 August, 1943, it became the most successful German remote controlled missile of the Second World War. By the end of the war, it had sunk about 440,000 tons of shipping and destroyed many bridges over the Oder.

The HS-293 was a powered glider bomb which had the advantage of sparing the mother aircraft the dangerous operation of overflying the target. The carrier aircraft used were the twin-engined He 111 and Do-217 bombers and the four-engined FW-200, Ju-290 and He-177. Further trials were carried out with the flying boat BV-222 and the Ar-234 jet bomber. As a military payload, the standard version carried a bomb warhead of 325-500 kilograms and used an impact detonator to explode the bomb.

The Allies could not understand why the Germans were so slow to deploy their HS-293. In actual fact the Henschel flying bomb, of which only a small quantity of the weapons produced were used in action, was also a victim of sabotae by senior German officers. One example of this is the story of the HS-293 D, equipped with the revolutionary 'Tonne' camera. As early as Autumn 1944, hundreds of these special missiles were already in store, but not a single one was ever used at the front. In his book *Verschwörung gegen Deutschland* (Conspiracy against Germany), the author Karl Balzer uncovered what happened:

"Work on the development of the weapon had been

carried out with enormous effort and individual commitment in Karlshagen, Jesau, Neu-Mecklenburg and Rechlin. Everything was ready to go into production. After this special section had been transferred into the Sudetenland, from Spring 1944 a combat squadron was requested to test these combat-ready weapons in combat.

"Incredibly, here, too, everything was delayed as a result of difficulties concerned with demarcation of responsibilities. Then, in June, when a squadron had at last been made available on the Adriatic to test this 'Tonne', there was a fresh delay, which was characteristic of deliberate sabotage. Special multiple plugs were required for connecting the cables in the aircraft. There were thousands of these plugs in Berlin-Straussberg. Then, when the multiple plugs were requested as a matter of extreme urgency and couriers had even been sent to Berlin to collect them, they were returned with the explanation that this depot was under the command of a senior Wehrmacht officer, who refused to release them. Instead of this, the visit of *General* Fellgiebel from the Wehrmacht Intelligence Service was announced, saying that he was on his way. The situation was described to the *General* from Intelligence when he arrived. We asked him, because of the urgency, to personally authorise the release of the required plugs, saying that we had only three days before the weapons test had been ordered. When the *General* is about to leave the factory after four hours of fruitless discussion, I [a production supervisor on the staff of Fernseh. GmbH: *author's note*] stand in his path and ask him very politely for the necessary signature. 'I've got more important things to do at the moment!' was his laconic reply. I point out to him the fact that the test operation of the 'Tonne', on which the greatest hopes are placed, is imminent, I point out that the technical formality of the signature is not much to ask … 'Outside my office, I don't sign anything. Come to my office in Berlin a week tomorrow. We'll see what we can do then. Besides, the war is going to last a long time, and you won't be too late!' … He leaves me standing there without another word and drives away in his car …"

"Shortly after this, the installations were transported away - not to be tested in action in the Adriatic - to a storage area in Klein-Machnow. I came across them there again in November 1945. The Russians had discovered them, thought they were radio sets, turned the knobs - and when no music came out immediately poured petrol over them and set fire to them. *General der Nachrichtentruppen* Fellgiebel, however, was executed on 4 September 1944 because of the part he had played in the 20 July asassination attempt."

As we know today, the so-called 'Tonne' was used for the first time in the Korean War. This supposedly American invention was then announced, saying that it had been one of the most important in recent years, and that its future implications could not yet be evaluated. But there were other versions of the HS-293, which could be far more dangerous for the enemy than the HS-293 D (…)

Because the HS 293 was a tried and tested system which worked well, it became the preferred test aircraft for all possible improvements and ideas. Although the official documents do not indicate this, we may be relatively sure that these included variants with special warheads, for example, gas or radiological warheads. The B and A-2 versions were to serve as the carrier systems for these. The H S 293 B was a wire guided glider bomb. It had the FuG-207 'Dortmund'/FuG-237 'Duisburg' wire guidance system, by means of which two wires, each 12 kilometres long, were deployed from the aircraft, these wires being wound round spools 100 mm in diameter and 130 mm wide. The missile itself also carried about 16 kilometres of wire in a similar configuration. 200 B-versions were produced in case the enemy succeeded in disrupting the guidance system for the H S 293A. The conversion of the A version could be carried out without any problem and the relevant operational airfields had already been supplied with a number of these devices. This simplified solution was used with conventional warheads in Italy, the Mediterranean area, and on the Oder front.

It was also planned to mount special warheads on this kind of wire guided missile. Gas or radiological warheads are most effective if, in contrast to the normal operation of the impact detonator, they explode in the air at a predetermined height. In this connection it was known that trials were carried out using the H S 293 with barometric detonators, which caused the warheads to explode when it the missile came below a certain height. This experimental series was called H S 293 H V 6.

The published literature has problems in explaining the development of such separation detonators in the HS 293, because they dispute the existence of special warheads within this weapon, which would be the only explanation why such tests were carried out of. Instead, it is suggested that the development of these expensive barometric detonators would have served to ensure that the test missiles were destroyed, in order to prevent intact examples of falling into the hands of enemy spies (!) after landing after impact-a somewhat ridiculous explanation for this expensive high-technology, but how could people otherwise explain that a weapon which, as was clear from its whole design, was intended to strike a small target (a ship or a bridge) precisely and destroy it, if it was now to be exploded far beyond its target?

Unfortunately, it is not known when the production of gas warheads for the HS 293 began and how far the development of radiological combat agent had progressed.

In action, the carrier aircraft would have approached the target in a dusk mission to a distance of about 12 kilometres, would have released the missile from a considerable height and then would have guided it by wire over the target (for example, a city or a bridgehead) and exploded it at a height of about 30 metres above the ground.

Whilst we are thrown back on suppositions with regard to the radiological variants of the H S 293, there is more concrete information relating to the gas versions of the HS 293. The effect of one single HS 293 armed with nerve gas would have been comparable to that of a small atomic bomb. The available indications all suggest that the such 'gas HS 293s' were standing by ready for action in Norway. In Trondheim there was a large HS 293 store, which had the appropriate conversion and servicing facilities. The nearby Trondheim/Vaernes aerodrome was intended to be the operational base. From February 1944, 3.'/KG 40 was stationed there, equipped with Heinkel He-177 A-5s. The notable thing about this unit is that it was dissolved in August 1944, that is, about the same time as the conventional anti-ship missile operations came to an end. The reasons for this were the increasing Allied defensive measures against conventional missile attacks on convoys and the increasingly desperate fuel situation. Herman Goring is said at this time to have issued the order to scrap all HS-293s. But this order was not obeyed.

Then something remarkable happened! 3./KG 40 was reformed in October 1944, although the conditions that had prevailed since August 1944 had by then considerably deteriorated.

There must therefore have been a particular reason why this unit which was responsible for remote-controlled weapons was reformed, although the prevailing conditions suggest that there was no longer apparently any purpose for it. The real reason for this reorganisation may well be that the special crews of KG40 who had been trained for long missions over the sea were now intended to be used for quite different operations.

According to reliable reports, the real reason for the unit being reformed was that the He-177 A5 was planned to be used in an annihilation attack against Britain, in the event that the Allies carried out a gas attack or an attack with nuclear weapons against Germany. Because such an Allied attack was never made, the special He-177s did not need to be deployed.

In February 1945 3/KG 40 was dissolved with the rest of the squadron. What happened after this as regards the aircraft and crews in Trondheim is unknown. Allied post-war reports speak of Heinkel bombers in Norway which at the end of the war were intended to carry out a decisive mission, the preparations for which had almost been completed (this episode is outlined in more detail in Volume 1). This then raises the question as to what extent are there are overlaps here. In this case too, the truth will only come to light after all the documents in the Allied secret archives are released.

B) Special versions of rockets and missiles which did not see active service

Project Gleitfläche: Zippermayr's bomb?

On a photograph dating from May 1945 which shows 'Enzian' rockets captured by the Americans at the Aviation Research Establishment 'Hermann Goering' in Braun-

schweig, another remarkable-looking weapon can be seen in the background. Although at the time separate photographs must certainly have been taken of this secret weapon, to date these have not been published. Why not?

As far as can be seen from the available photograph, this puzzling weapon is a large monoplane bomb with a fat fuselage and circular aerofoils. It is most likely to be something from the Gleitfläche project. Development on this project had begun in February 1945 at the DVL. What was new and revolutionary about the Gleitfläche was that it could be used both as a glider bomb and as container for supplies. This procedure had the advantage that the load to be carried could be a great deal larger than that carried by weapons of similar size of conventional design. Several versions of the Gleitfläche were developed. It is known of one of the last versions that it had a wingspan of 0.8 metres and a wing area of 0.805 square metres, and had an airborne weight of 600 kilograms. This looks to be about the estimated size of the weapon shown in the photograph.

As with Dr Lippisch's glider bomb, it was also planned to use nipolite explosive for the hull of the bomb version of the Gleitfläche.

It was as if Gleitfläche was tailor-made for Dr Mario Zippermayr, a guided weapons specialist (torpedoes, rockets), aircraft designer ('Pfeil'), and inventor of the 'artificial tornado' (Zippermayr carbon-dust explosive) who is largely unknown even to the present day.

Experiences with launching small bombs with 25 and 50 kilograms of Zippermayr carbon dust explosive had indicated that even these created explosion radii of several kilometres, so that because of the danger to the aircraft attacking from the air, missions with artificial tornadoes could probably not have been carried out with large calibre bombs, even if a parachute were used to slow them down.

Dropping larger bombs on a parachute was in this case less interesting, because a high impact velocity was absolutely essential to ensure that the Zippermayr explosive worked to best effect. This is why, instead of this, powered rockets such as the 'Enzian' or fast glider bombs with a flight radius of several kilometres may have been considered.

An additional argument in favour of the use of the Gleitfläche is that it had transpired and that the Zippermayr explosive payload could only be loaded immediately before the carrier aircraft took off, so that empty bomb hulls with large volumes and small dimensions seemed ideally suited for for this purpose.

Again, for the Gleitfläche project, as for so many developments at that time, it was a question of 'too little too late.'

X-8 Missile: The secret further development of the 'battleship killer'

The X-series comprised designs for remote-controlled bombs, missiles and rockets by the DVL under the direction of Dr Kramer. The best-known of these are the X-1 (Fritz-X) and X-4. In 1943, the X-1 got a name for itself as a 'battleship killer', and in 1944/45 was also used against land targets such as bridges (Normandy and the Oder front) and ports (Portsmouth). Nerve gas warheads are also said to have been developed for the X-1.

Up to this time it was thought that, with the X-7, a small wire-guided anti-tank rocket, had come to the end of the line. But French documents from the post-war period clearly show that the French Navy carried out experiments with former German X 8s! According to the documents, the X-8 was a project which the Germans had not been able to complete. Essentially, it seems that the X-8 was a variant of the FX 1400 bomb, the body of which had been altered into rocket form like the X-4 and equipped with a rotating stabiliser system. Whether, like the X-4, it also had a rocket motor to increase its range is certainly unknown, but extremely probable.

Documents which have recently come to light[166] indicate that in actual fact at the end of the war in the vicinity of Ohrdruf, work was being carried on on further developments of the X series. The X-8 may also have been among these secret developments.

After the war, the French Navy had a small series of X-8 produced and tested for its own purposes.

The unusual thing is that all the available data are only based on the French documents. Here too there are are still no more precise data such as drawings or photographs. On the basis of experience with similar events, this lack of data causes us to wonder whether behind the X-8 project something quite different was hidden.

Shipborne Vergeltungswaffe R-300 Bs

At the end of January 1945 the *Reichsfuhrer-SS* Heinrich Himmler had ordered the creation of the *Entwicklungsgemeinschaft Mittelbau*. The thermodynamics expert Professor Dr Alfred Buch was apointed as the director of this establishment.

Because of the seriousness of the war situation, immediate measures were necessary, which would be carried out in the newly-created rocket centre. to do this, Professor Dr Buch, Dr Wernher von Braun and SS *Standartenfuhrer* Dr Wagner decided to make available personnel from the *Elektromechanische Werke Peenemünde* for the production and deployment of the small rockets.

These rockets included the types HS-117, X-4, 'Typhoon' (flak and artillery version) and the shipborne rockets of the R series.

Only the types H S-117, X 4 and 'Typhoon' reached the stage of experimental tests.

But in Bleicherode, Professor Buch had developed a proposal which would have given the shipborne R- 300B rockets devastating explosive power. To achieve this, a three-dimensional gyroscopic system would be incorporated in the interior of the rocket, consisting of a motor-driven spherical assembly. In this way it was expected that the explosive power of the R-300Bs could be multiplied.

A single Arado Ar-234 C or Gotha Go-229 could carry up to four of these rockets, and thus would have had the firepower of an entire conventional squadron of aircraft, whether this was to be used to combat bomber streams or to take out bridgeheads.

It is surprising that during the post-war period no further development of this idea is known to have taken place on the part of the victorious powers.

Henschel HS 117H shipborne rocket 'Schmetterling' (Butterfly) - V-3?

How is it possible that a defensive weapon of medium-range is widely known as the V-3? This was the Henschel HS 117 *Schmetterling* anti-aircraft rocket. This rocket, weighing 440 kilograms, was the German anti-aircraft rocket which came nearest to being ready for front line service. Developed as early as 1941 by Professor Wagner, the development of the *Schmetterling* would also be delayed for years. Only in 1943 was the project reactivated, much too late, and was assigned the highest priority.

The range of the *Schmetterling* was 32 kilometres against high-flying targets and 16 kilometres against low-flying aircraft. At the end of 1944, as a result of being linked to the 'Würzburg' ground radar system, the system was rendered capable of operating in all weathers and at night. Some of the last rockets which came to be tested were also provided with approach detonators of the 'Fuchs' type. Otherwise, guidance was carried out from the ground or from aircraft via the 'Kehl-Strassburg' control system, or else the rocket was wire-guided as in the case of the HS 293.

After many delays, production of the *Schmetterling* was to have commenced in March 1945 with 150 missiles in Nordhausen, and to have increased to a rate of 3000 per month by November 1945.

It was planned to equip 60 anti-aircraft positions with *Schmetterling* rockets. Operational trials had been carried out as early as September 1944 by the flak rocket-testing unit LET 700. A week before the German collapse, the first regular operation took place with a salvo of *Schmetterling*s being launched against Allied aircraft, with devastating effect.[167][168]

Nevertheless the question remains unanswered why this purely defensive weapon was given the designation V-3 by contemporary and post-war sources. This is all the more surprising if it is known that the HS 117 *Schmetterling* was the lightest and smallest of the German air-to-ground guided rockets. Its payload of only 36 to 100 kilograms and its short range of made the *Schmetterling* unsuitable for long-range operations.

But there was a shipborne rocket designated as the HS 117 H which was a further development of the standard versions.

By 1945, considerable resources had been expended in testing the shipborne rocket. It is known that some 90 flight trials and launches of all versions of *Schmetterling* rockets were carried out using He-111 and D L Do-217 test aircraft.

The launch propulsion system was dispensed with in the case of the H S 117 H shipborne rocket and the upper half of the aerofoil was transferred to the underside of the rocket. When development ended, ranges of about 25 kilometres were being achieved.

The HS 117 H was also to be deployed as a *Vergeltungswaffe* under the likely designation V-3. The rocket would be transported by fast multi-seater combat aircraft (Ju-88S and Ju-388) into the target area.

A Zippermayr charge was planned as a special V-weapons combat agent for the H S 117 (see *Hitler's Miracle Weapons* Volume 3).

It can thus be seen why this former anti-aircraft rocket was designated as the V-3. To date, nothing is known concerning radiological isotope charges for the HS 117.

But the Henschel V-3 was never used in action! On 6 February 1945, the development of the HS 117 H was included among the weapons the development of which was ordered to be halted by the Commission under the direction of *SS-Obergruppenführer* Dr Kammler. By contrast, development work was to continue on the ground-based anti-aircraft version.

It is not clear why Dr Kammler had development of the V-3 aircraft version of the HS 117 halted. It might be supposed that either it was not expected that the Zippermayr rockets would be completed by the end of the 'six-month deadline', or that insuperable technical difficulties had arisen. In Spring 1945, the German planners assumed that they had another six months to bring their decisive weapons to combat readiness. As we know, for the Third Reich, this was a fatal mistake!

A further possible reason for the halting of development on this weapon might be that the suitable carrier aircraft were no longer available at the end of the war. At the end of the war there were only two prototypes of the Ju 88 S 5, the Ju 88 M and the Ju-388 J-2 were still under construction, so that for carrying the rocket only the Ju-188 remained, which was much more vulnerable to Allied air defences. In addition to this, the few Ju 188s which were available were suffering from the shortage of fuel, as were all the larger aircraft of the Luftwaffe. Even the missions of the Heinkel He-111 V-1 carrier aircraft against Britain had fallen victim to this shortage of fuel in January 1945.

For this reason alone, it could be understood why development on the HS 117H was halted.

Despite Dr Kammler's order to halt development on the H S 117 H, however, there are clear indications that Dr Mario Zippermayr in Lofer had continued to work on some test versions of the *Schmetterling* right up until the end of the war. The Henschel factory is said to have continued development work on the H S 117 H until the end. All this could suggest that it was only the H S 117 H air-to-air version which was halted, and not the air-to-ground V-3 version.

During the post-war period, in the 1950s, the Soviets provided Leningrad and Moscow with a girdle of HS 117 *Schmetterling* anti-aircraft rockets, some of which had been captured and some of which had been subsequently manufactured in Russia. When these were deployed against American reconnaissance aircraft, however, they were only equipped with conventional warheads.

Messerschmitt 'Enzian' shipborne rocket: sub-atomic V-weapon?

Why did considerable numbers of German experts show remarkable aversion to the Messerschmitt 'Enzian' rocket in their postwar interrogations? Even the specialist literature tells the story of the weapon in a nebulous and contradictory fashion.

The 'Enzian' was a rocket dvelopment carried out by the Messerschmitt company. The basic idea was to create an anti-aircraft rocket out of smaller version of the Messerschmitt Me-263. With an explosive charge of 500 kilograms, the 'Enzian' was planned to be used not only as a guided anti-aircraft rocket to break up bomber streams, but also as an airborne remote controlled rocket for launch against ground targets and as a shipborne weapon. Its explosive charge would have been half of that of a V-2 payload, but with significantly less cost. In addition, the large diameter of the 'Enzian' allowed warheads of many different kinds to be installed.

The appearance of the 'Enzian' which was planned to be launched from aircraft was not changed, only the auxiliary launch rockets were omitted. Guidance would have been carried out by the 'Kehl' procedure which had already been tried and tested with the Henschel H S 293. But because of the considerable weight of the missile, only larger carrier aircraft would have been suitable to launch it.

The colourful history of the ground-to-air version of the Messerschmitt 'Enzian' has already been dealt with in various books. Five different versions of the rocket, bearing the designations E-1 to E-5, were designed. 38 flight trials were undertaken in Peenemünde with the E-1 version from March 1944. The published literature is largely silent on the shipborne version. Does this mean that there was not anything of this kind?

The development of the 'Enzian' suffered as a result of the dilemma that the Walther propulsion system which was planned for it was not developed quickly enough. Only in summer 1944, therefore, was a new propulsion system commissioned from Dr Konrad's institute, which was largely to be based on the propulsion system of the 'Rheintochter II'I. This propulsion system was intended to be used both for the planned mass production E-4s and also for the supersonic E-5 version.

The E-4 version was the version that was considered as a *Vergeltungswaffe*! This was a 4.10 metre-long rocket with a wingspan of 4.05 m and a fuselage diameter of 0.876m. The entire construction, including the fuel tanks, was to be of wood. Three different wood production procedures had been developed for this purpose by the company Holzbau Kissing AG in Sonthofen, where some of the Messerschmitt staff had been 'outstationed'.

Construction of the E-4 began from January 1945, and although the entire 'Enzian' programme was halted by Dr Dornberger's committee with effect from 8 February 1945, development and construction work on the rocket still continued in the Alps. The first mass-production was to commence there from May 1945. Was the order to halt work on the 'Enzian' revoked, or did 'they' continue working on it for some other reasons?

Photographs dating from May 1945 show American soldiers inspecting captured 'Enzian' missiles in the valley station at Lofer.

From March 1945, Dr Mario Zippermayr worked in the valley station of Lofer. Among the projects on which he was working there were the anti-aircraft rockets 'Enzian' and *Schmetterling*. But Dr Zippermayr was also the inventor of the so-called 'Zippermayr principle'. This principle envisaged creating tornado-like effects by means of explosions of carbon dust (see Volume 3). It can be seen that these super explosives were also planned for the anti-aircraft rockets 'Enzian' and *Schmetterling*.

According to secret documents only released in July 1999,[169] [170] [171] Dr Zippermayr mentioned that rockets loaded with special carbon dust charges could be a launched by aircraft at cities and other installations and could create destruction equivalent to that caused by an atomic bomb, only with significantly less cost. In addition, it would also have been possible to add a mixture of radioactive isotopes to achieve a radiation effect. In actual fact, available documents indicate that work was being carried on on a radioactive version of the Zippermayr system.

The 'Enzian' was capable of transporting a 500 kilogram warhead and would have been the automatic carrier system for such sub-atomic attacks. It is also known that in later development phases of the 'Enzian' it was planned to incorporate target seeking warheads or approach detona-tors, which after the initial phase of flight under remote control would take over the guidance system in the final phase of the flight.

It is difficult to estimate how long it would have taken to develop the 'Enzian' to a state of combat readiness. Apart from the 38 test launches from converted 8.8 centimetre anti-aircraft gun carriages, no other 'Enzians' were used. There was not enough time to carry out test launches either from aircraft or from ships! It seems that there were also no operational trials. In the final analysis, here, too, everything was in vain. Could things have been different?

What is notable is that the 'Enzian', like other weapons connected with Hitler's nuclear weapons programme, were so trivialised and un-objectively described in post-war reports that one gets the impression that people had something to hide here.

But there are indications that some rethinking of this question is taking place. Thus, the underground chambers of the *Oberbayrischer Forschungsanstalt Oberammergau*, as the main development location of the 'Enzian', are today being expressly connected with the development of V-weapons.[172]

The ground version of the NCR would have been ideally suitable as a ground-to-ground remote-controlled rocket to defend the planned Alpine fortress. Launched from high-level positions, it would have been able effectively to hin-der Allied advances through mountain valleys by means of Zippermayr projectiles and approach detonators – that is, if the rocket had been ready.

In the post-war period, the USA designed the 'Rascal' nuclear missile, which was suspended under a Boeing B-47. Alert observers will be able to discover here, without too much imagination, certain similarities to a wartime project carried out by the Messerschmitt company …

3) Second generation V-missiles

Were there second-generation Flying Bombs?

The Fieseler Fi-103 is rightly regarded as the ancestor of our present day cruise missiles. In summer 1944, Germany's Fieseler robot bombs were a technologically new weapon, years in advance of other countries. But soon it proved that the flying bomb was by no means immune against well-organised enemy air defences. Anti-aircraft installations of all calibres controlled by radar, high-performance piston-engined fighter aircraft and the first Allied jet fighters of the Gloster 'Meteor' type saw to it that increasingly fewer numbers of the Fi-103 reached their target.

The German response to this was to exploit the develop-ment potential of the basic design of the Fieseler flying bomb to create the high-speed cell. In addition, efforts were made to bring the second generation of *Vergeltungswaffen* into service in the form of completely new flying bomb developments.

The Junkers Rocket Glider

On 16 April, 1945, many US Army Air Force (USAAF) bombers flew a devastating air-raid against the German airbase of Zerbst. But this air-raid seemed to have no purpose, because since 11 April 1945, Zerbst had been deserted by the Messerschmitt Me-262 jet fighters of KG (J)54 which had previously been based there. But possibly this American 'bomber hunt' was after quite different 'prey'!

This is because, according to witness statements, in Zerbst 14 Junkers rocket gliders had been based since October 1944. According to the statements, these missiles had delta shaped wings and rounded nose. The same informants state that the length of the missiles was about 10 metres. Launched as *Mistel* by carrier aircraft, they were to be guided by a special remote controlled guidance system which had been developed by Theodore Sturm. The Junkers rocket gliders, it was said, had been transported from Peenemünde to Zerbst, *Mistel*-fashion, on Ju-88s and were being held in readiness there in the surrounding woods for a special mission.

According to the then commandant of the airfield, the missiles were intended to be armed with uranium bombs. But these were never delivered. To control the mission, a special telephone line had been laid from the aerodrome at Zerbst direct to Martin Bormann in the Führer headquarters in Berlin. If this part of the account is true, it is clear that the alleged Soviet spy 'Werther' (alias Bormann) wanted to forestall and prevent deployment of these weapons.

The rocket gliders survived the heavy air-raid of April 1945 unscathed, but immediately before the Americans arrived, they were totally destroyed, leaving no remains, by explosive charges which had been brought there for the purpose. Before the airfield commandant left in a Heinkel aircraft, he had the guidance mechanisms and compasses of the missiles buried near the airfield with other sensitive material. After the war, the Russians carried out an intensive search for this material, but apparently had no success. Several sources suggest that after German reunification, the same district was also combed by the *Bundeswehr* and the US Army, in the effort to find 'something'.

What can we make of the whole story?

According to information given by witnesses, there was no similarity between the Junkers rocket gliders and any known German missile design.

Unfortunately, there has been no success to date in finding further confirmation or documentary evidence concerning the existence of the Junkers rocket gliders at Zerbst. Here, once again, we face the problem of the credibility of eyewitness accounts. But there are many parallels between the Junkers rocket gliders and other mysterious second-generation missiles.

That such developments did exist is proved by two sentences written by Rudolph Lusar in his reference work on German secret weapons: "At the end of the war some other glider bombs were ready for operational service. No further details are known".[173] Perhaps at the time he wasn't allowed to say any more than this!

Henschel HS 315 Long-Range Rocket Glider

During the last phase of the war, the Henschel company was working on a large long-range glider bomb, which in all probability was planned for use with non-conventional warheads.

According to available documents, work on this large glider bomb only began at the end of 1944. The planned weapon was to be carried by the high-level Henschel HS 130 bomber at a height of 16,000 metres, and dropped from there.

The body of the bomb, which was about 8.5 metres long, was to have stump wings with a wingspan of about 2.5 metres. The bomb, weighing about 6.4 tonnes, was accelerated to a speed of over 1000 kilometres per hour by means

of a di-glycol solid fuel propulsion system. Thus, this bomb, which it is said was to be called the HS 315, would be three times as heavy as the Fieseler Fi-103. It would be guided by a remote controlled guidance system. But a guidance procedure was considered in which the guidance transmitter would be placed in advance at the target by high-speed aircraft or by other means (via agents, or in ports by means of U-boats). In addition, a large number of different target search devices were examined to see if they would be suitable for this glider bomb.

There are however a series of circumstances which indicates that something special was also planned for this weapon. Thus, according to some documents, it was planned to be used with the Henschel high-level HS 130 bomber.

In February 1944, *Generalfeldmarschall* Erhard Milch ordered all work of the HS 130 to be immediately halted. Most of the HS 130s which had been built were to be scrapped. The HS 130 E-1s still under construction were to be dismantled and the material recycled.[174]

To what extent these instructions were actually followed is questionable. But afterwards there must have been only a very few HS-130s which were available for the testing and deployment of the planned high-level bomb. Other high-level aircraft, such as the Ju 388, did not have the same maximum height ceiling as the HS 130 and would thus have been less suitable for carrying the HS 315.

With this long-range glider bomb, was the Henschel company pursuing the intention of carrying on their HS 130 programme which had been axed at the end of 1944? Had parts been stored from which it would be possible to produce more HS 130As, Cs, or Es?

It is thus clear that the Henschel high-level glider bomb was from the outset only to be built in a very small production run. In terms of armaments economics, the expense of a project for producing such a new glider bomb with conventional warhead would have been completely uninteresting. It would also have been to a certain extent pointless to go to the great expense of bringing guidance transmitters to the target area only to guide some conventional warheads to the target. The remarkable thing is that in the case of the U-boat V-1, in all probability also a nuclear weapon, exactly the same target procedures were planned as for the Henschel high-level glider bomb. Coincidence? Despite the absence of further documentary evidence, the conclusion can be drawn with some certainty that from the outset the Henschel high-level glider bomb was a planned special weapon which would be produced at great expense and in very small numbers, in order to deploy a non-conventional, probably atomic payload.

The VU-weapon

A microfilm gives details of the existence of a further secret weapon which apparently had got to the flight tests stage as an early as 1944. This was the so-called Vu-weapon. In the text, this designation is possibly an abbreviation for the concept *Wurfwaffe*. This Vu-weapon would be launched from a catapult. Its overall weight was 10 tonnes, with the warhead weighing two tonnes and the remaining eight tonnes being comprised of the metal structure, propellant and guidance installations.

The experiments with the weapons were carried out at Bolovec near Pilsen. The target for the projectile would have been Hradec-Kralova.

The remote control equipment was produced in the Siemens-Schuckert factory near Vienna.

This weapon, which (according to the secret report) had already reached at least the flight test stage, did not ever turn up in wartime or post-war references. Nor are there any photographs or plans. Even the details relating to the weapon's weight on the microfilm do not match any of the known German secret weapons. But it is interesting that the Swiss aviation publication *Interavia* published a report after the war which stated that three Soviet long-range weapons launch ramps were at Hradec-Kralova. Were there connections here with the former German V weapon?

If this Vu projectile had actually existed, it must have been an SS development carried out in Pilsen by the Kammler group. This would also explain the fact that no documentation exists today.

The 'V-4' Duck-Wing Flying Bomb - Alias 'V-3'

In the vicinity of Swinemünde on the Wollin Peninsula, near to the village of Misdroy, there was a testing ground which today is principally connected with test firing of the HDP multi-chamber cannon ('Fleissiges Lieschen'). But other secret tests were also carried out there with weapons whose existence is generally denied today. It seems that these included second-generation flying bombs which even got to the stage of being flight tested.

Only long after the Cold War had come to an end did the former Polish soldier, Kasimir Browski, tell what he had discovered in 1948 during his summer holidays in Misdroy. In addition to two mysterious launch ramps, in simple dives without special equipment in 4-5 metres of water, he found a series of new missiles which had plunged into that Baltic Sea shortly after launch in failed tests during the war. If he originally expected to find down there the well known V-1s from Peenemünde, instead of these he discovered a completely different weapon which to all intents and purposes had at least been developed up to the stage of flight testing. Browski saw an unconventional missile which had a long fuselage with duck wings, with a propulsion system resembling that of the V-1 being fixed to the rear of the fuselage. The wings had control surfaces (this observation suggests that this new weapon was to be remote-controlled). It was painted grey green, while the propulsion system components were painted in a darker, more rusty colour.

One of these flying bombs, which Browski called 'V-4s', was still complete, while some of the others were damaged,

without propulsion systems and with buckled wings. Unfortunately the recreational diver had no opportunity to take exact measurements. However, he estimated that the diameter of the fuselage was about 80 to 90 centimetres.

If we assume that Browski's drawing is approximately correct in terms of proportions, this suggests a missile which looks like a smaller version of the later US Martin B-61 'Matador'.

It seems clear that some of the duck wing missiles had been tested in flight at Misdroy. Whether, and if so, how many of these were able to be successfully launched is not known today. And despite all subsequent research, their manufacturer and where they were manufactured remains a mystery.

Did the duck wing bomb, designated as a 'V-4', have something to do with the Vu-, D 6000 and Junkers rocket gliders?[175]

The propulsion system only showed a superficial similarity to that of the V-1. Up to the present we do not know whether the Misdroy missile was to use an Argus tube, another ramjet propulsion system or even a jet propulsion system. The known drawing and other information rather suggest that it would have been a new jet propulsion system in the 300 horsepower thrust class. The problem with this, however, is the fact that these more powerful propulsion systems were not ready on a regular basis until the end of the war. On the stern of the missile a rocket propulsion system had been installed to provide auxiliary launch power.

The published drawing of Browski's 'V-4' also shows auxiliary launch rockets under the fuselage, which would have enabled the 'V-4' to be launched from short catapults.

It is a subject of discussion that the 'V-4' was also to be used as the first stage in the two stage A-4 and/or the *Ross und Reiter* project (see relevant section). This is also confirmed by information from the circle of the Peenemünde scientist 'Dr X', who has already been quoted extensively. In accordance with his reliable information, the range of the remote controlled 'V-4' was to have been approximately 3500 kilometres, with the missile being equipped with a heavy warhead of approximately 2500 kilograms.

From October 1944, reports from Sweden spoke of a wave of 'ghost rockets' over Scandinavia. These could have been robot-like high-flying aircraft which produced 200 metre long white gas trails and made a noise as loud as that of a four-engined bomber. These reports were so numerous that there is no doubt that they had some basis in truth. Most of the reports came from the Swedish High Command and/or Government. Somewhat unnerved, the Swedish military authorities prepared a precise summary of the instances of a V-1, V-2 and V-3 overflights and crashes in their territory in order to be able to use them as the material for making a diplomatic protest in Berlin.

In connection with these events in Norway and Sweden, seen by many people, there was always talk of some secret new weapons developments. In the Allied press they were designated as 'flying shell', 'V-11/2' or as the 'V-3'. These must have all fairly probably referred to the same missile which Browski designated as a 'V-4'.

A Swedish expert reported in the Stockholm newspaper *Expressen* that the V-3 was a type of combination between V-1 and V-2: "It can fly at a great height, is very fast and can be guided more easily than the V-2, but it does not fly as high or as fast as the V-2". Many of the flying bombs could even change their direction during flight without crashing. Thus it was directly observed how some machines turned back on themselves and flew back again in an easterly direction. This is why the in 1944 the V-3s, and later in 1946 a second wave of 'ghost rockets', were also called 'boomerang bombs'. Many of the missiles crashed while overflying. Even today in Sweden you can hear rumours about such a crash in some lake or other. In Denmark, too, one of the missiles failed and even killed some people in the crash.

Initial vague indications suggest that this revolutionary missile could have been tested at least once against Britain (see 'V-weapons in the Far North').

For the British and the Germans it was clear that the boomerang missiles were ultimately to serve as carriers for atomic weapons.

The Italian star journalist Luigi Romersa, who visited Germany on behalf of Mussolini at the end of 1944, reported in this connection that Reich Propaganda Minister Dr Goebbels had also told him in a conversation about the new radio controlled V-bombs, "the latest of which will be an incredible surprise ..."

As early as the late summer of 1944, alarming reports from agents had reached Britain which stated that in Norway a German nuclear weapon was being prepared which was to be launched from catapults at Britain.

The mysterious trail of the V-3 alias V-4 missile can be followed through 1944 to the end of the war and beyond into the post-war period!

As early as 10 April 1945, the British warned of a new delivery of remarkable V-weapons which had arrived in Norway with the intention of being deployed against the United Kingdom. But this did not happen, instead the war came to an end. But from 1946, suddenly many missiles were once again spotted over northern Sweden, which by experts at the time were identified as radio controlled V-4s. A range of 1000 kilometres was ascribed to this weapon. These may have been Allied test launches with captured German weapons. Reports in circulation at the time suggested that the British launched captured V-4s from Norway, while the Russian missiles had come from Misdroy and the Leningrad area.

One day in 1948, however, these sightings of V-4s in the Far North suddenly ceased and since then nothing has ever again become known of them.

Possibly, even today, individual remains or even entire V-4s are lying some kilometres from the shore of the former testing ground at Misdroy in the Baltic Sea and are awaiting being salvaged by enterprising divers.

4) Special rocket developments

The 'Planet Project' and Prof. Orthmann's Special Warheads

Despite some six to seven metre-thick concrete covers on the bunkers, the problem of the vulnerability of fixed rocket launch positions to enemy mass air raids had turned up time and time again during 1944. The V-weapons installations in Watten, Wizernes and Mimoyeques had been severely damaged by large Allied bombs even before they were put into operation.

One of the defensive measures against such expected air-raids on specific targets may have been the project which involved using converted A-4 rockets to attack enemy bomber streams. Instead of the warhead in the nose cone, 427 small rockets each of 44.5 mm calibre to were accommodated in a container. The Reich Research Committee developed these small rockets with expandable folding aerofoils, giving the project the name of 'Planet'.

The anti-aircraft A-4s would have been guided by radar to the vicinity of the bomber stream. Then it was planned that the 'Planet' rockets would be released underneath the enemy bombers, with the rockets which did not score a direct hit at their first approach he repeatedly circling and penetrating the bomber stream.

The service ceiling and range of the 'Flak A 4' may have exceeded that of all other aerial defence rockets.

Some Peenemünde A-4 tests were known in which guidance equipment of the *Wasserfall* flak rocket had been installed in normal rockets. To date, such test launches have always been seen as simply assisting the development of the *Wasserfall*. But is it not more likely that these were perhaps test flights of the 'Flak A-4'?

The 'Planet' programme was run by the *Reichsforschungsrat* (RFR). The rocket and space pioneer Rolf Engel, who died in 1993, was a member of the RFR, and during the post-war period gave an account of a rocket warhead development carried out by Professor Ortmann, which would have precisely suited the small rockets in the Planet project. A coincidence? According to the information Engel outlined, the rockets were to be guided into a bomber stream and then then explosively expel a chemical combination which was to remove the oxygen from propulsion systems. Another version of this project planned to use a chemical substance with an effect similar to that of the oxygen bomb (see Volume 3). The ignition of this mixture comprising warhead payload and atmospheric air would thus destroy all aircraft in a given radius around the rocket.

Authority NND 750122
By [illegible] NARA Date 4/25/78

S E C R E T

PW INTELLIGENCE BULLETIN No 2/32

13.   Fantasia: German Secret Weapons   (Continued)

Second Story

On 6 Jan.44, between 1300 and 1400 hrs, PW saw a formation of four-
motored American Liberators flying over STETTIN. He heard a noise like that
of a V-2 taking off and saw a large red ball ascending rapidly toward the formation. It appeared to grow as it rose. There was a loud explosion and he
saw broken parts of planes falling.

PW comments that there were three divisions(?) of Flak in action at the
time (3 x 72 pieces), but when he returned to PEENEMUENDE he was told by a
friend who worked in the officers' club that this had been the first attempt
with a new secret weapon and that 47 planes were brought down by the single
shot. Another friend in Flak Regt 11, STETTIN, told PW that the Flak had
fired anti-personnel charges that day instead of usual Flak ammunition. When
PW asked why, he was told that the ammunition was left over from AFRICA and
had to be used up. PW's own comment (see also PW INTELLIGENCE BULLETIN 1/13
Item 17) is that it makes more noise and might be used to hide the noise of
the secret weapon.

(Source: S/Gefr Franz KRIEMER, 5 Para Mortar Bn 5 Para Div)

American document referring to a new aerial defence weapon.

If in previous published historiography, people had been of the opinion that this project never came to be implemented, the latest information prompts a re-evaluation of this assessment. According to this information, the 'Flak A-4' did go into production, being supplied with the reinforced Visol liquid propulsion system planned for the A 8. This made the 'Flak A4' capable of being stored even with full fuel tanks - an important criterion for aerial defence, because it was then not necessary to have to fuel rockets only when the air-raid sirens sounded, and thus lose valuable time.

According to an American secret report which was only released in 1998, the test mission of this weapon took place on 6 January 1944. A German who was captured by the Americans said that on that date between 1308 hours and 1400 hours a formation of four-engined American Liberator bombers was flying over Stettin. The man heard a noise like the launch of a V2 and saw a large red ball which quickly climbed in the direction of the aircraft formation. As it gained height, it seemed to grow, and then it gave a loud explosion and the eye witness saw shattered pieces of aircraft plunging to earth. When he later returned to Peenemünde, a friend who worked in the officers' club there told him that this was the first trial with a new secret weapon. 47 aircraft, he said, had been brought down with this single missile. Another friend, who was serving in Flak Regiment 11 in Stettin, told the later prisoner-of-war that on that day, instead of normal anti-aircraft ammunition, the regular flak units were firing anti-personnel charges into the air. When the man asked why this had been done, he was told that this ammunition have been left over from the African campaign and had to be used up. His own opinion, however, was that this ammunition which was unsuitable for aerial defence made considerably more noise, and in actual fact was used to to give the impression of a heavy flak bombardment to drown out the noise of of the secret weapon.

According to information provided by a reliable source, over 100 'flak A-4s' were able to be produced, and all these were stored. One of the phenomena connected with this weapon which has remained unexplained even until today is the fact that evidently this was the only successful test mission, and the other 'flak A-4s' must not have been used.

'Flying Man' Special Rocket Device

In Spring 1941, six high-ranking German generals expressed to Hitler their wish for a device to be created which would enable infantry to jump over enemy obstacles and the forward parts of the front when they were on the offensive. This involved creating a so-called 'flying man' by means of a belt of rockets. After two years of thorough development and experiment, the first flight of such a rocket belt took place on 2 May 1943. Initial tests flights exceeded all expectations.

The 'flying man' consisted of two tubes like the Schmidt jet exhaust tubes. Two devices of this kind were thus buckled onto chest and back, so that the stronger propulsion system was on the back and the weaker on the chest. To launch the device, both engines had to be ignited at the same time, as a result of which the soldier was lifted into the air and by the rocket belt and propelled forward by the stronger rocket tube on the back. The fuel consumption of this device, which could achieve speeds of 160 kilometres per hour, was small, and amounted to only 100 grams per second. In addition, the soldiers could carry 30 kilograms of payload at a height of 150 to 200 metres. The flying man was able to cover a distance of several hundred metres.

It is commonly agreed that it was possible to equip trial groups with such devices, which were also tested in front line service. One American report says that a special unit equipped with the special rocket belts succeeded in winning a fierce fight with American armed forces. In this engagement, American losses are said to have been 3,200 soldiers, 70 tanks and 57 artillery pieces. It is said that at the end of the war, rocket belts of this kind fell into the hands of the Allies and that even today one of them still exists in a secret steel room under the National Air and Space Museum in Washington. Will this report, which sounds like a science-fiction story, ever be able to be confirmed?

It is a fact that 17 years after the end of the war, in the USA, a rocket belt was developed by Bell Aerospace based on the model of the 'flying man' built in Germany. Despite extensive tests, the American army could not decide whether to introduce this device into service. Finally, one model of this device was used as an attraction in a James Bond 007 film. The performance criteria of the Bell device are said to have happened to be comparable to those of the German device.

PART III

Was there a threat of nuclear rocket attack and missile attacks in Europe in 1945?

In his speech 'Discorso della Riscossa' on 16 December 1944,
before the packed opera house in Milan, Benito Mussolini spoke
of the imminent German offensive on the most important Allied cities.
This was to be a 'definitive offensive' – with bombs and rockets of
inconceivable power: These bombs, Mussolini said, would be able
to destroy a city in a single moment …[1]

The odyssey of *Lehr- und Versuchsbatterie* 444, or why was Dr Kammler's elite unit moved to Peenemünde after it was evacuated?

One of the oldest and most experienced rocket units was *Lehr- und Versuchsbatterie* (Training and Experimental Battery) *444*. As early as July 1943 it was the first rocket unit to be formed, still with the name *Lehr- und Versuchsbatterie Köslin*. On 28 January 1945, *Lehr- und Versuchsbatterie 444* moved back to Germany at the height of Dr Kammler's V-weapons offensive. Before this, the unit had, together with *Art.-Abt. (mot) 485*, formed the large V-weapons unit *Gruppe Nord*.

It seems remarkable that Dr Kammler, only two days after he had been given command of the V-1 operational units, allowed his offensive power to be weakened by removing this experienced unit. There must have been good reasons for this.

Lehr- und Versuchsbatterie 444 was to be transported into the Peenemünde area to carry out a series of experiments with new improved A-4 rockets. Unfortunately it has never become known what these rockets were. But the nine special versions must have already been so far developed that it was possible to change over. At the same time the difference between them and the old version must have been great enough and important enough to justify withdrawing *Lehr- und Versuchsbatterie 444* from the front.

It has never become known how long the battery stayed in Peenemünde during the spring of 1945, and what it did there. Is another unexplained mystery here?

Because the new A-4 rockets could apparently afford to wait, *Lehr- und Versuchsbatterie 444* was finally transferred back to the West. At the beginning of March 1945 the battery finally received two rockets which were equipped with remote-controlled guidance. Was this the same kind of projectile for which the unit had been transferred to Peenemünde in the first place? The indication that a remote-controlled guidance system was to be installed suggests the conclusion that these special A-4s (with or without gliding wings) were to be deployed using the new 'Freya-Langlatte' procedure under radar control. They were then launched from Armsen (to the south-east of Werden) in the direction of the North Sea.

Later the rocket unit once again toWelmsbüttel in Schleswig-Holstein. There, on 6 April 1945 the last (officially known) German wartime rockets were launched, when two other experimental rockets of an unknown version were launched in the direction of the North Sea.

It is amazing that so shortly before the end of the war rockets were still being used for experimental purposes. Were there important reasons for this?

Unfortunately it remains unknown even today which new rocket version justified the transfer of the experienced *Lehr- und Versuchsbatterie 444* from the heavily pressed Western Front at the end of January 1945. That this was no trivial matter is shown by the fact that Dr Kammler had chosen his most experienced unit for this purpose. In addition, their transport to Peenemünde took place at the same time as Peenemünde was being 'evacuated'. Why had the otherwise coolly calculating *SS-Obergruppenfuhrer* had one of his most important units transferred into an exercise area which he had just ordered to be evacuated, if something important was not going on? If this was all no coincidence, then the potential significance of the unknown A-4 version appears even greater. Was it the intention to prepare for operational service, under the greatest secrecy, remote-controlled rockets with weapons of mass destruction?

The fact remains that the rocket battery was finally transferred back to the West, without bringing their new armament with them. The experimental launch of individual remote-controlled rockets over the North Sea in March and April 1945 is not likely to be the real reason why the unit was transferred from the Western Front at the end of January 1945.

As with so many units of the German Wehrmacht and the SS, the *Lehr- und Versuchsbatterie 444* had waited in vain for the promised new victory weapons.

Feldpostnummer 66791: The third V-weapons regiment – the first atomic rocket unit?

If we assume that the German rocket programme was at an early stage connected with the intended use of nuclear-armed weapons, then this raises the question as to which special military units were to operate them.

There is also already a hint of mysterious remote-controlled rocket units which could be connected with such plans:[2] On 25 January 1945, *SS-Obergruppenführer Dr Kammler* ordered the formation of the *Division z.V.* This reorganisation, concerning which only a fragmentary, scarcely legible written document has been preserved, was to completely re-order and reorganise the existing long-range rocket units, as part of which the units which previously had not belonged to the *Division z.V.* were to be included in it.

In addition to Artillery Regiments (mot) z.V. 901 and 902, a third V-weapons unit, *Artillerieregiment (mot) z.V.903*, was planned. The existing *Artillerieabteilungen (mot) 962* and probably also (*t. mot) 953* became part of the Division.

Artillerieabteilung (mot) 962 was a mysterious V-2 unit which, although it must have been considerably older, was never mentioned in operational reports up to that time. The unit was formed on 14 December 1943, and is said to have been finally stationed in Zwolle in Holland. Its role after 20 August 1944 is completely unclear. What is certain is that it was not directly connected with the other existing operational V-weapons units.

Research results suggest that *Artillerieregiment (mot) z.V.903* was also formed out of *Artillerieabteilung (t. mot) 953*. This long-range rocket unit, which was formed on 15 August 1943 with a staff in Greifswald and training facilities in Karlshagen, was part of the rocket units which were first formed. This unit, as unit 962 previously, is never connected with one of the other operational rocket units, and although the unit, which consisted of three batteries and the staff, was formed as early as summer 1943, no accounts of its wartime activities are known. It was officially dissolved on 15 December 1944, and in February 1945, that is, at the same time that *Artillerieregiment z.V.903* was formed, was removed from the *Feldpost* register.

The remarkable thing about *Artillerieregiment 903* is that this third V-weapons regiment was in no way connected with the other two operational regiments 901 and 902. This indicates that the two *Abteilungen* 962 and 953, and also Regiment 903 which was later formed out of these units, were units for which a special role was planned. Otherwise, in the light of the scarce resources in manpower and material, it would not have been possible to afford the luxury of a year's inactivity on the part of such expensive special formations.

So was the mysterious 'third V-weapons regiment' the unit whose batteries were intended to launch nuclear or radiological V2s A-4Bs and A 9/A 10 rockets? In any event, it is remarkable that almost nothing is known about the operational service and what finally became of *Artillerieregiment z. V 903*. Perhaps for reasons of secrecy, it is not to be found in the Army service directory, *Frontnachweiser des OKH/Chef Heeresrüstung und Befehlshaber des Ersatzheeres*, nor on the organisational chart *Organisationskartei des Allgemeinen Heeresamtes*, although its troops were, from mid-February, assigned *Feldpost* Number 66791. Even mysterious secret units must be able to get their post!

A) Victory Weapons target – London: 'The finest target in the world'

London's preparations for 'X-Day'?

With the possible exception of a few remaining shots, the battle for London is over. The godson of Winston Churchill, Duncan Sandys, proudly announced these words at a press conference on 7 December, 1944. He continued that there was now only a small threat of danger from individual German flying bombs launched from the air.

Although this statement meant that the official British view was that the battle of London was at an end, nevertheless since August 1944 precautionary measures had been developed which put all previous measures in the shade. Even the sudden evacuation of London was secretly prepared for! One of the measures necessary for this was the decision to create, in a radius of five miles around the centre of London, suitable collection points, which included mostly school buildings, cinemas, dance halls and - look on and be amazed - football stadiums. Requisitioned buses were to collect refugees wandering around on foot. 87 further escape routes were prepared, to enable a quick evacuation of the city centre in an emergency. Until the end of the war, the Londoners did not hear a word about these preparations made by their government. Probably, the government wanted to forestall any panic.

But why was the British government still preparing plans for the evacuation of London if at that time all V-1 bases on the French and Belgian coasts had already fallen into the hands of the Allies and the V-2 bombardment had not even begun? One reason which is suggested is that at this time the Home Office had received serious warnings from British agents in Germany and Sweden. These warnings concerned planned German V-weapons attacks, the expected strength of which made such radical measures necessary.

What sort of attacks did these have to be to force the British to take such precautionary measures? After the loss of launch bases on the Continent, the conventional German mass bombardment by flying bombs of the British capital had become a thing of the past. Therefore, what the government feared could have been individual attacks with devastating effect.

Were these preparations taken against the eventuality of a threatened nuclear attack on London? The evacuation distance of seven miles from the centre of London which was planned by the British government recalls the effective radius of the later Hiroshima bomb.

According to information in the Spanish newspapers *Pueblo* and *Las Provincias*, the extreme British protective measures were indeed being taken against the threat of a feared German atomic bomb attack.[3]

This attack was to take place from the same launch ramps which were being used for V-weapons. Then an area of three kilometres in radius would have been covered in death and destruction by every bomb. As early as March 1944, Hitler had told *Oberst* Hans Ulrich Rudel about these plans, and in this he was clear what was really meant by the special missions of the V-1s and V-2s: nuclear victory weapons were to be launched against Britain!

According to other reports from Allied agents,[4] the Germans are said to have also been experimenting with atomic weapons in Norway, the weapons being launched from a catapult and having an expected radius of destruction of more than two miles.

These warnings, entirely independent of each other, coming from German and Swedish sources, compelled the British to act.

It should raise some mistrust that the originals of these agents' reports are apparently even today still classified.

'Why U.S. President Roosevelt was not to travel to London' - Had the Allies got wind of the German plans?

On 15 July, 1943, the high-ranking OSS agent Allen Dulles had sent his famous telegram in which he informed his secret service chief Donovan about simultaneous atomic research and rocket activities in Peenemünde.[5] This was what set the alarm bells ringing among the responsible Allied authorities!

It was completely clear to the British and American experts that Germany's rockets and missiles, even if they were so superior in technological terms, were not significant enough to have decided the outcome of the war so long as they were armed with conventional warheads. But what would be the case if the Germans were ultimately to arm their rockets and missiles with atomic bombs?

Some time during December 1943, therefore, the later leading member of the ALSOS mission, Samuel Goudsmit, was charged by members of the British secret service with investigating whether the Germans were in a position to arm their rockets with atomic warheads. The director of the Office of Scientific Research and Development, Vannevar Bush, the American atomic General Groves and many other experts could not rest throughout the war at the possibility of the existence of a German rocket with atomic weapons.[6]

In Spring 1944, Vannevar Bush travelled purposely to Britain to warn General Eisenhower about the danger from German nuclear rockets. In doing so he pointed particularly to the possibility that they could be launched at the invasion ports of Plymouth and Bristol. At the end of his explanation, General Eisenhower said that Bush frightened him to death, and he asked him: "What should we do?"

One of the possibilities which were recommended was to increase the intensity of bombing raids on the V-weapons positions which were known to the Allies. In addition, many Geiger counters were delivered to Britain within the framework of Operation Peppermint, to guarantee that proper preparations were made for such attacks.

When, then, on 13 June 1944, the first V-1 flying bomb struck London, Goudsmit and a British scientist by the name of Stever immediately went to the impact site in order to scan the bomb crater which had been left behind by the Fi-103 with a Geiger counter to test for radioactivity.

Relieved, they confirmed that the V-1 bomb had simply been carrying a perfectly conventional explosive.

Although during the Normandy invasion and the V-weapons offensive, no deployment of German atomic rockets and nuclear-armed missiles had taken place, renowned American experts in particular reckoned with the possibility that this could happen. Philip Morrison, a leading member of General Groves' staff, therefore made the urgent recommendation to the security services that President Roosevelt should under no circumstances meet with the British Premier Churchill in London, because the city could be destroyed in an atomic bomb attack and both politicians could be killed. Evidently, President Roosevelt agreed with this recommendation.

From summer 1944, and for the rest of the war, Philip Morrison made it his habit to listen to the BBC World Service programme in the morning and in the evening in order to assure himself that London still existed!

But to those among the Allied specialists who knew the facts about the Allied Manhattan Project and the German rocket and missile project, it was entirely clear what the Germans' ultimate plans were.

Search for counter-measures: The first ventures in anti-rocket defence – The Allied forerunner of SDI?

Sooner or later every measure gives rise to its counter-measure. Thus, during the Second World War, considerations were already being given as to whether it might in fact be possible to develop a defence against ballistic rockets coming from the stratosphere at many times the speed of sound.

As a result of the expectations gained through Allied espionage that there might be an attack carried out by German A-4s, as early as 24 August 1944 the British anti-aircraft command proposed a method to defend against the V-2. Under the assumption that the flight path of the rockets could be predicted with radar, the air defence specialists planned to create a barrier of anti-aircraft fire around London in order to cause the warhead of the rocket to explode while it was still in the air.

This procedure is ominously reminiscent of the American rocket defence during the Gulf War, when an attempt was made to get the Iraqi 'Scud' rockets to explode prematurely using 'Patriot' anti-aircraft missiles.

But the British specialists recognised that to defend against every individual V-2 warhead would involve a gigantic expense: 320,000 anti-aircraft rounds would have to be fired in order to ensure that the missile was effectively destroyed! A great disadvantage of this method was also that, after being fired, about two per cent of anti-aircraft rounds equipped with approach detonators would fall to the ground and explode there. With a weight of approximately 14 kilograms per anti-aircraft shell, this would mean that every time the anti-aircraft barrier was deployed 98.6 tonnes of warheads might be expected to explode on the ground.

It was likely that the one-ton warhead of the rocket would thus cause less damage in the target area than the British anti-aircraft defence itself, and that the consumption of ammunition would, within a short time, quickly exhaust all anti-aircraft munitions supplies. In addition to this, of course, there was no guarantee that this method would definitely be able to destroy the rocket whilst it was in the air.

Looked at critically, then, the British rocket defence plans only actually make sense if they were in fact meant to serve as the last line of defence against attacks by individual nuclear victory weapons carriers. The winged rockets A-4 and A-9, because of their slower speed in flight, would have given the British defences a better chance of hitting them.

Despite all its disadvantages and a calculated chance of success of only 3 to 10 per cent, the plan was put into operation. The real reasons for continuing this uncertain procedure for defence against the V-2, which itself would endanger the British civilian population, were never revealed! Did the authorities regard this secondary damage caused by their own defensive fire as an acceptable risk in preventing an atomic attack?

The end of the war intervened before approval could be given to try this plan out for the first time.[7] We will never know how this forerunner of 'SDI' would have worked in earnest.

But with regard to developing a passive form of defence, it was tried to at least create a system of early warning of threatened rocket strikes. Therefore, special artillery observation units were sent to Belgium to observe the sky over Holland using light-sensitive measuring equipment and keep a lookout for traces of rockets being launched. The idea was to at least be able to transmit to Britain a minimum of warnings against rocket strikes. As a further measure, the Royal Air Force (RAF) sent the '108th Mobile Air Reporting Unit' to Belgium. These special troops were to try to get a precise radar fix on the V-2 launches. But this system also produced as many false alarms as it did genuine warnings and for the most part was unable to confirm the launch of any missiles.

During the whole of the Second World War, given the then state of technology, no organised defence was possible against the German long-range rockets.

The only known instance in which it was claimed that a V-2 which had already been launched was actually shot down occurred when during its lengthy launch manoeuvres the V-2 happened to fly through a group of four-engined B-24 bombers of the 34th Bomb Group and received so many hits from the defensive fire of the bombers that it plunged to earth again. But here, too, it will never be clear whether this was really a genuine kill, or whether the rocket simply failed to launch properly.

In any event, the four-engined consolidated B-24 bombers can claim to be the only aircraft to have ever shot down a ballistic missile in flight. This record has never been broken to the present-day.

The sinister threat: V-weapons in the Far North

To the present day, the events relating to the stationing of V-weapons in the Far North are surrounded in mystery.

As early as summer 1944, the British had been warned of the imminent danger that the Germans were testing types of weapons which could be launched by catapult and from there reach London. Was this a genuine threat, or was the whole thing just an old wives' tale?

On the basis of statements from witnesses, it is relatively certain that there was a special hangar at an airfield near Stavanger in which large crates were stored.[8] Only a Luftwaffe *Hauptmann* named Kern was allowed to enter the hangar. When his driver one day looked through the *Hauptmann's* attaché case unobserved, he saw that there were various documents in it relating to V-1s. Some time - as yet unknown - in autumn 1944, large crates were taken from the same hangar to the port of Sandnes, to be taken by ship back to Germany. While the crates were being loaded, one crate fell and broke apart. This left a V-1 visible.

Because no V-1s were produced in Norway during the war, it must be assumed that their presence in Stavanger was connected with plans to use them later from Norwegian bases. In this case, then, the store must have been an interim store for Fi-103s for U-boats stationed in Norway.

Certainly there are reports in the British newspaper the *Daily Mail*, based on Norwegian sources, that 50 miles west of Oslo and on various high plateaux between Oslo and Bergen, a series of German V-weapons bases had been constructed. Members of the Norwegian resistance, from whom this information is said to have come, believed that these bases were mainly planned for the V-2, but that they could also be used for long-range models of the V-1. It was said that the Germans were working night and day installing concrete and iron in these positions and had even constructed light mountain railways and cable ways to provide supplies. Each launch position, the report said, consisted of a large concrete hall which was dug deep into the cliffs. The roof was semicircular and consisted of reinforced concrete. A long launch rail track was said to lead out in front of each bunker entrance.

What the experts at the time did not understand was why the Germans were taking such efforts to construct these V-weapons bases on mountain summits which were so out of the way, because neither the V 1s nor the V-2s needed to be at such a height to be successfully launched. It was therefore assumed that perhaps these bases were intended for the V-3.

As is outlined in the section concerning the V-4 alias V-3 missile, these were the same weapons as the boomerang

bombs which were tested by Germany in Norway in 1944/45.

According to a report in the British newspaper the *Daily Express* of 15 January 1945, the missiles sighted over southern Sweden the previous day had been launched from Hardangervidda, the Hardanger plateau in Norway.

There was also a gigantic building project on the Gaustad summit, the purpose of which is contested even today. This could have been a massive radar installation, an ultra-modern radar installation for guiding advanced missiles and/or A 9/A 10 rockets, concreted launch installations or even a combination of all these types of installation.

The building project was surrounded by extremely high degree of secrecy and security. Only German workers were employed, entire districts were sealed off and also under surveillance from the air day and night. Were the installations built in high locations which were difficult to access, because in this way the Germans would be able to protect themselves better from commando operations carried out by the Norwegian resistance?

Because the Gaustad was quite near to the famous Rjukan heavy water plant, in 1997, the Spanish researcher Antonio Chover wrote to some Norwegian local authorities and asked what had been happening in that area during the Second World War. Chover received several replies which all asserted that in Norway there were never any launch bases for V-weapons and that moreover nothing at all had happened on the Gaustad. Even Klaus Helberg responded. He was one of the heroes of Telemark who tried to sabotage a German heavy water transport. He assured Chover: "In Gaustad the Germans had an observation base for aerial observation. I am sure that there were no plans to build rocket launch bases there. Also I have never heard anything of the Germans having any such plans for other districts in Norway". But eventually the Spanish researcher received a letter from the Museum Director of the Norwegian Industrial Workers Museum in Vermonk. This museum is located in the building of the former Rjukan heavy water power plant. Herr Frode Saeland told the Spaniard something quite different - something which was finally the truth: "The Germans began their construction work on the Gaustad summit in autumn 1944. The local commander referred to the location as a V-position and rumours had it that this was connected with a secret V-weapon … In a book published in 1946, the construction on the Gaustad summit was seen as the largest and certainly the most expensive radio installation that the Germans left behind. Even the suggestion that it might have been a radar station was rejected. During the war the resistance and the British suspected that the Germans were building radio stations there for remote control of the V-weapons. This resulted in discussions between the British specialists: Was it possible in any event to reach Britain from Norway with remote-controlled flying bombs? Consideration was therefore given to mounting an air-raid on the entire installation. The Germans had prepared themselves for this eventuality. On the other side of the valley they had, with great effort, brought up aerial defence equipment. The whole end station of the cable way to the summit and the surrounding area was a real confusion of gun positions, ammunition stores and barracks".

So what is to be made of this? From the description, the concrete launch bunkers in Norway could have been intended for missiles of the long-range V-1 type (or further developments of these missiles). The V-2 did not require any launch tracks and could have been launched from any flat piece of ground.

Recently, Antonio Chover discovered that perhaps there could in actual fact have been German attacks from Norway on Britain with advanced missile developments. It is known that in the early hours of 24 December 1944 there was a surprising large-scale raid by 50 high-altitude Heinkel He-111s from KG 53, which crossed the British coast between Skegness and Mablethorpe with the loss of only one aircraft to British night fighters, and one which crashed in an accident. They were able to launch 31 V-1s in the direction of the industrial centres of northern Britain. All missiles launched by KG 53 struck their targets between 5:28am and 6:45am.

Reports, which must be taken seriously, also suggest that on the previous day, on 23 December 1944, attacks took place on Manchester! At this time, the He-111s from KG 53 were not in the air and V-1s and V-2s from Holland did not have sufficient range. The weapons which attacked Manchester were evidently something else!

According to reports from the news agency Reuters and the Swedish newspaper *Südsvenska Dagbladdet*, it was possible that the bombardment on northern Britain came from the area or from the Hardangervidda (Hardanger plateau) in Norway! While the V-1 attacks of 24 December 1944 and their impact sites are precisely documented, to the present day nothing has ever been published concerning the weapons impacts in northern Britain on 23 December. The press simply confirmed that "casualties were caused and many buildings were destroyed".

The Germans never mentioned these separate attacks, which is not surprising, because similar secrecy can be seen regarding the initial operations of the V-1s and V-2s.

There are however indications from the Axis powers that during the Christmas period in 1944 Manchester was not only attacked by He-111s launching V-1s. Thus on 26 December 1944, the Italian newspaper *La Stampa* in Turin reported: "German long-range weapons hit Manchester. Five German scientists are honoured by the Führer for inventing and developing the new long-range weapons".

The new weapon must therefore have been a success. And a day previously, the *Corriere della Sera* in Turin reported that the *Duce* had been disappointed to have found out about the use of a new German weapon on the Western Front not from the *Führer* himself, but from a newspaper correspondent accredited to the Allied High Command.

It seems clear, then, that this new German weapon was not the He-111/Fi-103 combination, which had actually been in operation since July 1944.

Will we ever be able to shed any light on what happened over northern Britain on 23 December 1944? It seems that this alleged trial attack with missiles from Norway was not followed by any other V-attacks against Britain during the rest of the war. Yet the danger from German V-weapons in Norway worried the British until the end. As late as 10 April 1945, the *Daily Mail* reported that a secret consignment of '25 ft missiles' had arrived in Norway which were to be launched by the Germans against Britain. They were transported by rail to Sorlandbeg in south-eastern Norway.

The V-weapons consignment reported in the *Daily Mail* thus arrived in Norway at the same time as the last German victory weapons were being prepared for action on the Eastern and Western fronts ... We recall in this connection the words of Hanns Schwarz: "Towards the end of the war, several new weapons with long-range effect were almost completed. Some of them were in the so-called Fortress Norway. There, thre were bases for the production of the most important weapons, of which we only knew that they were the weapons with unprecedented range and that they were to be armed with a quite new explosive substance..."[9]

Previously, such formulations have always been taken to refer to the A 9/A 10. But it is almost certain that, apart from the V-1, the Third Reich was able to develop even more advanced medium-range rockets. With the A 9/A 10 it would have been possible to strike the distant regions of Russia and America, but to bombard Britain and the parts of Europe which were occupied by the Allies something else was needed!

Unfortunately it never became known what the British found in Norway when they occupied the country from May 1945.

Winged rockets for special operations? The vanished rockets of Mobiler Schiesszug P VII

How far could the mobile deployment of A 4 B winged rockets have progressed? Here, too, misinterpretations during the post-war period seem to indicate how this question might be answered.

Right at the beginning of the evacuation of Peenemünde in February 1945, Wernher von Braun and Dr Kammler had ordered their colleague Dr Debus to take his *Mobiler Schiesszug Prüfstand VII* to the area of Cuxhaven. The withdrawal of this mobile unit is remarkable because the other launch crews had to remain in Peenemünde.

The official purpose of this move was the continuation of the test launches for the *Mittelwerk Produktion* on the Artenwalde naval test area near Cuxhaven. Certainly the *mobiler Schiesszug P VII* took with them a number of A-4 rockets from Peenemünde which had already been tested. Evidently, however, at the end of the war none of these rockets was left, because when the British took over the area some weeks later, they only found a few scant fragments of V-2 rockets. What had happened?

During the postwar period, the transfer of the mobile unit to Cuxhaven was seen as a kind of technical pledge on the part of Wernher von Braun that he planned to defect to the Americans. This, as might have been expected, was the view taken by many former colleagues from Peenemünde, although it did not make any sense to transfer the mobile launch unit to the British zone in the north instead of to the American southern zone. How the occupation zones were to be divided up among the Allies was something which the responsible German authorities had known for a long time. Things might have looked different if the mobile launch unit in actual fact was intended to be used for a special military operation. The members of the unit were familiar with launching the newest Peenemünde experimental rockets and evidently had some of the most up-to-date missiles with them, which at the end of the war had all disappeared.

So far as we can judge today, there are three possible versions of what happened in the meantime: In the first scenario, the mobile unit actually took special A-4s with them and lost them on the way to Cuxhaven, or some other similar explanation. This assumption is hardly satisfactory! According to the second version, the mobile unit, as they retreated, met a part of *Artillerieginement z.V.901* which was also breaking through to the rear. This training unit from Regiment 901 had previously been stationed in the Tucheler Heide.

According to the third version, these two units were joined by another important section of *SS-Werferabteilung 500*, whose training regiment was also retreating from Poland. According to this version, the fact that the units met and combined did not come about by chance. *Wereferabteilung* 500 then took military command of the other two units and ordered the launch of the special rockets they had with them.[10]

One can only believe that the fact that the three units met was purely coincidental and that the rockets were somehow lost in the confusion of the general German collapse.

But it becomes interesting if we assume that the retreat of *mobiler Schieszug P VII* from Peenemünde, the fact that it met with the two other units and the fact that the rockets which they had with them were launched was a well planned special operation. In this connection, it should not be forgotten that in Peenemünde at the end of the war there was intense interest in the development of the winged rockets. Thus considerably more winged rockets of the Type A 4 (Bastard) had been produced than has previously been assumed. The last photographs from Peenemünde also show quite clearly brightly painted A-4Bs on mobile Meiller trailers which, unlike their predecessors in the black and white experimental colour scheme, were painted in RLM 76 (light blue). This was the colour scheme for combat versions, and this was the colour scheme in which the last known A-4 operational rockets were painted on the photographs from April 1945.

Did the mobile launch unit in actual fact take with them these long-range rockets with a range of 750 kilometres which had already been thoroughly tested in Peenemünde?

Dr Kammler and Wernher von Braun would have sent the mobile launch unit, the unit best familiar with launching the A 4 B, to the West for operational launches. In view of the poor military situation there may not have been enough time available to retrain one of the normal V2 launch units on the use of the A-4B.

What would have been more likely, then, than to combine the technically expert experimental personnel directly with the new experimental rockets and the units which had already been trained for operating rockets?

It is remarkable that *Artillerieregiment* 901 also appears in connection with this supposed special operation. The name of the unit turns up repeatedly whenever there is any mention of planned special operations with V-weapons in Spring 1945. This is the case in connection with both operational V-2 plans on the Eastern Front and the secret V-1 launch ramps near to Berlin.

SS-Werferabteilung 500 had great experience with guiding the V-2 and with using the radio guidance system. This was indispensable if any success was to be achieved with the A-4B!

According to reliable information, more than 20 versions of the improvised long range A4 B (Bastard) rocket were produced, of which at least six were launched in operational conditions.

The impact of six individual A-4Bs would not have changed anything. But things would have looked different if this was only the background for the planned use of considerably more effective warheads. Was the new unit comprising P-VII-Abt. -500-Rgt-901 expecting a delivery of such warheads, which, as it turned out, did not arrive? Were the A-4B winged rockets deliberately transferred from Peenemünde or to the West an operation of this kind which in the event turned out not to be possible? Positive answers to these questions would explain why A-4B experimental operations during the post-war period are denied even up to the present day.

B) February 1945: Victory Weapon launches against French ports and Paris?

On 23 February 1945, Adolf Hitler made his last speech to the German people and once again promised final victory. At the same time the government of neutral Spain was informed by Germany that some Spanish cities close to the French border could suffer collateral damage if the new weapons were deployed at the last minute. In this case, it was said, this would not be a hostile action against Spain, but it was simply be a last defensive measure on the part of the Germans. In connection with this, wrote the former German Press correspondent Hermann Jung in July 1945 in his book, published by Javier Morato Editor, *Por que perdio Hitler la guerra* (why Hitler lost the war), the 'incorrigible optimists' in Germany of the time began to whisper something about splitting the atom.

The target of the planned German attacks may well have been French ports on the Mediterranean and Atlantic coast. Either the Germans were not clear how accurate their rockets would be, or they were expecting extensive side-effects after the rockets were used (such as, for example, nuclear fall-out) depending on the prevailing weather situation. According to information provided by the Chief of the *SS-Hauptamt*, Gottlob Berger, Paris too was in danger of being attacked by victory weapons carried by rockets.

Here, as in the case of Sweden, this could have been a deliberate German propaganda manoeuvre to keep a neutral state from hostile activities against the Third Reich, which was growing increasingly weaker. But because Franco's Spain by the end of the war was still largely pro-German, as far as it was possible to be, such a threat seems to be counter-productive. It is therefore a lot more likely that the events of 23 February 1945 represented a serious German warning to a friendly neutral state, so that Spain could take suitable protective and evacuation measures in the endangered border areas. We recall here the British plans to evacuate London in summer/autumn 1944 for fear of German nuclear attacks.

Curiously, Herman Jung's book appeared several weeks before the atomic bomb was dropped on Hiroshima! But in the book there is open talk about atomic bombs and their possible effects on the target areas … It will only be possible to come to a balanced judgement of this event if the exact text of the German letter to the Franco Government (and that Government's response?) is placed in the public domain.

Finally, in Spring 1945, the Third Reich had further cause to fall back on the goodwill of the Spaniards, if they wanted to rescue material and personnel from the increasing threat of Allied capture.

As with so much else concerning Spanish involvement in the Second World War, here, too, there seems to be a continuing veil of secrecy.

C) How far advanced were the preparations for rocket operations for Hitler's 'Last-minute All-round Defence'?

The 'Last Strike'? Ssecret last-minte V-weapons plans in the West

On 16 March 1945, *Art.Rgt.z.V.901* had launched the last V-2s at Antwerp from the Westerwald, and afterwards had to evacuate the positions there because of the American units rapidly advancing from the Rhine.

After the last V-2 had been launched at Britain from Holland on 27 March 1945 and the last V-1 on 29 March 1945, this was the definitive end of the German V-weapons campaign in the West.

But as the result of his research, the author Karsten Porezag asks the question whether after this the overall commander of all German V-weapons units, *SS-Obergruppenführer* Dr Kammler, was not planning a decisive action to bombard the advancing US troops in a zone 50 kilometres along the Rhine.

German leaflets dropped over the Westerwald and Siegerland required the population to evacuate this district by 1 April 1945 before new German weapons were deployed which would decide the outcome of the war and promised final victory. These leaflets are connected with the planned deployment of So-BF-109s armed with small nuclear bombs (see Volume 1). But it is possible that this victory weapons operation was to be carried out using V-2s.

If it was hoped to prevent the Western Front from collapsing after the surprise crossing of the Americans over the Rhine at Remagen, perhaps the last opportunity of doing this would have been a combined victory weapons operation against the Americans, who in the meantime were advancing along the Lower Rhine. This fact may not have escaped Kammler, but his activities now threatened to become an almost hopeless race against time.

According to Dr Dornberger,[11] conventionally-armed V-1s had already intervened in the fighting in the Ardennes and in the Rhineland.

For a long time, the reports of Allied front line soldiers in the Ardennes concerning V-1s striking in the vicinity of road crossings, marching routes and in the open field were thought to be chance crashes of faulty flying bombs on the way to Liege or Antwerp. In actual fact, from 16 to 30 December, 1944 about 100 V-1s were launched directly against Allied troops during the Ardennes offensive. Their targets were traffic junctions, important bridges and ammunition depots in the hinterland.

In view of the poor accuracy of the flying bomb, the German planners may have placed less reliance on direct hits than on achieving effects on morale, and gathering experience in operating these weapons on the ground.

A lot of research has also yet to be carried out on the subject of the V-1s used a few months later in Spring 1945 against the troops of the Western Allies in the Rhine valley. Remarkably, there are no further reports from other authors, so that something special could be being suppressed which later could no longer be mentioned: test operations for the all-round defence, which was to be assisted by the flying bombs carrying victory weapons, when these became available. In the opinion of the present author, this particularly applies to the V-1 operations in the Rhine valley, which are said never to have taken place. Possibly, here, when no warheads for victory weapons could be delivered, in desperation normal flying bombs were launched against the targets which were originally planned for victory weapons. It goes without saying that after the war not another word was spoken about this whole subject!

Let us trace the steps of the V-2 units on the Western Front. In this connection, it is notable that *Gruppe Süd* suddenly began constructing new V-2 launch positions in the Schelderwald near Wallau - Breitenbach - Biedenkopf and at Marburg/Kirchhaim. As late as 18 March 1945, heavy V-2 transport trains were directed via Rehe and Driedorf to Herborn and in the direction of Marburg. On 19 March the Staff of *Art.Rgt.(mot)z.V.901* moved to Tringenstein, where the previous day soldiers of *Heeres Abt.705* turned up.

After the units, severely weakened in the withdrawal, had moved into the Marburg area on 26 March 1945, as early as 28 March, all operational plans for *Art.Rgt.(mot)z.V.901* were abandoned because of the rapid American advance, and most of their equipment blown up. Whatever Dr Kammler had perhaps intended to achieve with a last V-weapons strike on the Western Front, now it was too late! When the advancing Americans captured the remains of the V-2 transport trains, they realised that everything was complete, including propellants and service connections, but not the warheads! Thus the great mystery remains as to what sort of warheads Kammler intended to use for these last operations in the West. If there were any written orders or plans concerning these, these documents must certainly have been among the first to be destroyed at the end of the war.

If we believe other Allied secret documents, there were also V-weapons operational bases in the area or on the periphery of the planned Alpine Fortress. Even the last refuges of the Third Reich were not to be left without V-weapons!

Thus an OSS report dated 7 February 1945 states that 10 kilometres north-west of Friedrichshafen there was a V-1 launch ramp directly beside a V-weapons factory. Another OSS reports confirms that this was not the V-2 weapons factory in Unterradach, which was already known to the Allies.

In addition, an undated OSS document reports the construction of launch ramps for flying bombs or similar weapons by the Organisation Todt in the district of Daisendorf on Lake Constance. Directly in the central area of the Alpine fortress, on 26 February 1945, the OSS reports the construction of launch bases for V-2s being carried out by companies from the Vienna area. Are there are parallels here to similar construction projects in Norway?

In a Gmunden too, in the Traunsee area, there were said to have been launch positions for V-2s. The latter report had indeed been known for many years, but to date no further details have become known.

It is unclear which targets it was hoped to strike from such remote launch areas and what form of armaments these rockets and flying bombs, based in the last refuges of the Third Reich, were intended to use.

It may be certain that mass attacks were no longer possible from here. So this again raises the question whether, instead of conventional weapons, victory weapons were to be deployed.

Mysterious V-weapons activities on other fronts too?

Germany's rockets and missiles became known as a result of their attacks against London, Antwerp, Liege and other targets in the hinterland of the Western Allies. Although this already showed that the Third Reich, despite all its efforts, did not have sufficient conventional V-weapons to achieve a decisive success, nevertheless there are clues that there were other V-weapons activities for direct deployment against the advancing Allied ground troops. Traces of this intention can be seen in all European theatres of war during the last year of the war. Some of these events took place weeks before the end of the regular V-weapons bombardment in the West. What was behind it all?

It is notable that, apart from one photograph, none of the many people who wrote memoirs of Peenemünde after the war said anything about preparations for using V-weapons on the war fronts, although some of them must have been directly concerned with this. For the most part, details concerning these plans only became known in recent years as a result of the release of former American microfilmed secret documents. Can people have been concealing something here for so many years?

V-weapons in Italy

The idea of using V-weapons from Italian soil was developed relatively early! As early as May 1943, *Reichsmarschall* Goering was planning to bombard the North African ports of the Allies with Fi-103s from southern Italian positions. This operation may have been based on the idea that perhaps it could prevent an invasion of Italy.

Before the Fi-103s, after many delays, were finally ready for service in summer 1944, southern Italy was to have long since been lost.

New plans for using V-weapons on the Italian front, however, became ever more apparent at the end of 1944. Thus an Allied RIP Special Interrogation Report dated 1 December 1944 reports that, in Hitler's words, V-weapons would be used in Italy very shortly.[12]

This announcement was followed by a series of disquieting reports which all pointed to the fact that something unpleasant seemed to be brewing here! Thus it was reported that 10,000 V 1 bombs were expected in Pola, which were to be launched against the Po plain. It was said that some of these projectiles would contain gas.

Newly-created launch bases for the ones were confirmed in San Sieste, Sant' Erasmo (near Venice), Noventa-Vigintina (north-west of Rovigno), Ponte Oleggio, Lonate Pozzolo, Pizzoleta (south of Villa Franka), Legino, Ghedi and Rappallo.[13 14 15 16]

An alarming OSS report dated 6 February, 1945 then gave information concerning the arrival of the German command to prepare the flying bomb offensive in the area or of the River Piave.

But the plans for large-scale construction of other positions in the Po plan and the Piave estuary had to be abandoned again from 20 February 1945. But still this was not yet the end of German efforts to use V-weapons in Italy.

Thus there exists a report dated 24 March 1945, which states that in the mountains north-west of Savona in the region of Legino, a German unit was continuing to construct V-weapons launch bases.

Another G2 (G-2:American Secret Service, *author's note*) report dated the same day, which was also classified as reliable, described the existence of remarkable V-weapons based on the south-western side of Monte Rosa or in the vicinity of Rappallo. This launch position, according to a report, was already completed and had a platform which was 60 metres long and 25 metres high. Four tunnel-like openings near the platform led into the mountain. The whole position, the report went on, was well camouflaged against observation from the air.

In response, the Allies ordered increased aerial surveillance of the district around Rappallo. Nothing further was published concerning the results.[17]

The tunnel like openings in Monte Rosa or could have perhaps been a Regenwurm project operation, which was pursued with greater urgency from the middle of 1944.

Were there also large-scale projects in Italy which recall the German rocket bunker projects in Normandy? An Italian study group for fortifications research in Milan under Dr Carlo Clericia a few years ago found out that a former suspected V-weapons base in bunkers had existed in

Possible remains of the bunkers of the V-weapons position at Ghedi aerodrome (Brescia, Italy). (Photo: Carlo A. Clerici, July 1999)

the area of the Ghedi airfield. The complex is located some 10 kilometres south of Brescia. The secret installations had walls about five metres thick, and in the opinion of the researchers displayed a certain similarity of with the planned V-weapons bunker of Sottevast in France.

This information makes us sit up and listen, because it is precisely the position at Sottevast which is mysterious even to the present day! It was one of the four large rocket launch bases in bunkers which were planned in France. When the Allies captured the area it had only been about one quarter completed and, if it had been completed, would have been bigger than the gigantic rocket launch bunkers in Watten and Wizernes. The British researcher and atomic rocket specialist Philip Henshall is firmly convinced that the Sottevast bunker was to play a special role in the planned nuclear or radiological victory weapons operations against Britain. Was this also the case for Ghedi?

Unfortunately it is not known when work began on the bunker at Ghedi, which is so similar to Sottevast. Today, the district is largely under water because of an artificial lake. What secret is concealed under the surface of the water? The fact is that no V-weapons operations actually took place from Italian soil. According to the available data, at the end of February, the idea for a mass deployment of V-1s, some armed with gas, in Italy was abandoned and, instead of that, work was carried on only on individual selected bases for V-weapons.

This could mean that even on the Italian front Hitler intended to use V-weapons within the framework of the all-round defence to stabilise the fronts. But this plan also never came to be implemented. Even before the preparations for the deployment of V-weapons in Italy in Spring 1945, surrender negotiations had already long since begun between SS General Wolff and his American counterpart Alan Dulles in Switzerland. To date, not all the background to the premature surrender of *Heeresgruppe Italien* has been sufficiently explained. At the time, the Western Allies even allowed German elite units to keep their weapons for a while after the surrender, and among the Allies there was talk with the Germans of a joint attack on Russia. It is probable that under these circumstances, deployment of victory weapons against the Western Allies in Italy would not have been possible with the senior SS commanders who were stationed there!

Fortunately for all those involved, on the southern front there was never this dilemma between 'orders and obedience'.

V-weapons on the Yugoslavian front

If recently released Allied secret reports are to be believed, plans also existed for deployment of V-weapons on the Yugoslavian front. Thus, on 27 December 1944, information was received that in the area of Rosenbach between Jessenice and Willach, V2 launch positions were being built, and that already 10 train loads of rockets had arrived. On 15 January 1945 and on 22 February 1945 other reliable reports were written which asserted that an additional V-2 position would be created at Lake Basko (Bokinjso), but that this was not yet completed. One of the reports described that the area in question was heavily wooded and that all access to it was forbidden. But there was even one drawing (now disappeared) which showed this V2 base under construction. Here too, no V-weapons came to be launched against Tito's troops. It would also have been pointless to wish to use such projectiles, which had been planned to be used as ground weapons again cities, against groups of partisans. But things would have looked very different if the V2s on the Yugoslavia front had actually carried radiological or nuclear warheads to achieve stabilisation of the fighting front here. In this case, too, it could be interesting to be able to have a look at the observations made by the Allies in the form of notes after they captured this area.

Rockets and missiles as Victory Weapons for the 'All-round Defence'

Although missing from official German orders and documents, there is evidence that during 1944-45 the V-1 and V-2 were to be used for purposes other than Hitler's stated doctrine of utilising them as vengeance weapons striking Allied cities. Although in the spring of 1944 Hitler continued to categorically withhold permission for the use of the V-1 in a direct role against enemy harbours or bridgeheads, there are indications that in reality, plans were afoot to depart from such a policy.

From Autumn 1944 Allied supply dumps and harbours on the European mainland were already under such effective attack that their usability was strongly affected, although unfortunately this was at the cost of many civilian casualties adjacent to the target areas.

The direct use at the front of V-weapons occurred in limited numbers - a handful of V-1s during the final battles in the Ardennes and the Rhine Valley, and V-2s against the Remagen bridge. The question is: were these launches made only in individual instances caused by the desperate military situation, or was a wider policy at work?

The entire concept of 'all-round-defence' was enumerated by Henry Picker. According to this plan, at the final moment victory weapons would be used on all German fronts to stabilise the situation. Rockets and flying missiles were to play a major part. Unfortunately, these ideas cannot be corroborated in any existing official documents. However, that such a policy existed cannot be doubted. It

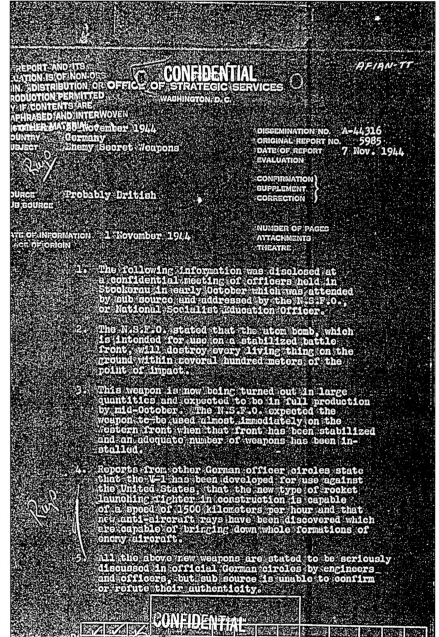

Document of the American OSS secret service dated 7 November 1944 concerning the planned tactical deployment of German atomic bombs. These were expected to be completely ready for production in October 1944. The document also mentions the development of production plans for the German U-boat V–1, rocket-launching fighters capable of a speed of 1500 kilometres per hour, and anti-aircraft rays.

was certainly being discussed at an officers' conference at Stockerau in October 1944 (see volume 1).

Nevertheless, there were simply too few miracle weapons available at the front to make such a policy possible. One thing the Germans may have been attempting to do is to contaminate tracts of land, thus blocking the Allied advance.

The final opportunities for such a policy to have been launched were as the Western Allies advanced from the eastern banks of the Rhine whilst on 16 April 1945 the Soviets launched their offensive against Berlin. In Italy, the River Po remained until April 1945 the final German bulwark against the Allied advance, whilst the Brenner Pass was much too late to act as the 'Alpine fortress'.

'VE' instead of 'V–2'? – The development of the military situation in the battle against the Allies after the 'All-round Defence' had failed to materialise in April 1945

Without the deployment of victory weapons, things happened in Italy as they inevitably had to happen: on 5 April 1945 the last Allied offensive in Italy began, with the Allies breaking through into the Po plain on 20 April. Only

a few German soldiers managed to cross the Po, most of them having had to leave their heavy weapons behind. Before the remnants of German troops were able to gather for the last battle on the southern flank of the Alpine fortress, on 2 May 1945, *Heeresgruppe C* finally concluded the surrender which had been planned months before. Without the southern flank, the Alpine fortress which was being developed was doomed.

In the West, where deployment of victory weapons also failed to materialise as part of the all-round defence, similar developments were taking place! At the end of March 1945, after the Anglo-Americans had crossed the Rhine, the collapse of the German Western Front came about relatively quickly.

Since January 1945, after the end of the Ardennes offensive and the successful Russian breakthrough, all large German units with any fighting strength, together with most of the German Luftwaffe, were transferred eastwards to stop the red flood. VE (Victory in Europe), the Allied war aim in the fight against the Axis powers, was approaching closer and closer!

Until today it is a subject for discussion whether the German High Command, or at least important parts of it, allowed – or tolerated – the Western Allies to march through to Berlin, despite all the casualties which the stubborn but pointless deployment of individual German units in the West were causing.

After this, the last aim of the German leadership was to withdraw their own units into the area of the Alpine fortress whilst at the same time preventing the Russian advance in the East until the Western Allies arrived at the Oder. It was hoped on the German side that this might allow the possible fracture of the enemy coalition to come about.

Then, by 12 April 1945 the Anglo-Americans had actually succeeded in advancing as far as the Elbe and thus marching deep into the later zone of occupation which had already been promised to the Russians. In mid-April 1945, the Western Allies were only 79 miles away from Berlin. Only individual German holding forces lay between the Elbe and Berlin, while from the stubbornly defended Oder front to Berlin there was still a distance of 120 miles. Could they have gone further?

As early as 21 March 1945, however, the Allied Supreme Commander Eisenhower had decided not to continue the advance to Berlin. The Americans feared that this would cause a confrontation with the victorious Soviets. Senior Allied officers maintain until today that one of their main concerns was what would happen if the Soviets continued their advance through the Americans and British to the French Atlantic, a Russian advance against which the Anglo Americans could offer very little resistance.

The Anglo-Americans therefore advanced as far as a bridgehead at Barby (just in case …), but not any further across the Elbe, and thus left it to the German army in the East to mount its defensive battle against the Russians. If the Anglo-Americans had not halted their advance and had pushed further eastwards, this would certainly have led to the immediate collapse of the German defence against the Russians. Was it precisely this that the Western Allies wanted to avoid?

Today much is made of the peace-like celebrations as the Americans and Russians met at Torgau on the Elbe. But what is not mentioned is that the Americans and British were at the same time making defensive preparations on the banks of the Elbe, were stationing artillery positions directly controlled by reconnaissance aircraft and allowing some of the German troops going into captivity to retain their weapons for a little while longer.

Was it the secret intention of the Anglo-American commanders that Germany and Russia would so weaken themselves in the expected battle of annihilation on the Oder that the Russians would afterwards have no taste for the further advance to the Atlantic which the Western Allies so much feared?

The Germans were very well informed what the Allied demarcation lines would look like after the war, and when the Allies had not advanced further over the Elbe to Berlin, it must have been clear to the German High Command that the hoped-for joint action of Germans and Western Allies against the Russians on the Oder would come to nothing. The only way out of this situation for the German side would have been the option of stabilising the Eastern Front by using victory weapons, and thus at least gaining a little more freedom of movement in negotiations (with both sides?). How would the Western powers have reacted to this?

But even in such a hypothetical case, the question would have still existed as to whether the German leadership, which had already been involved in many individual negotiations with the Allies, would in any event have been in the position to carry out such annihilation attacks.

After the V-weapons offensive in the West had ended: Victory Weapons on the Eastern Front

More recent American works give accounts of German plans to deploy more of the V-1 and V-2 launch units against the advancing Russians. But these works do not admit that to date there are no definite reports concerning V-1 or V-2 launches on the Eastern Front.

By contrast to this, after the war the former armaments Minister Albert Speer stated that it had never been planned to use the weapons against Russia. The flying bombs and rockets were, in his words, to be used as vengeance weapons exclusively against soft targets, such as the population of the Western democracies.[18] It could not, he said, be expected that the Russians would be influenced by this type of action. The deployment of V-weapons against the Soviet Union was thus regarded as pointless from the very outset.

But what if in 1945 in the East it was planned not to fly terror attacks as had been flown against London, but something completely different? In this regard, Hitler gives certain hints. Thus, on 13h April 1945, he said that he was

SS-Obergruppenführer Dr. Kammler's radio message of 23 April 1945.

convinced that on the Oder because of the strength and formation of the artillery there would be an enormous defensive victory.

But the German artillery on the Oder was by no means out of the ordinary as far as concerns their numbers and the nature of their formations, but with their many anti-aircraft guns often drawn by Berlin trams and milk floats, they rather represented the last levy. The remnants of the German field artillery on the Oder was only able to be equipped with a pitifully small amount of ammunition to enable it to survive the expected massive battle. Instead of forces of this kind, for an enormous defensive victory they would have needed new weapons with devastating effect.

Were Hitler's comments in any event intended to refer to normal artillery units or did he mean the V-weapons units

which belonged to the same arm of the service under the designation *Artillerieabteilung zur Vergeltung (z. V.)*?

The development of events points in this direction: on 16 and March 1945, *Gruppe Sud* launched its last V-2 in the West at Antwerp and a little later, on 27 March 1945, the bombardment of London by *Gruppe Nord* ended. After this, as a result of the collapsing Western Front, both V-2 units withdrew into the centre of what remained of the Reich. A terrible massacre took place when Dr Kammler's rocket troops withdrew from Holland! In this operation, SS members of *Gruppe Nord* murdered more than 200 Russian volunteers who had been working for them, including their women and children. Were they hoping in this way to silence (as potential witnesses) this workforce which was no longer needed? Perhaps they knew too much about Dr Kammler's victory weapons plans?!

Then the V-weapons offensive in the West quickly came to an end. As early as 3 April 1945, Hitler had all deliveries of explosives to the West halted, because the Americans were approaching the *Mittelwerk* with enormous strides and it could be expected that the production of all V-weapons would soon cease.

But what happened afterwards to the launch units?

Art.Rgt.z.V.901 of *Gruppe Süd* had withdrawn, with great losses of material, from its launch area in the Westerwald to about 10 km west of Celle in Lower Saxony. This was a planned withdrawal within the framework of the so-called Blücher Operation. Regiment 901 was now to launch rockets from Celle against *Festung* Küstrin, which was approximately 110 kilometres north-east of Berlin. But this order of 29 March 1945 could no longer be obeyed because of the military collapse of the Third Reich which was now developing more rapidly. Thus, as early as 7 April 1945 all the equipment of *Gruppe Süd* was destroyed so as not to let it fall into enemy hands.

One day later, the war diary remarked with defiant pride: "With the destruction of all our special equipment, any sign that the Group was involved with long-range weapons has been removed. The time of our proud operation of the long-range weapon is finally being replaced by the time of *Gruppe Süd* as a close-quarters combat group."

At about the same time, the V 1 operations in the West carried out by *Gen.Kdo.A.K.Z.V.* also came to an end. Thus on 29 March 1945 the last flying bombs were launched against Britain and on 30 March the last operation against Antwerp came to an end. On the same day the Divisional Commander *Oberst* Wachtel ordered the withdrawal from Holland under the code word 'Lützow'. This was carried out without great losses and with the recovery of almost all the equipment. Here, too, the plan was to resume operations. For this purpose the line Varel – Wolfsburg – Clockenburg was reoccupied. Because of the constantly deteriorating war situation, however, *Gen.Kdo.A.K.Z.V.* issued the order on 5 April 1945 to destroy its all these special equipment associated with the V-1s because of the imminent threat from the enemy. All war diaries had to be closed on 8 April 1945 and delivered to *Gen.Kdo.A.K.Z.V.* On the same day, the war diary of the 5th Flak Division (W) noted that it was no longer possible to deploy V-weapons against worthwhile targets because of the rapid advance of the Anglo-Americans.

On 4 May 1945 the former V-weapons Division of the Luftwaffe went into British captivity at Bad Sägeberg , after previously being used during the last month of the war for ground operations as an anti-tank commando using flak and infantry weapons.

But contrary to all reports, none of the missile rocket units which it had been planned to use for close combat was actually involved in action on the ground. Instead of this, attempts were still made to re-deploy them on the Eastern Front with V-weapons. Thus there exists the statement of the former adjutant of an infantry battalion, who

on 25 April 1945 witnessed the erection of several 'remarkable ramps' in his battalion's sector close to Berlin, which must have been V-1 catapults. According to his statement, the unit responsible for this operation was *Art. Rgt. 901*, that is, the same unit which was to launch rockets from Celle against the Eastern Front.

The catapults were in the village of Linum, north-west of Berlin. Typically, the Eastern Front launch bases were close to railway lines which led westwards to the V-1 depot at Tramm near Lüchow/Danneberg …

But in this case too it was no longer possible to deploy V-1. A supposed radio message from *SS-Obergruppenfuhrer* Dr Kammler on 23rd April, 1945, which was sent at 1658 hours to *SS-Oberstumfuhrer* Schürmann in Berlin contains the following words: "Blow up V-1 devices in Berlin immediately, *SS-Oberstumfuhrer* Schürmann to immediately set off to Reporting Station München-Obervöhring, Muspilistr. 19."

So what conclusion can be drawn from this? Weeks after the end of the conventional V-weapons offensive in the West, attempts were evidently being made to mount a renewed operation with the few remaining *Vergeltungswaffen* against the Russians. This is all more amazing when the National Socialist leadership had previously considered that normal operation involving *Vergeltungswaffen* would have no chance of success against the Russians. How much smaller must now the German chances have been to achieve a decisive success on the Eastern Front with the few remaining resources after it had not been possible to achieve this against the more sensitive Western Allies? In addition, in the light of the military situation in April 1945, it seems to have been pointless to hope for further support.

Even the Russians began during this late stage of the war to show the first signs of exhaustion, and thus Stalin threatened the death penalty for all those who could not obey the order to advance. Such measures had not been customary in the Russian army since 1942. This shows how seriously the situation was taken.

On the evening of the third day of the defensive battle, however, *Heeresgruppe Weichsel* had to report to the OKH in Zossen that now there were no more reserves which they could throw into the battle. According to this report, the only thing which could be expected was to discover whether on the fourth day of the defensive battle the enemy would try to break through at the weakest point of the front by mustering all their forces, or whether they had suffered heavy losses and were nown no longer capable of doing this.

The latest publications of Allied secret documents also state that the Germans succeeded, by the end of the second day of the battle on the Oder, in destroying half of the Russian armour. Would this not have been the moment to bring about the decisive turn of the tide by launching victory weapon V-1s and V-2s against Küstrin?

The Supreme Commander of the 9th Army on the Oder front, *General* Busse, whom Hitler had ordered to hold the

Eastern Front until the new weapons were ready for deploymen , sent this radio message to his exhausted troops: hold on for another two days, then everything will be sorted out!

A possible explanation, worth considering, why nothing happened can be found in the statement of former *Flak-Oberleutnant* Hans Pfau: His unit, the '125th' (Heavy Railway Flak *Abteilung*?) had to hold a 'huge testing area' in Berlin/Lichterfelde. *Oberleutnant* Pfau was not allowed to enter the area. This order, he said, also applied to more senior officers. Nevertheless, while going about his duties he found out that atomic warheads were supposed to be stored there, and that the detonators for them were still to be delivered by aircraft. The aircraft, it was said, had not arrived because it had been shot down by traitors!

Are there any clues today about the sabotage of the detonator transport aircraft shortly before the end of the war? It is true that remarkable things were going on in April 1945. Thus, in 2002 the *Polizeipräsidium Oranienburg-Land Berlin* tried to explain the case of an He-111, which on 23 April(!) 1945 crashed about 70 km north-west of Berlin and was completely destroyed. According to eyewitnesses, the aircraft is said to have been shot down by a Bf 109 fighter aircraft! In addition to information about the flight destination and the persons on board who were killed, the police were interested in finding any indication of what cargo the He-111 was carrying. A series of other unusual events makes the last flight of the He-111 at Ganz a mystery.

Here, either there is a dreadful combination of coincidences or it must have been an instance of treason involving high-ranking German people with a well-functioning organisation. Perhaps some day, despite the chaotic circumstances during the last days of the war, it will be possible to clarify what happened to the betrayed aircraft carrying the detonators.

According to Pfau, new detonators would only have been ready three to four months later, but in the meantime the end of the war intervened.

The statement of this reliable witness (he is a holder of the German Federal Cross of Merit) raises the question as to whether the nuclear warheads were not intended for the V-1s set up near Berlin. This would also explain why at the decisive moment they were not used.

Thus it can be assumed with some probability that this afternoon of 23 April 1945 was the time when the responsible authorities in the Third Reich definitely renounced the possibility of using victory weapons on the Eastern Front. In the chaos of the last days of the Third Reich, however, it is also conceivable that even after 23 April 1945 in the Berlin area work continued to be carried out to the last moment on building the V-1 ramps, because a contemporary witness says that he saw work going on as late as 25 April. Were they waiting there for missiles and special warheads which never arrived?

In any event, at the beginning of May *Art.Rgt.z.V.901* withdrew westwards from the Eastern Front and after crossing the Elbe surrendered to the American army waiting on the opposite bank.

All-round Defence - Summary

In his book, *Hitler's Table Talk*, Henry Picker asks how many more dead, war injured, refugees there would have been and how much more destruction would have been suffered if Hitler's opponents had not, as Churchill said, been victorious at five minutes to midnight and thus in Spring 1945 rendered futile Hitler's all-round defence plan in which a Germany's rockets, uranium bombs (with their power of completed destroying everything within a radius of three kilometres) and isotope weapons would have played a crucial role.

The warheads for the Enzian and HS 117 H rockets, which worked on the Zippermayr principle, were not yet ready for operational service and the HS 293s, BV 246s and V-1s armed with nerve gas were not allowed, on Hitler's orders, to be used as first strike weapons.

In order to achieve a decisive and permanent success at the front, a simultaneous deployment of a large number of these weapons would have been necessary. In view of the desolate state of the Reich, this was no longer possible. A more realistic possibility in 1945 would have been devastating attacks with individual victory weapons again special targets such as Allied river crossings, bridgeheads, supply junctions and command posts. The opportunity for such decisive attacks would have been available in spring 1945 on all fronts, as the Allies tried to cross the Rhine, the Oder and the Po. Was Hitler's promised 'deployment of miracle weapons at the front' in actual fact a plan for deploying tactical nuclear warheads and isotope charges on rockets and missiles? Despite the many smaller and larger conflicts since the end of the war, to date, fortunately, there has never been a tactical front-line deployment of nuclear weapons and missiles. It is therefore not possible to judge how great were the prospects of success in the event of a limited German deployment in spring 1945.

There are many indications that from the Far North to Yugoslavia attempts were made during the last months of the war to prepare for such an attack. Would Hitler's victory weapons have achieved what the armies, now bled dry, could no longer manage? In order to get even an opportunity for stabilising the fronts, nothing other than the deployment of 'more unconventional' charges would have been sufficient. But from spring 1945 these would have to have been for the most part on German territory, which in the meantime had been occupied by the Allies. Was this one of the reasons why the new weapons were not deployed, or was it rather that in technical terms they were not yet ready? Today, a clear answer to this question cannot be given. And it is also to date unclear to what extent

Hitler's all-round defence was hindered by treason and sabotage. Possibly all the factors which have been mentioned, together with the chaos of the last weeks of the war, had resulted in the race against time being lost by Germany in this case too.

After deployment of the weapons in the West no longer had any chance of being implemented because of the Anglo-American sudden rapid advance, the danger that unconventional rockets and missiles would be deployed on the Eastern Front existed until the end of April 1945. On the same day when Hitler, contrary to his original intention, decided not to go south to the Alpine fortress, but to stay in Berlin, *SS-Obergruppenführer* Dr Kammler also ordered the destruction of all the special V-1s in Berlin which had been retained for the 'all round defence' in the East.

The end of all these hopes had come! Or was there something else that we know nothing of? The author hopes to be able to explore and answer this question further in a future book.

Conclusion

How dangerous really were Germany's V-weapons? It is beyond dispute that Hitler's former rocket and missile programme changed the face of the 20th century. Without atomic technology, no other technological achievement would have brought about such widespread changes in our lives.

Permitted by one of the (few) loopholes in the Versailles treaty, Germany's rocket and missile programme was created as early as during the Weimar Republic, and after Hitler seized power gained a dynamic which became stronger and stronger until the end of the war.

After many unnecessary delays, the first V-1s were launched against Britain from June 1944. This was the beginning of a bitter campaign which extended over nine months. Contrary to the opinion often advanced today, Germany's conventional V-weapons had a great influence on the further course of the war. Would mass deployment of the new flying bombs and rockets against the Allied embarkation ports in Britain and the bridgeheads in Normandy have even been able to bring about a turning-point in the war on the Western Front, as the Allied Supreme Commander General Eisenhower wrote after the war, or had it become clear to the German leadership even before the weapons were deployed that there was really no possibility of this?

What is certain is that ultimately the V-weapons were planned to be used as carriers for weapons of mass destruction. The Third Reich promised that victory in Europe would be achieved at the last minute by means of this rocket surprise. Work had been doggedly and deliberately carried on for years for just this purpose.

Recently discovered documents from the former *Reichssicherheitshauptamt* (RSHA) indicate that at the beginning of 1945, the American President Roosevelt, still conscious of the German counter-offensive in the Ardennes and in the northern Vosges, was considering whether to withdraw from the European theatre of war in order to commit the United States in the future in Asia and in other parts of the world. Fear of the devastating effects of (unconventional?!) V-weapons played a significant part in these considerations.

In his secret report number 28/44 of 6 February, 1945, the German secret agent 38622 reported that on 31 January 1945 travelling via Tangiers from the USA, a Vatican courier arrived with important documents in Madrid, which he was to bring to the Pope after discussions in London. Agent 38622, who was one of the closest colleagues of Cardinal Faulhaber, wrote that the alarming news had come to the Vatican from America that Roosevelt intended, under quite specific conditions, to withdraw his troops the following year from Europe.

38622 listed the following significant conditions: "1. There is the possibility that Germany will in fact succeed in holding its *Westwall* and the Rhine line in the West ... (...) 7. By means of its V-weapons, Germany will possibly bring about the collapse of Britain, and in France and Belgium will disrupt the lines of supply of Allied units to such an extent that America will be compelled to leave Britain itself, together with French and Belgium, to Bolshevism and withdraw American troops from Europe ... 8. America will try to agree this withdrawal of its troops from Europe on a peaceful basis with Bolshevism, namely in the form of finally leaving Europe to Bolshevism and committing America to a policy of non-involvement in Bolshevik reconstruction in Europe."

If this report is to be believed, it is clear that the informed circles of political leadership in the USA at the beginning of 1945 were apparently firmly expecting the possibility of a devastating German (nuclear?) knockout strike in Europe and in this case would have withdrawn from the European theatre of war. What purpose would there have been in liberating a Europe of nuclear devastation with the millions of dead and a destroyed infrastructure which were to be expected in this event?

But in spring 1945, Germany succeeded neither in holding the Rhine line and the *Westwall*, nor in managing to deploy really devastating V-weapons, so that the fears of the Vatican were not fulfilled and the US troops could remain in liberated Europe.

Something which is not mentioned in the agent's report is the fact that significant circles of the Americans at that time had just as overwhelming a fear of German V-weapon attacks with nuclear warheads on their own homeland. We will be dealing with this subject in Volume 3.

Notes

Notes to Introduction

1. Walter Dornberger, *Der Schuss ins Weltall* (The Launch into Space), p. 112, Bechtle, 1952.
2. C. Lester, "Secrets by the Thousands", p. 329ff, *Harper's Magazine*, October 1946.
3. Michael J. Neufeld, *The rocket and the Reich*, pp. 272-9, The Free Press, 1995.
4. Dieter Hölksen, *V-Missiles of the Third Reich*, pp. 304-11, Monogram, 1994.

Notes to Part I

1. A. R. Weyl, *Fokker - The creative years*, pp. 349-51, Putnam, 1962.
2. Peter Gray, Owen Thetford, *German Aircaft of the First World War*, p. 571, Putnam, 1962.
3. Bill Gunston, *Die Illustrierte Enzyklopädie der Raketen und Lenkwaffen*, pp. 104/5, Bund und Zeit, 1981.
4. Olaf Gröhler, *Geschichte des Luftkriegs von 1910 bis 1980* (History of Air Warfare from 1910-80), pp. 70, 86, Militärverlag der DDR, 1981.
5. Alfred V. Verville, "Germans & Rockets 1922", CUOHR, USAF Microfilm, reel 43811.
6. Benjamin King, Timothy Kutta, *Impact - The History of Germany's V-Weapons in World War II*, pp. 26-33, Sarpedon, 1998.
7. J. Miranda, P. Mercado, *Die geheimen Wunderwaffen des III Reiches* (The Secret Miracle Weapons of the III Reich), p. 66, Flugzeug Publications, 1995.
8. Walter Dornberger, op. cit., p. 198.
9. Peter Korrell, *TB-3 - Die Geschichte eines Bombers* (TB3 - The History of a Bomber), pp. 131-2, Transpress, 1987.
10. Dimensione Cielo, 4, *Bombardieri, Ricognitori* (Bombers, Reconnaissance), pp. 47-9, Edizioni Bizarri, 1972.
11. Cesari Gori, Ali d'Italia 11, SIAI, p. 79, 2nd part, pp. 47-9, La Bancarella Aeronautica, 1999.
12. Peter C. Smith, *"Pedestal" - The Malta Convoy of August 1942*, pp. 106-7, 2nd ed., William Kimber, 1987.
13. During the war, work on remote-controlled missiles was also carried out successfully in the USA and Japan. But these robot weapons only came into operational service after the V-1.

Notes to Part II

1. Volkhard Bode, Gerhard Kaiser, *Raketenspuren-Peenemünde 1936-1996*, (Rocket Trails) pp. 44-6, Bechtermünz, 1997.
2. Werner Budeler, *Geschichte der Raumfaht* (History of Space Travel), pp. 258-60, Sigloch Edition.
3. Heiko Zeutschner, *Die braune Mattscheibe - Fernsehen im Nationalsozialismus* (The Brown Screen - TV under National Socialism), pp. 82/83, Rotbuch, 1995.
4. Arthur T. Wheeler, *The WuWa! Wunderwaffen - The Nazi Atomic Project*, p. 8, summary in Spanish, 2001

5. David Irving, *Die Geheimwaffen des Dritten Reiches* (The Secret Weapons of the Third Reich), pp. 45-6, Sigbert Mohn, 1965.
6. Stefan Lauscher, *Die Diesellokomotiven der Wehrmacht*, p. 145, Eisenbahn-Kurier 1999.
7. Roland Hautefeuille, *Constructions Speciales*, p,7, Jean-Bernard, 2nd ed., 1995.
8. Here, the generals also mentioned that deployment was to commence at the beginning of 1943, and that at that time (the end of 1942) development work had already been underway for eight months.
9. Walter Dornberger, op. cit., pp. 218-225.
10. Otto Skorzeny, *Meine Kommandounternehmen* (My Command Operations), p. 156, Universitas, 1993.
11. Mark Wade, 'Peenemünde' in: astronautix. com, 2001.
12. Philip Henshall, *The Nuclear Axis - Germany, Japan and the Atom Bomb Race 1939-45*, Vorspann, Alan Sutton, 2000.
13. Michael Derrick, *Geheimwaffen des Dritten Reiches und deren Weiterentwicklung bis heute* (Secret Weapons of the Third Reich and developments based on them up to the present day), p. 94, König, 2000.
14. Arthur T. Wheeler, op. cit., pp. 7/8.
15. Ference A. Vadja, Peter Dancey, *German Aircraft Industry and Production*, pp. 102-4, SAE, 1998.
16. Ibid., p. 83.
17. After the success of the Allied invasion of France and the collapse of *Heeresgruppe Mitte* in Summer 1944, this plan was finished (see also Friedrich Georg, *Hitler's Miracle Weapons Volume 1*).
18. David Irving, op. cit., p. 205.
19. ibid, pp. 213, 224.
20. Otto Ernst Remer, *Verschwörung und Verrat um Hitler* (Conspiracy and Treason in Hitler's Circle), pp. 277/8, Remer Heipke, 5th ed., 1993
21. Kurt Grasser, 'Projekt Zement' in: *IBA-Informationen*, p. 39, Vol. 19, 1992.
22. H. A. Koch, *Flak*, pp. 283/4, 2nd ed., Podzun, 1965.
23. David Irving, op. cit., pp. 342-58.
24. Wilhelm Helmold, *Die V-1*, pp. 294-303, Bechtle, 1988.
25. Benjamin King, Timothy Kutta, op. cit., pp. 324-7.
26. Richard Overy, *Die Wurzeln des Sieges - warum die Alliierten den Zweiten Weltkrieg gewannen* (The roots of victory - why the Allies won WW2), p. 393, DVA, 2000.
27. David Irving, op. cit., pp. 267-8.
28. Ralf Georg Reuth, *Joseph Goebbels Tagebücher 1924-45* (Diaries), Vol. 5, pp. 2058-9, 2069, 2nd ed., Piper, 2000.
29. Benjamin King, Timothy Kutta, op. cit., p. 200.
30. Bob Ogley, *Doodlebugs and Rockets - The battle of the Flying Bombs*, p. 168, Froglets, 1995.
31. Benjamin King, Timothy Kutta, op. cit., pp. 3, 122, 210-12, 244-6, 271-4, 316-323.
32. Thomas Powers, *Heisenbergs Krieg - Die Geheimgeschichte der*

deutschen Atombombe (Heisenberg's War – The Secret History of the German Atomic Bomb), p. 470, Hoffmann und Campe, 1993.

33. Bruce Lee, *Marching Orders – The Untold Story of World War II*, pp. 226-7, Da Capo, 2001.

34. Thus, for example, 240 of Air Marshal Harris' four-engined bombers bombed Darmstadt on 12 September 1944, and left behind them 12,000 to 15,000 dead (according to David Irving, *Und Deutschlands Städte starben nicht* (And Germany's cities did not die), Weltbild, 1989).

35. Adolf galland, *Die Ersten und die Letzten – Jagdflieger im Zweiten Weltkrieg* (The First and the last – Fighter Pilots in the Second World War), pp. 325-6, Schneekluth, 1953.

36. Joachim Engelmann, *Geheime Waffenschmiede Peenemünde* (Secret Peenemünde Weapons Makers), pp. 112/3, Podzun-Pallas, 1972.

37. Rudolf Lusar, *Die deutschen Waffen und Geheimwaffen des Zweiten Welkriegs und ihre Weiterentwicklung* (The German weapons & secret weapons of WW2 and their further development), p. 200, 6th ed., J. F. Lehmanns, 1971.

38. Statement made by Hitler to Jodl on 26 June 1944, quoted in David Irving, *Die Geheimwaffen des deutschen Reiches*, p. 268, 294, 337/8, Sigbert Mohn, 1965.

39. James McGovern, *Operazione Crossbow & Overcast*, p. 289, U. Mursia, 1970

40. Olaf Groehler, op. cit., pp. 447-453.

41. David Irving, *Und Deutschlands Städte starben nicht*, pp. 253-6, Weltbild, 1989.

42. Charles Messenger, *Blitzkrieg – Eine Strategie macht Geschichte* (A strategy makes history), p. 293, Bechtermünz, 2000.

43. General Spaatz papers, in: USAF Microfilm 43811.

44. J. Engelmann, *Raketen, die den Krieg entscheiden sollten* (Rockets which were to decide the outcome of the war), pp. 146-150, Podzun-Pallas.

45. On 13 November 1939, the HWA reduced the Peenemünde budget from 50 to 25 million *Reichsmarks*.

46. Henry Picker, op. cit., pp. 683/4, Propylaen, 1997.

47. Max Klüver, *Den Sieg verspielt – Musste Deutschland den Zweiten Weltkrieg verlieren?* (The chance for victory missed – Did Germany have to lose WW2?), p. 298, 2nd ed., Druffel, 1984.

48. Roger Ford, *Germany's secret weapons in World War II*, p. 75, UBI, 2000.

49. Richard Overy, Goering, pp. 138-150, Phoenix Press, 2000.

50. Benjamin King, Timothy Kutta, op. cit., pp. 2, 37, 39, 60-68, 80-81, Sarpedon, 1998.

51. According to Dornberger, this exchange of heavy for light flak took place the night before the great air-raid (see Dornberger, op. cit., p. 177, Bechtle, 1952) The question as to who gave the orders for this remains unanswered even today!

52. Louis Kilzer, *Hitler's Traitor* – The twice-winner of the Pulitzer Prize Louis Kilzer, on the basis of released secret documents, provides a convincing picture of the unimaginable degree of treason and conspiracy prevailing in wide circles of the Third Reich leadership. Presidio, 2000.

53. Roland Hautefueille, op. cit., pp. 164/166, Jean Bernard, Auflage 1995.

54. David Irving, *Geheimwaffen*, pp. 98/99, Sigbert Mohn, 1967.

55. Walter Dornberger, op. cit., pp. 112-115, Bechtle, 1952.

56. Joseph Mark Scalia, *Germany's last mission to Japan*, pp. 138/139, Chatham, 2000.

57. David Irving, op. cit., p. 254, Sigbert Mohn, 1965.

58. Uli Jungbluth, 'Hitlers Geheimwaffen im Westerwald – Zum Einsatz der 'V-Waffen' gegen Ende des Zweiten Weltkriegs' (Hitler's secret weapons in the Westerwald – On the deployment of the 'V-weapons' towrds the end of WW2), in: *Werkstatt-Beiträge zum Westerwald* No. 2, Geschichts- und Kulturwerkstatt Westerwald, 2nd ed., 1996.

59. Henry Picker, op. cit., pp. 42, 586, 683/4, Propyläen Taschenbuch, 2nd ed., 1997.

60. David Irving, op. cit., p. 200, Sigbert Mohn, 1965.

61. L/C Bot 1945, German long range missiles – August 1944, in: USAF Microfilm 43811.

62. Hans-Ulrich Rudel, *Trotzdem*, pp. 134-135, K. W. Schulz, 1996.

63. *Hitlers Berghof 1928-1945*, p. 135, Arndt-Verlag 2000.

64. Hitler's statements concerning the beginning of V-1 operations may be connected with a conversation which he had had previously on 5.3.44 with *Generalfeldmarschall* Milch. In that conversation, Milch informed the disillusioned Hitler about the developing success of the V-1 programme (source: J. Engelmann, op. cit., p. 75.)

65. In fact, *Oberst* Max Wachtel's *Flugregiment 155 (W)* was ready as early as March 1945 to launch the first flying bombs against London. Source: David Irving, op. cit, p. 229.

66. Henry Picker, to whom we owe this inside information about Hitler's attitude to the rocket, expressed regret in his book that for reasons of secrecy he had not gone into this subject in more detail.

67. David Irving, op. cit., p. 348.

68. Dieter Hölksen, op. cit., pp. 151-2.

69. Theodor Bennecke, *Karl-Heinz Hedwig*, op. cit., p. 88.

70. Information given by the Kammler researcher Tom Agoston to the author in 1989.

71. Headquarters Mediterranean Air Force Target Intelligence Section – Sheet U3, 923185.

72. Dieter Hölksen, op. cit.

73. J. B. King, John Batchelor, *Deutsche Geheimwaffen*, p. 43, Heyne, 1975.

74. CIOS Report XXXII – German Guided Missile Research, quoted in: Edgar Meyer and Thomas Mehner, *Hitler und die Bombe*, pp. 189, 192, Kopp Verlag, Rottenburg 2002.

75. Heinz J, Nowarra, op. cit., Vol. 4, pp. 110-111, Bernard & Graefe, 1988.

76. Wilhelm Helmold, op. cit, Appendix.

77. Kyrill von Gerdorf, Kurt Grasman, Helmut Schubert, *Flugmotoren und Strahltriebwerke* (Aircraft engines and jet propulsion systems), p. 267, 3rd ed., Bernard & Graefe, 1995.

78. J. R. Smith, Anthony Kay, *German Aircraft of the Second World War*, p. 672, 3rd ed., Putnam, 1978.

79. King/Kutta, op. cit., p. 295.

80. Botho Stüwe, *Peenemünde West – Die Erprobungsstelle der Luftwaffe für geheime Fernlenkwaffen und deren Entwicklungsgeschichte* (The testing station for secret remote-control weapons and the history of their development), p. 791, Bechtle, 1995.

81. Philip Henshall, *Vengeance – Hitler's Nuclear Weapon – Fact or Fiction?*, pp. 75-82, Allan Sutton, 1995.

82. Philip Henshall. *The Nuclear Axis*, op. cit., pp. 95, 109, 130.

83. Bob Ogley, op. cit., p. 148.

84. Office of the Director of Intelligence, An Evaluation of German Capabilities in 1945, Headquarters US Strategic Air Forces in Europe, p. 35, 19 January 1945.

85. Jürgen Michels, *Peenemünde und seine Erben in Ost und West _ Entwicklung und Weg deutscher Geheimwaffen*, pp. 49-50, Bernard & Graefe, 1997.

86. Walter Dornberger, op. cit., pp. 151-2.

87. Information from the papers of 'Dr X' of 22.11.2001. Remarkably, in the postwar period the leading staff at Peenemünde insisted that 'calculations would have shown that not much would have been gained by enlarging the

rocket'. What is known is that the R-2 derivative then had alsmost twice the range of the normal R-1.

88. Gerhard Taube, *Deutsche Eisenbahn-Geschütze* (German Railway Guns), p. 157, Motorbuch, 2001.
89. Jürgen Michels, op. cit., p. 71.
90. Information from papers of 'Dr X'.
91. Michael J. Neufeld, op. cit., pp. 157, 282.
92. Heinz J. Nowarra, op. cit., p. 63.
93. Walter Dornberger, op. cit, p. 140.
94. ibid.
95. Dr Walter Dornberger, *V-2*, p. 140, Hurst & Hackett, 1954.
96. 'Brief Interrogation Report on Prof. Dr Wernher von Braun' op. cit.
97. Geoffrey Brooks, *Hitler's Nuclear Weapons*, pp. 185, 188-9, Leo Cooper, 1992.
98. Ron Miller, The *dream machines - A pictorial of the spaceships*, p. 363, Krieger, 1993.
99. Mark Wade, Nuclear/Ammonia, in www.astronautix.com, 2001.
100. Jim Wilson, 'America's Nuclear Flying Saucer', p. 68 in: *Popular Mechanics*, November 2000.
101. Reinhard Haunhild, Hellmut H. Führing, *Raketen - Die erregende Geschichte einer Erfindung* (Rockets - the exciting story of an invention), pp. 117, 123, Athenaum, 1958.
102. Fritz Hahn, op. cit., pp. 137/139.
103. Jürgen Michels, op. cit., p. 209.
104. Ron Miller, op. cit., p. 255.
105. Tom Agoston, *Teufel oder Technokrat - Hitlers graue Eminenz*, p. 18, Mittler, 1993.
106. Michael J, Neufeld, op. cit., pp. 248-51, 256.
107. Ian V. Hogg, *German Secret Weapons of the Second World War*, p. 40, Greenhill, 1999.
108. Jürgen Michels, op. cit., pp. 74/5.
109. H. A. Koch, op. cit., p. 276.
110. Fritz Hahn, op. cit., p. 169.
111. Howard A. Bueckner, Wilhelm Bernhart, *Hitler's Ashes - seeds of a new Reich*, p. 162, Thunderbird, 1989.
112. Heinz J. Nowarra, op. cit., p. 63.
113. PMP Aescala 'EMW A-9'
114. Jan V. Hogg, op. cit., pp. 40-1.
115. 'Dr X' papers.
116. Mark Wade, 'R-11' in: astronautix. com, 2001.
117. Antony L. Kay, *Monogram Close-up 4: The Buzz Bomb*, p. 10, Monogram Aviation Publ., 1977.
118. Dieter Hölksen, op. cit., pp. 188-9.
119. Günther Gellermann, *Der Krieg, der nicht statfand* (The war that never took place), pp. 103-4, Bernard & Graefe, 1986.
120. David Myrha, *The Horten Brothers and their all-wing aircraft*, pp. 23-4, Schiffer, 1998.
121. DDK Pers. Files (1916-52), 'Eisenhower suggests, Try out new rocket-assisted bombs against Bergen or Trondheim' in: USAF Microfilm 43811.
122. Express Staff Reporter: 'V-Bombs on New York inside 60 days', via David Monaghan on 21 January 2002.
123. J. Engelmann, op. cit., p. 70.
124. Fritz Hahn, op. cit., p. 183.
125. Brief Interrogation Report, op. cit.
126. Fritz Hahn, op. cit., p. 183.
127. Michael J. Neufeld, op. cit., p. 293.
128. Headquarters Mediterranean Allied Air Forces, Target Intelligence Section APO 650, Report HI 182 dated 19.9.44.
129. Richard Overy, op. cit., pp. 308-9.
130. Mark Wade, 'R-2' in: astronautix. com, 2001.
131. Mark Wade, R-5., ibid.
132. CIB-1, IBO-1 (18 March 1949) Conference of CWS officials with Ing. Mario Zippermayr.
133. Philip Henshall, personal letter to the author dated 8 January 1996.
134. Mark Wade, op. cit., 'R-5'.
135. Henry Picker, op. cit., p. 683.
136. Pat Flannery, Virus House German Nuclear Weapon in: www.Luft46.com, 2000.
137. David Myrha, *The Horten Bros*, op. cit., pp. 225-7.
138. Helenes T. Freiberger, Investigations, Research, Developments and Practical Use of the German Atomic Bomb, APW/U 96/45.
139. Geoffrey Brook, op. cit., pp. 186/9.
140. Chuck Hansen, op. cit., pp. 121-2.
141. Philip Henshall, *Nuclear Axis*, op. cit., pp. 167-8, 208.
142. Al Christmass, *Target Hiroshima*, pp. 176, 178-9, Naval Institute Press, 1998.
143. When the ALSOS Mission arrived in November 1944 in Strasbourg, just after the town had been captured, they found in the 'physikalisches Institut' there detailed information about the atomic reactor laboratory in Stadtilm (source: Ulrich Brunzel, *Hitlers Geheimobjekte in Thüringen*, p. 55, H- Jung-Verlag, Zella-Mehlis, 1993.
144. Franz Kurowski, *Unternehmen Paperclip*, pp. 13, 134, 137, Bastei-Lübbe, 1984.
145. Luigi Romersa, *La Defensa*, No. 76/77, p. 130, August-September 1984.
146. Franz Kurowski, 'Von der bedingungslosen Kapitulation bis zur Mondorfer Erklärung' (From unconditional surrender to the Mondorf Declaration), in: GFP e.V. Conference Minutes 1985, *Jalta und Potsdam überwinden* (Yalta and Potsdam overcome), p. 22, Bassum, 1985.
147. Mark Wade, 'RSA' in: astronautix. com, 2001.
148. William Lyne, *Space Aliens from the Pentagon*, p. 39, Creatopia, 1993.
149. Dr Walter Dornberger, op. cit., pp. 191-4.
150. Roland Hautefueille, op. cit., pp. 17, 21.
151. David Irving, *Geheimwaffen*, op. cit., pp. 246, 265.
152. Roland Hautefueille, op. cit., pp. 229-34.
153. Ibid, p. 280.
154. Philip Henshall, *Vengeance*, op. cit., pp. 106, 109.
155. Roland Hautefueille, op. cit., p. 285.
156. Dr Walter Dornberger, op. cit., pp 268-9.
157. Karsten Porezag, op. cit., p. 152.
158. Steven V. Zaloga, *The Scud and other Russian Ballistic Missile Vehicles*, p. 4, Concord, 2000.
159. Bernd Henze, Gunther Hebestreit, 'Raketen aus Bleicherode' in *Schriftenreihe: Spuren der Vergangenheit*, Vol. 1, pp. 46-47, H&H Verlag, 1998.
160. Robert Gardiner, *Conway's All the World's Fighting Ships 1947-1982, Part II: The Warsaw Pact and Non-Aligned Nations*, pp. 473, 492, 493, Conway, 1983.
161. Steven V. Zaloga, op. cit., pp. 352, 353, 340 (other V-weapons).
162. Henze/Hebestreit, op. cit., p. 40.
163. Philip Henshall, personal letters to the author dated 10.3.97, 9.12.97.
164. Renato Vesco, *Operazione Pleniluno*, pp. 71, 74, 96, Mursia, 1972.
165. Tom Agoston, op. cit., pp. 18, 22-29.
166. Thomas Mehner, Document 'Klipper' (unpublished).
167. Benecke/Hedwig, op. cit., Vol. 10, pp. 154-163.
168. Miranda/ Mercado, op. cit., p. 91.
169. CIC Report, 4 August 1945.
170. Klaus-Peter Rothkugel, *Das Geheimnis der deutschen Flugschreiben*, pp. 166-7, VDM, 2002.
171. CIC 75, 191, 23 July 1945, 'Report on Talstation Lofer'.
172. Heinz-Jürgen Bardella, personal letters dated 1.5.96, 13.6.96, 11.8.96, 15.9.96.

173. Rudolf Lusar, *Die deutschen Waffen und Geheimwaffen des Zweiten Weltkriegs iund ihre Weiterentwicklungen* (The German weapons and secret weapons of WW2 and their further development), p. 216, 6th ed., J. F. Lehmanns, 1971.

174. Manfred Griehl, *Dornier Do-217 - 317 -417*, p. 171-188, Motorbuch, 1987.

175. Suggestion made to the author by Antonio Chover on 1 March 2002.

Notes to Part III

1. Edgar Meyer/Thomas Mehner, op. cit., p. 86.
2. Karsten Porezag, op. cit., pp. 138-147.
3. *Las Provincias* (Valencia), 12 August 1945, p. 7, Valencia.
4. *Daily Telegraph*, 11 August 1945, p. 5.
5. Thomas Powers, op. cit., pp. 372-3, 483, 485-6.
6. James McGovern, op. cit., pp. 50, 51.
7. Bob Ogley, op. cit., pp. 128, 149.
8. Karsten Porezag, op. cit.,
9. Mayer/Mehner, op. cit., pp. 27-8.
10. Daniel Velazco, information given to the author on 20 March 2001.
11. Walter Dornberger, op. cit.,, p. 287.
12. RIP Special Interrogation Report No. 31, 1.12.44.
13. CX, OP04, 11.1.45.
14. JSLD 462/3 20, 1.1.45 and OSS J-3028, 20.12.44.
15. ISLD. BR0098, 7.2.45.
16. OSS J-3509, early Feb., 1945.
17. Fifth Army G2 report No. 1046 II PW, 24.3.45.
18. Dieter Hölksen, op. cit, the V-1 and V-2, statement made by Albert Speer on 18.12.80, quoted in: Monogram, 1994.